ALSO BY NAOMI DUGUID
(all cowritten with Jeffrey Alford)

Beyond the Great Wall: *Recipes and Travels in the Other China*
Mangoes & Curry Leaves: *Culinary Travels Through the Great Subcontinent*
Hot Sour Salty Sweet: *A Culinary Journey Through Southeast Asia*
Seductions of Rice
HomeBaking: *The Artful Mix of Flour and Tradition Around the World*
Flatbreads and Flavors: *A Baker's Atlas*

ARTISAN
NEW YORK

Studio photography *by* Richard Jung
Location photography *by* Naomi Duguid

NAOMI DUGUID

BURMA

RIVERS OF FLAVOR

Published by Artisan
A division of Workman Publishing Company, Inc.
225 Varick Street
New York, NY 10014-4381
artisanbooks.com

Library of Congress Cataloging-in-Publication Data
Duguid, Naomi.
Burma: rivers of flavor / Naomi Duguid.
p. cm.
Includes bibliographical references and index.
ISBN 978-1-57965-413-9
1. Cooking, Burmese. 2. Cooking (Spices). 3. Food—Burma.
4. Burma—Social life and customs. I. Title.
TX724.5.B93D84 2012
641.59591—dc23
2011052121

Food styling by Linda Tubby

Printed in China
First printing, September 2012

10 9 8 7 6 5 4 3 2 1

PAGES ii–iii: *Children in a train compartment, traveling back to Mandalay from a festival in Lashio.* **OVERLEAF** (PAGES iv-v): *Ruins at sunset on the plains near Bagan.* **OPPOSITE:** *Offerings at Shwedagon, a temple complex in Rangoon.*

To the people of Burma, whose resilience in hard times, and generosity to a stranger, are remarkable and moving. And to Dom and Tashi and my extended family of friends, with love and thanks.

Bicycle and shopfront in the early morning, central Hsipaw.

CONTENTS

PREFACE

THIS BOOK CELEBRATES THE CULINARY CULTURE and traditional foodways of Burma, using recipes, stories, and photographs to engage with life there in all its richness, both in the kitchen and out.

My first trip to Burma was in 1980. Nine years later, I went from Thailand into a border area controlled by the Karen Independence Army, and in 1998 I traveled to Shan State and Mandalay. Since starting work on this book in late 2008, I've made many more trips into Burma. I've spent time in Rangoon but have also been able to travel widely around the country. I've slowly gained an understanding of the local food by hanging around: photographing; eating (and eating!) in markets, tea shops, and small restaurants; and having conversations with people.

For more than twenty years, I've been exploring food as an aspect of culture. I've co-authored six cookbooks that focus on home cooking—in the Indian Subcontinent, in the outlying areas of China,

One of many roadside restaurants in Kachin State, between Myitkyina and Bhamo. When the buses stop every day around noon, the women hurry to feed passengers their rice meal from a huge array of prepared curries, salads, and condiments.

and in the Mekong region—and also on staple foods such as flatbreads and rice. In my travels for those books I've learned how to be a beginner in a new place, slowly starting to decipher how things work, what the patterns of daily life and food might be.

When I poke around in a market with my camera, taking shots to remember what produce is there or the techniques used by a street vendor, people in Burma are often cautious at first. They wonder why I am photographing everyday items like piles of shallots or rice or leafy greens. But they soon get used to me. And once they feel at ease, I can start asking questions about the food: how and where it's grown, how it's prepared, and so on. Tea shops have open kitchens, as do most small restaurants, where I can watch and learn. Occasionally I have been lucky enough to be in the kitchen of a private house, invited by a friend, or brought along by a cousin.

I'm now hooked, not just on Burmese food, but also on the country. I'm convinced that the more foreigners who travel to Burma mindfully, the better. The country is opening to democracy after having been closed off by repressive government policies for several generations, and the political picture is improving. People in Burma are now optimistic about the future. They're happy to have a chance to engage with the outside world.

You may want to use this book just for armchair travel and cooking. However, I'm hoping that the stories, recipes, and photographs give you a sense of personal connection to the people of Burma and an urge to go and meet them and see their country for yourself.

INTRODUCTION

SHAPED LIKE A KITE WITH A LONG TAIL, Burma is the largest country in mainland Southeast Asia. It lies between the giants of Asia—India and China—and it has a long border with Thailand. For centuries it's been a cultural crossroads, a destination for traders and travelers from India and China and the rest of Southeast Asia. Buddhism traveled here from India about two thousand years ago and then spread eastward. The Mongols invaded Burma in 1271, then retreated back to China.

In this well-watered land of huge rivers and fertile valleys, kingdoms flourished and distinctive food traditions developed over the centuries. As a result, Burma's culinary scene today is rich and multilayered. From the brilliant salads, sparkling condiments, and easy curries of the Bamar people living in the central river valleys, to the inventive aromatic dishes of the peoples in the hills, Burma has a mother lode of delicious and accessible food traditions.

In the last 150 years, the people of Burma have seen invasions, conquests, war, and civil strife. Through it all they have maintained their culture, their pride, and their sense of self-respect. But the news stories Westerners read about Burma deal with large-scale events and rarely touch on the warmth and humanity of individuals.

Let me take you there, to that more personal layer of life in Burma. Food is an inextricable part of daily life and local culture everywhere in the world, and as an artist friend said to me a couple of years ago, "Food is the last refuge." The kitchen and the dinner table are places where people can relax and feel safe, where they can take a break from the challenges of the world outside. That's especially true for people in Burma, where government has until recently been more of a threat than a support. So the Burmese army and government are not invited into the kitchen in this book, nor will you find discussions of human rights mixed in with the recipes here.

Instead, political and historical details about the country can be found in the section called Burma over Time (page 306). There's also an Annotated Bibliography (page 351), so that you can engage with travelers, historians, novelists, and memoirists who have explored aspects of Burma's past and present. And you'll find a detailed Glossary of ingredients, cooking terms, ethnographic terms, and place-names (page 322). Finally, I've included Traveling in Burma (page 319), which gives some suggestions for those who would like to learn more about Burma with their own eyes and ears. There's nothing like immersing yourself in daily life in a new place to give you a sense of other people's lives and culture.

In the meantime you can travel in your imagination—and in your kitchen —using these recipes, photographs, and stories to transport you. The subtle hiss and delicate aroma of turmeric as it fizzes in hot oil will connect you to the people of Burma and to the mysteries and pleasures of their culture: the processions of monks as they collect food offerings at dawn; the colors and sounds of markets from Myitkyina to Hpa'an; the generosity of the noontime rice meal, with its enticing array of curries and condiments; the gleam of a golden pagoda on a hilltop near Mandalay; and much more that I hope will seduce you in the pages that follow.

A NOTE ON PRONUNCIATION AND PLACE-NAMES

In Burmese, the combination "ky" is pronounced "ch," and "gy" is pronounced like the soft "g" in the name George. The currency, written "kyat" in English, is thus pronounced "chat," and the sarong-like garment worn by men, spelled "longyi," is pronounced "lungee."

In 1989, the government —then a repressive military regime—decreed that the country's official name would no longer be Burma but Myanmar. The government said that "Burma" was a relic of colonial times. But in fact Burma is the only name that has ever been given to the whole country, because historically the name "Myanma" was used for only a small area, the central valleys where the dominant Bamar population lived. It's a name that excludes the huge outlying areas that make up the rest of the country, and it excludes the people (Shan, Kachin, etc.) who live there. Therefore, I use Burma in this book.

The government also changed the names of many places. In general I try to use the name that I think readers will find easier. For example, I use the more familiar Rangoon, Irrawaddy, and Moulmein rather than the replacement names Yangon, Ayeyarwady, and Mawlamyine.

For a list of place-names old and new, see page 340.

OPPOSITE: *A market vendor in Mandalay puts an offering into the bowl of an older nun.* OVERLEAF: *Two monks walk down the main street in Dawei in the early morning, before the shops are open, each with his begging bowl and umbrella.*

THE PLACE AND THE PEOPLE

AT 262,000 SQUARE MILES (678,000 SQUARE KILOMETERS)
Burma is 30 percent larger than its neighbor Thailand, and almost
exactly the size of the state of Texas. The population is about 60
million, compared with Thailand's 65 million and Vietnam's 85 million.

The Irrawaddy, Burma's longest and most important river, ranks
as one of the great rivers of Asia. It starts as a small trickle just north
of the border in Tibet and flows south through the center of Burma,
growing with water from its tributaries, until it reaches its broad
delta and the Andaman Sea, south of Rangoon. The Irrawaddy Valley
is where Burmese kings established their various capitals over the
centuries and where **Bamar** culture developed and flourished in all its
rich complexity (see Burma over Time, page 306). The Bamar people
make up nearly 70 percent of the population of Burma and dominate
the country both culturally and politically.

As the Irrawaddy flows south out of the mountains, its valley

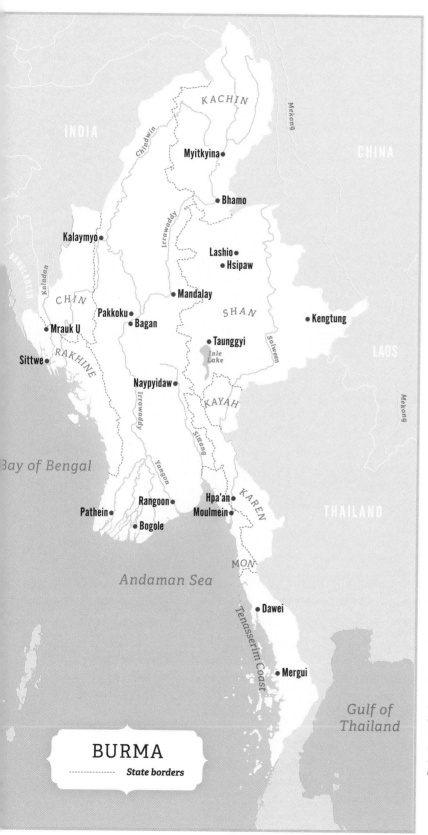

INDIA

BANGLADESH

CHINA

KACHIN

Chindwin

Mekong

Myitkyina•

•Bhamo

Kalaymyo•

Irrawaddy

Lashio•
•Hsipaw

CHIN

Kaladan

•Mandalay

SHAN

•Kengtung

Pakkoku•
Mrauk U•
•Bagan

•Taunggyi

Inle
Lake

Salween

LAOS

Mekong

Sittwe•

RAKHINE

Irrawaddy

Naypyidaw•

KAYAH

Sittang

Bay of Bengal

Yangon

Rangoon•

Hpa'an•
Moulmein•

KAREN

Pathein•

THAILAND

•Bogole

MON

Andaman Sea

Tenasserim Coast

•Dawei

•Mergui

Gulf of
Thailand

BURMA

------------- *State borders*

The majority of the population of
Burma is Bamar ("Burma" is derived
from the name of this ethnic group).
In the heart of the country (its large
cities, the central fertile valleys,
and the Irrawaddy Delta), Bamar is
the dominant culture. In the hills
and outlying areas, many other
(non-Bamar) peoples have lived for
centuries, each with a distinctive
culture and way of life. These include
the Shan, Mon, Kachin, Chin, and
Karen. All of them are citizens of
Burma (or Myanmar, as it is now
officially called).

widens. By the time it reaches Mandalay and the ancient capital of Bagan, the valley's fertile farmland yields peanuts that supply cooking oil to the whole country. Green vegetables grow everywhere, and so do subtropical fruits such as bananas and papayas. In the rich flatlands near Rangoon, the country's major city (and its capital until 2005), and south in the huge Irrawaddy Delta, where rainfall is much more abundant, rice is the main crop.

The mountains in the north and the ranges of hills that frame central Burma on the west and the east roughly mark the boundaries between the Bamar-majority heartland and the outlying non-Bamar regions of the nation.

The upper triangle of Burma, with its steep mountains and fast-flowing rivers, is Kachin State, which lies between India and China. It's a frontier area and its capital, Myitkyina (pronounced "*Meet*-chee-na"), reflects that: the population is predominantly **Kachin,** but there are also communities of Chinese and Shan, as well as people of South Asian descent living there.

The hilly neighboring state to the southwest is Chin State, which has borders with both India and Bangladesh. Its main river is the Chindwin, a huge tributary of the Irrawaddy. **Chin** people speak a number of related Tibeto-Burman languages and are renowned for their woven textiles.

South of Chin State and running along the west coast on the Bay of Bengal lies Rakhine State (formerly called Arakan), separated from central Burma by the Arakan Hills, a north-to-south range. Several wide rivers flow westward from these low mountains across the coastal plain to the sea. The **Rakhine** people speak a language closely related to Burmese.

To the east of central Burma and the Irrawaddy Valley rises the Shan Plateau, also known as the Shan hills (the latter is a more descriptive name, for the region consists of ranges of hills interrupted by river valleys, including the deep valley of the Salween River). It extends all the way east to the Mekong River (which marks the border with Laos). This is Shan State. The dominant people here are the **Shan** (the Burmese name for this ethnicity; in their own language, they are **Tai Yai**). Smaller populations of Chinese, Wa, Pa-o, Palaung, Intha, and others also live in Shan State. Another Tai people, the **Tai Koen,** live in the far eastern part of Shan State, in and around the old city kingdom of Kengtung.

Running south from the Shan Plateau, and parallel to Burma's border with Thailand, are ranges of beautiful limestone hills. This inland region is home to the **Karen** and the **Kayenni,** as well as other smaller populations, including the Palaung and the Pa-O. Hpa'an is the capital of Karen State (recently renamed Kayin State). (Rather confusingly, there is also a large population of Karen in the

In the morning in Mrauk U, there's a light mist as children walk to school and cattle are herded out to the edge of town to graze.

Bamar-majority Irrawaddy Delta, who moved there in colonial times.)

The Salween, another of the great rivers of Asia, flows south from China through eastern Burma—Shan, Kayah, and Karen States—until it reaches the coast at Moulmein, the capital of Mon State. The **Mon** are the first recorded inhabitants of the area around Rangoon and the coast south of there.

South of Moulmein is the Tenasserim coast. As mentioned earlier, Burma is shaped like a kite and the kite's narrow tail is the strip of land between the Andaman Sea and the limestone mountains that mark the Burmese-Thai border. The majority population in this region is Bamar, but there are also Mon as well as many Chinese who have been there for generations. The Moken, commonly called sea gypsies, live on their boats in and around the Mergui archipelago off the Burmese coast.

FLAVORS AND DISHES

COOKS ALL OVER BURMA WORK WITH LOCALLY GROWN
ingredients and generally prepare dishes from scratch. As a result,
flavors are fresh and food is seasonal. The basic pantry includes fried
shallots and shallot oil; dried red chiles, both whole and powdered;
turmeric; roasted chickpea flour; dried shrimp ground to a coarse
powder; and fermented shrimp paste, as well as fish sauce. Most
of these keep well, so they can be bought or prepared ahead and
stored in the cupboard. **Burma Basics** (see page 19) sets out the easy
fundamentals and techniques of the Burmese kitchen, in order to help
you get started.

Salads in Burma are spectacular, one of the glories of the cuisine.
They are made of raw or briefly cooked vegetables, or acidic fruits such
as green mango and pomelo, or cooked seafood or meat. Ingredients
are finely chopped or shredded, then dressed with flavorings and
carefully and thoroughly blended together. Lime juice, chopped roasted

*Asian shallots whole, peeled, and sliced; and garlic, with a bunch of fresh coriander behind. Shallots
are the essential basic flavoring in many Burmese dishes.*

peanuts, toasted chickpea flour, fried shallots, shallot oil, and fresh herbs, in enticing combinations, bring the salad ingredients to life.

Soups play a big role in Burma. Soup is an essential part of the central Burmese rice meal (see page 16), often a slightly tart clear broth that is a refreshing contrast to rich curries and is sipped throughout the meal. Outside central Burma soups often include meat and vegetables. Other soups are made of chickpeas or other legumes.

"Curry," the Anglo-colonial word that refers to dishes of meat or vegetables (or a combination) that are simmered in a sauce, is still used on English-language menus and in conversation in Burma. Central Burmese curries are generally made of meat, fish, or vegetables cooked in plenty of oil with simple flavorings: sliced shallots and turmeric, sometimes garlic, a little chile pepper (usually in powdered, dried form), and possibly ginger. Kachin and Shan curries use more fresh herbs. Most curries are mildly hot compared with those in neighboring Thailand.

Vegetables play a vital role in the Burmese kitchen. Main meals usually include a plate of raw or steamed vegetables, or a combination, to balance richer fare. One or more vegetable dishes, such as the curries and stir-fries in **Mostly Vegetables,** will also be served. Vegetable dishes are often flavored with a little meat, fish, or dried shrimp.

Although chicken and meat have a place at the table, apart from vegetables the most common dishes are fish- and seafood-based. Ocean fish are of course wonderfully fresh in coastal towns and villages, from Sittwe all the way south to Dawei (formerly called Tavoy), but for most Burmese, freshwater fish are the most appreciated. Dried shrimp and dried fish are staples, used as flavorings. In the **Fish and Seafood** chapter, you'll find recipes for crispy fried anchovies and a festive whole fish, as well as an array of fish curries. You'll also find fish in the **Salads** and **Noodles** chapters.

Shan meat dishes often include lots of vegetables (and, by the same token, Shan vegetable dishes may be flavored with a little meat), while central Burmese chicken and meat curries don't include many vegetables. Generally in a rice meal there will be only one or two meat dishes among many others, so that the proportion of meat served is not high. Although some Buddhists in Burma avoid beef, and others steer clear of pork, both meats are part of the cook's general repertoire. The **Chicken** chapter features several takes on chicken curry and fried chicken, as well as a succulent steamed Kachin chicken curry. In the **Beef and Pork** chapter, you'll find mouthwatering central Burmese and Shan curries, an unusual Kachin spiced pounded beef, and Shan recipes for meatballs and for spiced jerky.

Whenever outsiders eat Burmese food, the wide array of condiments and sauces that are on the table is a source of wonder and pleasure. Some are punchy with chile and garlic, others milder; some are tart with tamarind, others sweeter. **Condiments and Sauces** presents many options that can add pizzazz to any dish, along with palate-freshening chutneys, which often accompany a simple home-cooked meal.

The literal translation of the Burmese words for "to eat"—*thamin sa*—is "to eat rice." In other words, rice is embedded in daily life (see Rice Meals). In most of the country, the staple rice is similar to Thai jasmine, a slightly clinging tender white rice. The number one rice in Burma is called *nyi nyi thaw*. In the eastern part of Shan State sticky rice is the staple for the Tai Koen people. **Mostly Rice** includes recipes for breakfast favorites, including Fried Rice with Shallots and an oven-baked tender flatbread, as well as two fascinating versions of rice crepe.

Noodles are another daily essential, often served in a meat or fish broth and accompanied by a choice of condiments. *Mohinga* is a Burmese specialty, a cross between soup and stew made with fine rice noodles; I provide two versions, but there are many regional variations of this touchstone dish. Egg noodles, elastic and a little chewy, are the base of *ohn-no khaut swe*, a much-loved noodle dish dressed with a coconut sauce. From the Tenasserim coast comes a satisfying rice noodle–seafood stir-fry.

Sweet Treats has an assortment of delicious, inventive dishes, from fried bananas to semolina cake. In Burma they are usually eaten between meals, as a sweet snack with tea or coffee. They also work beautifully as a dessert at a Western table.

A NOTE ON COOKING TOOLS

There's no need for any special equipment to cook dishes from Burma. Although you would find a stone mortar and pestle useful, and a pleasure (see "Tools," page 209), it's not necessary: a food processor or a knife works fine. The food processor is great for grinding dried shrimp to a powder, and for chopping roasted peanuts. I often use a spider, a mesh basket that's like a small colander with a long handle (see photograph, page 301), to lift food out of hot oil, but you can also use a slotted spoon or tongs. A wok is ideal for stir-frying; I also use mine for deep-frying because its size makes it nice and stable on the burner. You can get by with a large heavy skillet and a heavy pot for recipes that ask you to stir-fry or to slow-cook. And you can deep-fry in a deep-fryer or a wide heavy pot.

For cooking plain rice, I use a straight-sided pot with a tight-fitting lid; you can also use a rice cooker. Sticky (glutinous) rice is cooked in a steamer.

It's helpful to have a cleaver for chopping up chicken and fish, but you can ask your butcher or fishmonger to do it for you. Chicken shears are another option for cutting up whole birds.

BURMESE FOOD IN A WESTERN CONTEXT

I'm assuming that as you embark on making dishes from Burma, you'll be incorporating them into your cooking gradually. I've made serving portions larger than they would be in a multidish Burmese rice meal, where so many dishes come to the table at once. The serving suggestions in the recipes are open-ended, rather than tied to a Burmese style of meal planning. For example, many of the salads and vegetables fit happily into a Western meal, and a lot of the main dishes can be served with Mediterranean or other non-Burmese sides.

Here are some recipes for different occasions for you to choose from. Those who are inspired to make a complete rice meal should see page 16.

WEEKNIGHT SUPPER COMBOS
Perfumed Coconut Rice
   WITH Broccoli Rabe with a Hint of Pork
Lemongrass-Ginger Sliders
   WITH Long-Bean Salad with
   Roasted Peanuts
Fish with Tart Greens
   WITH Eggplant Delight
Kachin Rice Powder Soup with Chicken and
   Ginger WITH Traveler's Eggplant Curry
Village Boys' Chicken
   WITH Everyday Cabbage-Shallot
   Refresher
Saucy Spiced Meat and Potatoes
   WITH Okra-Shallot Stir-Fry

FOR LOVERS OF INTENSE FLAVORS
Punchy-Crunchy Ginger Salad
Tart-Sweet Chile-Garlic Sauce
Sour-Plum Chutney with Chile Oil
Chile-Oil Fish

FOR THOSE WHO LIKE MILD
Silky Shan Soup
Eggplant Delight
Fried Rice with Shallots
Perfumed Coconut Rice
Noodles with Peanut-Rice Sauce,
   WITH Raw and Cooked Vegetable Plate
Seafood Noodle Stir-Fry
Fluffy Lemongrass Fish
Pale Yellow Shan Tofu
Deep-Fried Chayote Fingers

FOR MEAT LOVERS
Curried Chicken Livers
Sweet-Tart Pork Belly Stew
Pork Strips with Star Anise
Spice-Rubbed Jerky
Lemongrass-Ginger Sliders
Kachin Pounded Beef with Herbs

FOR VEGETARIANS
Shan Tofu Salad
Tamarind-Pumpkin Curry
Noodles with Peanut-Rice Sauce
Perfumed Coconut Rice
Silky Shan Soup
Paneer in Tomato Sauce
Golden Egg Curry
Chickpea Soup with Lemongrass and Ginger

BREAKFAST AND BRUNCH COMBOS
Easy Coriander-Tomato Omelet
   WITH Tender Greens Salad with Crispy
   Fried Shallots
Golden Egg Curry WITH plain rice
   AND Shallot Chutney with Cucumber
Breakfast Rice and Peas
   WITH a fried egg on top
   AND Sour-Plum Chutney with Chile Oil
Peanut and Rice Porridge
   WITH Intensely Green Spinach and
   Tomato Salad with Peanuts AND Fresh
   Red Chile Chutney
Mandalay Noodles with Chicken Curry,
   broth, and accompaniments
West Coast Mohinga

The market in Hpa'an, in Karen State, is one of the most colorful in Burma, with women in painted and colored hats and a huge array of produce as well as flowers and prepared foods.

rice meals

Most people in Burma have at least one daily meal centered around rice. Usually it's the main meal of the day, eaten at noon. The diversity of flavors and textures in a rice meal is wonderful. Even if I order only one curry at a little bus-stand restaurant it will come with not only rice, but also an array of condiments and sides, from a clear soup to fresh and steamed vegetables to chile pastes and more. They're taken for granted—like salt and pepper in North America—but they're a much bigger part of the meal, and more interesting.

The best way to eat a rice meal is with other people, whether at home or at a café or restaurant. It's more fun, of course, but also if you're eating out, with more people to share you can order a wider variety of dishes. All the dishes, from salads and meat curries to fried fish and soup, come at once, and they can then be eaten in any order or any combination, with the rice. Each person gets a bowl of clear soup, which can be sipped occasionally, for a change of texture and as a mild thirst quencher. You might take a spoonful of rice with meat curry, and then your next taste might be a bite of salad, followed by a spoonful of soup.

And by the way, people in Burma traditionally eat with their hands, but many in the cities now eat with a fork and spoon, as they do in Thailand, using the fork in the left hand to push food onto the spoon. Chopsticks are used only for eating noodles.

RICE MEAL SUGGESTIONS

If you want to dive in and assemble a more traditional rice meal feast for friends, here are some ideas for going about it. (Remember that in a rice meal a beef curry or other main dish will feed more people than if it is served Western style, because there are so many side dishes on the table.)

- Start by picking your "main dishes" (pick 3 if you're serving 4 to 6, 4 or 5 for a larger group): perhaps a spicy beef dish, a well-sauced fish or chicken curry, and a stir-fried vegetable, as well as a vegetable curry. Try to balance textures and flavors, the crisp with the tender, the well-sauced with the dry, the hot with the mild.

- Then consider what other flavors and textures you want, and use that to guide you in picking one or two salads and several condiments.

- Finally, choose a soup and the vegetables you want to include on a plate of steamed and raw vegetables.

- Rather than making dessert, put out fresh fruit and a bowl of palm sugar chopped into bite-sized pieces.

- For drinks, have pale clear tea for guests to sip as they eat. Beer is a good accompaniment to these strong flavors—a pale ale, for example. And you can also offer rum or blended whiskey with plenty of soda water, served over lots of ice. Serve black tea, green tea, or milk tea with the fruit and sweet.

Portrait of a rice meal: When I was in Bagan I ate almost every day under a big tree by the old city gate in Old Bagan. The choices at this open-air "restaurant" were astonishing; the dishes here include a tender beef curry, a vegetable plate (okra, carrots, eggplant, and more), simmered dal-like beans, a tangy clear soup with floating greens; and balachaung (crispy shallot and dried shrimp relish; see page 210).

BURMA BASICS

IF YOU HAVE A FEW PANTRY BASICS ON HAND, almost all the recipes in this book will be very easy, even the first time you make them. To get comfortable with Burmese food, start by going shopping. Most of the ingredients will be familiar: you can find all of them in Southeast Asian groceries and most in large supermarkets too.

The pantry list is not long. There are bottled or preserved ingredients—peanut oil, dried red chiles, turmeric powder, dried shrimp, fish sauce, shrimp paste, and tamarind pulp—and long-keeping perishables such as limes, shallots, garlic, and ginger.

Apart from the pantry staples, there are a few prepared ingredients that I make ahead and keep in glass jars, handy for whenever they're needed. They are used in all kinds of Burmese dishes, but I also rely on them when cooking foods from other places.

(The one recipe in this chapter that is more complicated is for Soybean Disks, for which miso paste is a good substitute.)

Recipes for all the Burma Basics follow. Please don't be intimidated:

you can put together your basic cook's pantry in an hour—that's right, you can make all these recipes that quickly. Then leap right into the Salads chapter, or whatever else catches your eye, and cook with ease.

I also like to keep a jar of Tart-Sweet Chile-Garlic Sauce on hand. It's my favorite everyday condiment, so it's here too. You'll find recipes for many more condiments in Condiments and Sauces (page 199).

THE BUILDING BLOCKS

Turmeric

Cooks in Burma use ground turmeric, a bright yellow-orange powder, in many dishes. They add it in small quantities to the oil at the start of cooking. It fizzes a little as the oil heats, and then once it's dissolved, in go the shallots and other ingredients.

Turmeric is an ancient ingredient from India, one long believed to have powerful medicinal qualities. It's antibacterial (so it's often rubbed on meat or fish before cooking), antiflatulent (it's usually added to legumes in South Asian cooking), and anti-inflammatory. Now the West is discovering the truth of those beliefs: turmeric is being talked of as an "anti-aging" food because of its anti-inflammatory properties.

Thus adding a pinch of it to cooking oil not only makes culinary sense but is also a healthy practice. This isn't surprising, for like cooks from India to China, cooks in Burma are very aware of health when they cook. It's instinctive wisdom. And it starts with a pinch of turmeric.

Shallots

Shallots are fundamental to Burmese cooking. They're thinly sliced and added to salads, and they form part of the flavor base in curries. Fried, they give sweetness and crisp texture to dishes of all kinds, from salads and condiments to street snacks. (Fried shallots are also an irresistible snack on their own.) Shallot oil—peanut oil that is flavored by the frying shallots—is a wonderful kitchen staple.

Asian shallots are smaller than European ones, with warm reddish brown skin. Beneath the skin, they're pale purple (see photograph, page 11). Preparing them is easy: Cut off both ends and discard, then slice lengthwise in half. It's easier to pull off the outer skin once they are halved. To slice them, lay the flat side on the cutting board and slice crosswise very thin to give you attractive half-moon-shaped slices.

Peanut Oil and Sesame Oil

Peanuts, or groundnuts as they are called by most English-speaking Burmese, thrive in hot, dry climates, which makes them an ideal crop in the central area around Mandalay and Bagan. Sesame is the other major oil crop grown in Burma. The oil is pressed out of the seeds, but there's no roasting involved; it is raw sesame oil, pale yellow, not dark like the roasted sesame oil used as a flavoring in some Japanese and Chinese cooking. Both peanut oil and sesame oil are stable at high temperatures and so are good for frying. In this book I call for peanut oil because it is more widely available but if you prefer, substitute unroasted sesame oil. Store peanut oil and sesame oil in a cool, dark place.

After using oil for deep-frying, I strain it and refrigerate it in a clearly labeled jar. If the oil was used to fry neutral ingredients (vegetables, for example), it can be reused for stir-frying. Once the oil darkens or if it has a strong odor, discard it.

OVERLEAF: *Having jars of Burma basics made and ready to be used in recipes gives me a rich, "my cupboard is full" feeling and makes cooking food from Burma very easy. From left: Fried Shallots, Shallot Oil, Toasted Chickpea Flour, and two versions of Red Chile Oil—one strained and, behind it, one with the chile residue still in the oil.*

fried shallots and shallot oil

MAKES A GENEROUS ¾ CUP
FLAVORED OIL AND ABOUT
1¼ CUPS FRIED SHALLOTS

*Photographs on
pages 22–23 and 227*

Here you get two pantry staples in one: crispy fried shallots and delicious shallot oil. Drizzle shallot oil on salads or freshly cooked greens, or onto soups to finish them. You can fry up shallots each time you need them, but I prefer to make a large batch so they're around when I need a handful to flavor a salad.

The trick with fried shallots is to cook them slowly, so they give off their moisture and get an even golden brown without any scorched or blackened patches. Once they're removed from the oil and left to cool, they crisp up.

1 cup peanut oil
2 cups (about ½ pound) thinly sliced Asian or
**   European shallots**

Place a wide heavy skillet or a large stable wok over medium-high heat and add the oil. Toss in a slice of shallot. As the oil heats, it will rise to the surface, sizzling lightly. When it's reached the surface, add the rest of the shallots, carefully, so you don't splash yourself with the oil, and lower the heat to medium. (The shallots may seem crowded, but they'll shrink as they cook.) Stir gently and frequently with a long-handled wooden spoon or a spider. The shallots will bubble as they give off their moisture. If they start to brown early, in the first 5 minutes, lower the heat a little more. After about 10 minutes, they should start to color. Continue to cook, stirring occasionally to prevent them from sticking to the pan or to each other, until they have turned a golden brown, another 3 minutes or so.

Line a plate with paper towels. Use tongs or a spider to lift a clump of fried shallots out of the oil, pausing for a moment to shake off excess oil into the pan, then place on the paper towel. Turn off the heat, transfer the remaining shallots to the plate, and blot gently with another paper towel. Separate any clumps and toss them a little, then let them air-dry 5 to 10 minutes, so they crisp up and cool. (If your kitchen is very hot and humid, they may not crisp up; don't worry, the flavor will still be there.)

Transfer the shallots to a clean, dry, widemouthed glass jar. Once they have cooled completely, seal tightly. Transfer the oil to another clean dry jar, using all but the very last of it, which will have some stray pieces of shallot debris. (You can set that oil aside for stir-frying.) Once the oil has cooled completely, cover tightly and store in a cool dark place.

fried garlic and garlic oil

MAKES ABOUT ¼ CUP FRIED
GARLIC AND ⅓ CUP GARLIC OIL

You can use a similar technique to make garlic oil, but slice the garlic thicker (a scant ¼ inch), rather than into thin slices, since it cooks much more quickly than shallots. Heat ½ cup peanut oil over medium-high heat, add ⅓ cup or so sliced garlic, and fry over medium heat until just golden, about 5 minutes. Lift out the garlic and set aside to crisp up. Store the oil as above. Fried garlic does not keep as well as fried shallots; refrigerate and use within 5 days.

red chile oil

MAKES ABOUT 1 CUP

*Photographs on
pages 22–23 and 29*

Chile oil is quick to make and keeps well at room temperature. You'll be happy to have it on hand to add a dash of heat and color to many dishes. It can also go on the table as a condiment, with a small spoon so guests can scoop out a little to drizzle on their soup or noodles or whatever. Be sure to warn them that it's very hot.

**1 cup packed dried red chiles, soaked in
lukewarm water for 20 minutes**
1 cup peanut oil

Drain the chiles and remove and discard the stems. Put the chiles in a food processor and process to a coarse paste.

Pour the oil into a nonreactive pan and set over medium heat. Add the chile paste and bring to a bubbling boil, then remove from the heat and let stand until cooled to room temperature.

You can store the oil with the chiles in it, but in Burma the oil often is served on its own. For clear oil, drain the oil through a sieve into a clean, dry glass jar and seal with the lid. Store away from heat and light. You can keep the chiles in another glass jar for a spicy condiment, or discard them.

AT MARKETS ALL OVER BURMA there are piles of chiles on offer, and women selling powders in many shades of red. These powders, made of dried red chiles that have been ground, come in many forms and qualities, so when recipes call for powdered dried red chile, the cook in Burma has many choices.

A friend of a friend in Rangoon, very particular about her dried chile powders, travels all the way to Bagan, a day's drive north of the city, to buy them. One of her chile powders is a brilliant, clear orange-red. It's fine textured, with no seeds, and is made from red chiles that have been sun dried, then trimmed of their stems, emptied of seeds, and finely ground. The taste is hot, with no smokiness. Another of her powdered dried chile options is a darker brown-red. This one is made from chiles that have been dried over a fire, and it has a lovely smoky aroma and taste.

If you don't like much heat, cut back on quantities called for and/or use a dried red chile powder that is milder. Remember that you are free to choose the amount and kind of chiles that you prefer, since there is no hard-and-fast rule. Another friend in Burma dislikes chile heat, so she substitutes sweet paprika for dried red chile powder in most of her cooking and has the color without the heat.

CLOCKWISE FROM TOP: Fresh red chiles for sale at the market in Hsipaw; these are hotter than cayennes, like a version of Thai bird chiles. Mild green chilies in Pathein market. Dried red cayenne chilies and sweeter dried round red chilies, as well as an assortment of dried red chili powders.

red chile powder

MAKES ABOUT ½ CUP Cooks in Burma tend to have a light hand with chiles, leaving guests to add more heat at the table by adding condiments such as chile oil, chile powder, and various sauces.

This powder packs a punch, so use only small amounts of it in recipes. The dried red chiles are dry-roasted for a few minutes in a skillet or over low heat on a grill. It's important to not let them scorch, which would make them bitter. I grind mine with the seeds, using a food processor; you can also remove the seeds before you grind the chiles. The with-seeds version has more heat and is coarser looking.

It's worth making a large batch of this.

2 cups loosely packed dried red chiles

Place a large cast-iron or other heavy skillet over medium-high heat. When it is hot, lower the heat to medium and add the chiles. Keep moving them around in the pan to help them roast evenly and to prevent charred spots. After about 3 minutes, they will be softened, aromatic, and a little darkened. *Alternatively,* grill the chiles briefly on a charcoal grill over a low flame, turning them frequently to prevent scorching, until softened and aromatic. Remove from the pan or grill and set aside to cool for 10 minutes.

Break off the stem ends of the chiles and discard. You can empty out and discard the seeds or keep them for a hotter powder. Using a food processor, or working in batches in a spice grinder or clean coffee grinder, grind the chiles to a powder (be careful not to inhale it). Store in a clean, dry jar.

Chile variations (clockwise from the bottom): large dried red cayenne chiles, lightly roasted; finely ground chile powder and next to it, chile oil; coarse dried red chile powder including seeds, in a mortar; and a heap of regular dried red chiles.

dried shrimp powder

MAKES ABOUT 1½ LOOSELY PACKED CUPS

Dried shrimp are an important source of flavor as well as protein through most of Southeast Asia. In Burma they are often used powdered. The soft powder gives a subtle depth of flavor and also thickens sauces.

Look for largish dried shrimp, more than ½ inch long if possible, and the darker-colored (more red than pale pink or beige), the better. Try to get shrimp that are a little soft rather than completely hard. The easiest way to grind them is in a food processor (traditionally, they are pounded in a mortar).

1 cup or more good-quality dried shrimp (see the headnote)

Place the shrimp in a bowl with water to just cover and set aside to soak for 10 minutes (20 minutes if the shrimp are very hard and dry). Drain and pat dry.

Transfer to a food processor and process until reduced to a slightly uneven, fluffy powder, from 1 to 3 minutes, depending on the toughness of the shrimp. Pause and wipe down the sides of the bowl occasionally if necessary. Store in a glass jar.

A display of dried shrimp for sale at the Yegyaw Market in Rangoon, with the vendor putting weights on the scale.

THE JAPANESE WORD *UMAMI* refers to a category of flavor, a fifth taste, after salt, sweet, sour, and bitter. It's the taste that is "meatiness," which we associate with ripe tomatoes, deep-flavored mushrooms, soup stocks, grilled meats, and more. English speakers have adopted the word, since there is no exact English-language equivalent.

In the cooking of Burma there are a lot of "umami ingredients," whose major role is giving a dish meaty depth of flavor. They include fish sauce, shrimp paste, fermented soybeans and soybean disks, fermented fish, dried shrimp, soy sauce, and oyster sauce (all these ingredients are described in the Glossary), as well as meat and fish. Burmese cooks also use MSG for meatiness, especially in soups; I usually substitute fish sauce for MSG. When I ask cooks in Burma what they or their mothers did before the arrival of MSG, they tell me that there was more use of fish stocks, and sometimes broths from meat bones, to give depth of flavor.

Substitution of one umami ingredient for another is always possible: If you have a recipe that calls for fermented soybeans, for example, and you don't have them available, or a recipe that calls for shrimp paste and you don't like the taste of it, you can substitute another umami ingredient, keeping in mind that the seasoning may have to be adjusted.

The issue of substitution also comes up if you are adapting recipes for vegetarians or vegans. Instead of fish sauce, use salt (1 teaspoon salt is approximately equal in saltiness to 1 tablespoon fish sauce); instead of Dried Shrimp Powder (opposite), use Toasted Chickpea Flour (page 32) for its thickening effect and agreeable taste, and add a little soy sauce or miso paste. Adding dried mushrooms to a dish also increases depth of flavor just as shrimp paste and fish sauce do. Best of all, follow the Shan approach to umami and use fermented soybeans in place of shrimp paste and other fermented or preserved fish ingredients. The Shan use *tua nao*—soybean disks—but in North America, brown miso paste (see Glossary) is more readily available. If you want to make your own Soybean Disks, see page 40.

toasted chickpea flour

MAKES 2 CUPS For this distinctively Burmese pantry staple, which is very easy to make and store, chickpea flour is simply lightly toasted in a skillet. Chickpea flour is made from ground dried chickpeas (garbanzos) and contains no gluten (see the Glossary for more). The flour is available in South Asian groceries (the common name for it in India is *besan*), some health food stores, and specialty stores. Keep it in a well-sealed bag in a cool place, as you would any flour.

Make this in any quantity you wish; I usually make 2 cups at a time. Use in salads to add a layer of flavor and texture, and also to thicken sauces and soups, as directed.

2 cups chickpea flour

Place a cast-iron or other heavy skillet over medium-high heat, add the flour, and use a wooden spoon to stir it frequently as it heats and starts to toast. Lower the heat to medium if it starts to brown quickly, and keep stirring to expose all the flour to the heat. After about 6 or 7 minutes, it will start to change color. Lower the heat a little and continue to stir as it gets a little more color, then remove from the heat and continue to stir for another minute as the pan starts to cool. The whole process takes about 10 to 12 minutes.

Transfer to a wide bowl and let cool to room temperature. Store in a clean, dry glass jar, well sealed.

toasted sesame seeds

Toasting sesame seeds is like roasting peanuts, except that the process is very quick. Make sure your sesame seeds are fresh; taste them before you use them. Set a cast-iron or other heavy skillet over medium heat. Add the sesame seeds and let them heat, shaking the skillet from time to time to ensure that they aren't scorching; or use a wooden spoon to stir them. After a few minutes, you will start to smell their lovely aroma; keep stirring so they don't scorch. Cook for another minute or two, until they are lightly touched with gold. Transfer to a wide bowl and let cool completely. Store, once completely cooled, in a clean, dry glass jar.

At the top, whole ginger and a couple of slices; in the middle, a bowl of dried shrimp sitting in a bowl of shelled peanuts without their skins; at the bottom, turmeric rhizomes, showing their brilliant orange insides, and a bowl of Toasted Chickpea Flour.

chopped roasted peanuts

MAKES A SCANT 1 CUP These are handy to have when you are making Burmese salads, so it's worth making a cupful or more at a time and storing them in a jar. Buy raw peanuts (in their papery skins or not, it doesn't matter)—you'll find them in Asian groceries and health food stores.

1 cup raw peanuts, with or without their papery skins

Place a cast-iron or other heavy skillet over medium heat, add the peanuts, and cook, stirring them frequently with a wooden spoon or spatula to prevent burning. Adjust the heat if necessary so they toast and change color gradually, in patches; as they heat up, the skins, if still on, will separate from the peanuts. When they have firmed up a little and are dotted with color, remove from the heat, but keep stirring for another minute or so.

If using skin-on nuts, carry the skillet over to a sink or a garbage can and blow over it gently to blow away the loose skins. Rub the nuts between your palms to loosen the remaining skins and blow again; don't worry if there are still some skins on your peanuts. Pick out and discard any nuts that are scorched and blackened.

Transfer the nuts to a wide bowl and set aside for 10 minutes or more to cool and firm up.

Once the peanuts are cool, place them in a food processor and process in short, sharp pulses, stopping after three or four pulses, before the nuts are too finely ground. You want a mix of coarsely chopped nuts and some fine powder. *Alternatively*, place the nuts in a large stone or terra-cotta mortar and pound with the pestle to crush them into smaller pieces. Use a spoon to move the nuts around occasionally; you don't want to pound them into a paste, just to break them into small chips.

Transfer the chopped nuts to a clean, dry jar; do not seal until they have cooled completely. Store in the refrigerator.

tart-sweet chile-garlic sauce [NGA YOKE THEE ACHIN]

MAKES ABOUT 1¾ CUPS

A standard hot sauce on tables in Burma, this condiment for every occasion is hot, tart with vinegar, and a little sweet. If possible, make it at least a day before you first want to serve it, because when you make it the sauce will seem watery, but it thickens and the flavors blend after a day.

I reach for this sauce whenever I am eating rice or noodles, and I drizzle it over fried eggs. It's also a great complement to grilled meat and deep-fried snacks. Once you have a stash of it in your refrigerator, you'll never want to bother with store-bought Sriracha or other commercial hot sauces again.

1 cup packed dried red chiles
¾ cup water
¼ cup coarsely chopped garlic
¼ cup fish sauce

¼ cup sugar
¾ cup rice vinegar, or substitute apple cider vinegar

Break the chiles in half, break off the stems, and empty out; if you wish, discard some or all of the seeds. Place the chile pieces in a small pot with the water. If your garlic is somewhat dried out and harsh-tasting (in the winter months), add it too. Bring to a boil, cover, reduce the heat, and simmer for 3 to 5 minutes, until the chiles are softened and have swelled up a little. If your garlic is young and fresh, add it for the last minute of cooking.

Combine the chiles and garlic with their liquid, the fish sauce, and sugar in a food processor, and process or grind to a coarse paste; scrape down the sides of the processor bowl as necessary with a rubber spatula. Add the vinegar and process again.

Transfer to a clean, dry glass jar and store in the refrigerator, preferably for at least a day before using. It will keep in the refrigerator for several weeks.

In the large bowl, Tart-Sweet Chile-Garlic Sauce; in the jar, Fresh Red Chile Chutney (page 203).

FERMENTED SOYBEAN PASTE AND DISKS

If you are cooking for vegetarians or are interested in the repertoire of fermented flavorings, then you'll want to explore these soybean disks.

The Shan pantry staple called *tua nao*, made of fermented soybeans, is sold in markets in northern Burma and northern Thailand, wherever there are Shan people. *Tua nao* are flat, thin, brown disks (friends in Thailand have heard them called "*tua nao* CDs"), sold in stacks of three, five, or ten.

Most people rely on cottage or village *tua nao* makers for their supply, but the process of making the fermented beans is not complicated—it just takes time. Soybeans are cooked in plenty of water, allowed to ferment for several days, and ground to a smooth paste. The fresh paste can be used as a flavor base in stir-fried or simmered dishes, or grilled or steamed and served as a topping for rice. But it doesn't keep long without refrigeration, so generations ago the Shan figured out that the best way to preserve fermented soybeans was to dry them.

The paste is flattened into thin disks, which are placed on racks and air-dried for two or three days. Both the disks and the fermented soybean paste are sometimes called "Shan *ngapi*" by people in Burma; they give a depth of flavor (see "Umami," page 31) to all kinds of dishes, just as *ngapi* (shrimp paste) does.

Although the fermenting bacteria are different, *tua nao* paste is a close cousin of Japanese miso, which can be used as a substitute. It has a similar fermented salty taste, but its flavor is much stronger, so substitute 1 teaspoon miso for 1 tablespoon *tua nao* paste; fermented soybeans, available from Chinese groceries, are another possible substitute.

I'd seen *tua nao* disks for years and written about them in *Hot Sour Salty Sweet*, but it was only a few years ago that I learned how to make them. It's a bit of a commitment, since you have to let the cooked beans ferment for several days, and rolling out the paste takes patience. Nevertheless, once you have a stack of flavor disks, it all feels worth the effort. And doing it gives an intimate sense of what it's like to create your own flavorings for yourself.

The basic recipe is for plain *tua nao* disks. You can also add flavorings (ginger, lemongrass, sesame seeds, wild lime leaves, dried chiles) to your paste or your disks (see page 40).

fermented soybean paste

MAKES ABOUT 3 CUPS The *tua nao* makers I know all let their cooked beans ferment in a rice sack, woven bamboo, or straw basket, so I use a basket. I assume it helps with fermentation. I have also left them in a little of their cooking water in a pot, and they fermented just fine.

½ pound (scant 1½ cups) organic soybeans, well washed

Spring water
About 2 teaspoons salt

Place the beans in a large pot, add water to cover by about 3 inches, and bring to a boil. Lower the heat to maintain a gentle boil and cook, half-covered, until the beans are completely softened, about 3 hours. Remove from the heat, drain, and using a slotted spoon, transfer to a basket. Let stand, loosely covered in a basket topped with a cotton cloth, in a warm place (but not in direct sunlight) to ferment for 2½ to 3 days.

When you smell an agreeable, slightly sweet fermented odor, you'll know you're there. (If it smells bad or you see mold, discard the beans. I haven't had this experience, but Mother Nature is sometimes fickle!)

You will have about 5 cups cooked beans. Working in batches, grind the beans to a smooth, thick paste in a food processor or a mortar. Add a little water as you grind the beans if you need to: I find I need to add a couple of tablespoons into the beans when using the processor. Transfer the paste to a large bowl.

Stir in the salt, allowing about ½ teaspoon salt per cup of paste; taste and add a little more salt if you wish. The paste will keep in the refrigerator, sealed in a glass jar, for about a week. Use it in cooking as a flavoring in place of shrimp paste; do not eat it raw.

soybean disks

You'll need several heavy-duty sheets of plastic or flat plastic bags, such as Ziploc bags (as you would for rolling out corn tortillas), or else damp cheesecloth, as well as a large fine-mesh metal rack or a woven bamboo mat, or even a flat basket, for air-drying the disks.

These instructions produce disks that are about 3 inches in diameter, smaller than those sold in most markets, and therefore easier to shape and handle. Once you are comfortable with the process, you may want to work with a scant 2 tablespoons per disk and pat the paste out to a 4½-inch disk (which will dry to a disk just under 4 inches across).

Set the rack or mat for drying near your work surface. See the note about flavorings below and prepare any flavorings that you wish to try. Using a spoon, scoop up 1 packed tablespoon of the paste and turn it out onto one of the plastic sheets or bags. Press it lightly in the center with your lightly moistened fingertips to flatten it a little more. Lay another plastic sheet or bag on the flattened paste and tap it lightly to encourage it to spread out and thin. Go on tap-tapping until you have a thin disk about 3 inches in diameter.

Holding the disk in the palm of one hand, delicately, and without rushing, peel off the top plastic. Gently flip the exposed surface of the disk onto the rack and peel off the second plastic with great care. Repeat with the remaining paste.

Place the rack in the sun to dry; cover it loosely with a cotton cloth at night, or bring indoors. Let the disks dry until they are completely dry and light; timing will depend on the thickness of the disks and the drying situation. The disks will shrink as they dry and may crack a little. *Alternatively*, if you live in a damp climate, you may need to air-dry these on a fine-mesh metal rack in a 150°F oven.

Store stacked in a cool, dry place; a cookie tin is a good option. They should keep indefinitely.

NOTE ON FLAVOR OPTIONS: *You can add flavorings to the soybean paste or disks. Options include dried red chiles, ground in a mortar or grinder; fresh wild lime leaves, finely sliced crosswise and then minced (see Glossary); sesame seeds; minced ginger or galangal (see Glossary); or a combination. Start by flavoring the paste disk by disk, to explore which combinations you prefer. Allow a scant ½ teaspoon flavorings per disk, and mix them in well before you start shaping it.*

In a basket at Hsipaw market, soybean disks (tua nao) sit next to some mint sprigs.

COOKING WITH TUA NAO: *The disks can be used as a flavor base for curries and soups (pounded to a powder and combined with aromatics to make a flavor paste that is cooked in oil), or they can be lightly toasted (over a flame or in a dry heavy skillet), then pounded to a powder. Tua nao powder is an essential flavoring in a number of salads (see Chinese Kale with Pork Cracklings, page 54) and vegetable dishes (Simmered Cabbage, Shan Style, page 116); it gives a nutty toasted undernote. The moist soybean paste can be fried in oil as part of a flavor base in curries and stir-fries. It can also be wrapped in a banana leaf or in foil, grilled or steamed, then used as a condiment for rice.*

SALADS

SALADS ARE ONE OF THE BEST ENTRY POINTS into Burmese cuisine. Their special quality is the balance of flavors and textures between tart and sweet, crunchy and tender, fresh and cooked. There are no heavy-handed dressings here, just an enticing lightness of touch. The word for "salad" in Burmese is *thoke*, meaning "mixed or blended by hand."

Burmese cooks are incredibly inventive; they can transform almost any ingredient into a salad, from banana flowers and green mango to poached fish. All it takes is the addition of flavorings from Burma Basics (pages 19–41), such as roasted peanuts, fried shallots, and toasted chickpea flour, as well as lime juice and seasoning. Vegetable-based salads include Intensely Green Spinach and Tomato Salad with Peanuts (page 44), Long-Bean Salad with Roasted Peanuts (page 50), and Roasted Eggplant Salad (page 56). Then there are salads made of shrimp (see page 68), Shan tofu (see page 51), grapefruit (see page 45), and more, each one distinctive.

intensely green spinach and tomato salad with peanuts

SERVES 3 OR 4

Photograph on pages 46–47

This is an attractive salad for a summer's day, the tomato brilliant against the rich green of the cooked spinach. Although it is dressed with both powdered dried shrimp and fish sauce, there is no fishiness to it, just a pleasing depth of flavor. The fried shallots give a hint of sweetness.

¾ pound spinach, trimmed of coarse stems
1 medium to large ripe tomato, cut into ½-inch dice (about 1 cup)
1 tablespoon Dried Shrimp Powder (page 30)
2 tablespoons Chopped Roasted Peanuts (page 35)

1 tablespoon Fried Shallots (page 24)
1 tablespoon Shallot Oil (page 24)
1½ teaspoons fish sauce
½ teaspoon salt, or to taste
¼ teaspoon Red Chile Powder (page 28), or a pinch of cayenne, or more to taste

Wash the spinach thoroughly in several changes of water. Place in a skillet or wide heavy pot over medium-high heat, cover tightly, and cook until the spinach is wilted and just tender, about 3 minutes. Remove from the heat, drain, pressing out as much water as possible, and set aside to cool. (You will have about 2 cups cooked spinach.)

When ready to proceed, coarsely chop the spinach and place in a shallow serving bowl. Add the chopped tomato, dried shrimp powder, roasted peanuts, and fried shallots, then add the shallot oil, fish sauce, salt, and chile powder or cayenne. Toss lightly to mix.

succulent grapefruit (or pomelo) salad

SERVES 4

Photographs on pages 46–47 and 164–65

A real triumph, this fresh-tasting salad is another instance of a Burmese dish that is greater than the sum of its parts. Pomelos are much larger than grapefruits, with thick skins and less juicy pulp; look for them at Asian and other produce markets. (Another version of this salad uses citrons.)

In Burma, pomelos (and citrons) are much more common than grapefruits. In North America, the reverse is true, so the easiest way to make this is with ripe grapefruit; pink ones make an especially beautiful salad. Serve as a refreshing foil to rich meat dishes.

2 medium grapefruits or 1 small pomelo
Scant ¼ cup thinly sliced shallots, soaked in cold water for 10 minutes and drained
1 teaspoon Dried Shrimp Powder (page 30)
1 tablespoon Toasted Chickpea Flour (page 32)

2 tablespoons Fried Shallots (page 24)
1 teaspoon fish sauce, or to taste
1 teaspoon Shallot Oil (page 24)
Salt (optional)

To segment the grapefruits or pomelo, using a sharp knife, peel the fruit, cutting deeply, so that you are cutting the peel and white pith off together and the fruit inside is exposed. (You may feel that you are wasting some of the fruit, but in fact this method saves more fruit in the end.) Hold the fruit in one hand, working over a bowl, and slide a sharp paring knife along the surface of one of the membranes. Twist the knife a little to flip the segment free from the membranes, and let it drop into the bowl. Work your way around the fruit like this, freeing each segment in turn. Squeeze any remaining juice from the membranes into the bowl.

Transfer the grapefruit or pomelo segments to a wide shallow bowl. (Drink the juice or set aside for another purpose.) Add the shallots, shrimp powder, toasted chickpea flour, and fried shallots and toss. Add the fish sauce and the shallot oil and toss. Taste and add a little more fish sauce or some salt if you wish.

OVERLEAF, CLOCKWISE FROM LOWER LEFT: *Intensely Green Spinach and Tomato Salad with Peanuts (opposite); Punchy-Crunchy Ginger Salad (page 48); Tart-Sweet Chile-Garlic Sauce (page 36); Succulent Grapefruit Salad (above); and Fresh Red Chile Chutney (page 203).*

punchy-crunchy ginger salad [GYIN THOKE]

SERVES 6

Photograph on pages 46–47

A salad made of pickled ginger is a good substitute for Burmese Tea-Leaf Salad (page 64) when pickled or fermented tea leaves are hard to find, because it delivers a similar refreshing lightly pickled taste. Use Japanese pickled ginger, or make your own (see Glossary). If you don't have the soybeans, just increase the amount of peanuts; use some whole and some chopped for a variety of textures. The tomato should be cut into long thin wedges, almost like shavings.

Serve as a snack or as a salad.

1 cup pickled ginger, rinsed thoroughly in cold water, drained, and sliced into fine strands
½ cup toasted pumpkin seeds (optional)
½ cup roasted or fried split soybeans or split peas, store-bought or homemade (see Glossary)
½ cup Chopped Roasted Peanuts (page 35)
½ cup lightly toasted sesame seeds (see page 32)

¼ cup Dried Shrimp Powder (page 30)
½ cup thin wedges of Roma or other fleshy tomato
1 cup shredded Napa cabbage
¼ cup Fried Garlic (page 25)
1 to 2 tablespoons fresh lime juice
2 tablespoons Garlic Oil (page 25), or to taste
2 teaspoons salt, or to taste

Place all the ingredients except the garlic oil and salt in a bowl and mix together with your hands, blending well. Add the garlic oil and salt and mix again. Taste and adjust the seasonings as needed.

intense ginger salad

I sometimes serve a nontraditional version of ginger salad with no greens or tomato. It's more of a chutney-like taste hit than a salad, and it is delicious.

tender greens salad with crispy fried shallots

SERVES 4 TO 6

Photograph on page 55

I learned this central Burmese version of the Shan dish Chinese Kale with Pork Cracklings (page 54) from a friend in Rangoon. It's very quick to make if you've got your pantry basics on hand, and it's an easy and flexible dish to turn to when you have plenty of greens around. Start with any tender greens, briefly boil them to soften, and then chop and dress them. This dressing also works well for uncooked greens such as watercress or lettuce leaves (omit the fried garlic and reduce the dried shrimp powder slightly).

About 1 pound tender greens, such as Taiwan bok choi, baby bok choi, pea tendrils, spinach, or pumpkin or cucumber vine tendrils, trimmed of tough stems and well washed

2 tablespoons thinly sliced shallots, soaked in water for 10 minutes and drained

2 tablespoons Fried Garlic (page 25), or a mix of Fried Garlic and Fried Shallots (page 24)

2 to 3 tablespoons Dried Shrimp Powder (page 30)

2 tablespoons Chopped Roasted Peanuts (page 35)

1 to 2 tablespoons Toasted Chickpea Flour (page 32)

1 tablespoon Shallot Oil (page 24), or more to taste

2 tablespoons fresh lime juice, or to taste

1 tablespoon fish sauce, or 1 teaspoon salt, or to taste

About 2 tablespoons Fried Shallots

Bring a large pot of water to a rolling boil. Toss in the greens and boil until just tender; timing will vary with the greens, but it should take no more than 5 minutes, and in many cases (spinach, for example) much less than that. Drain the greens and press out the excess water.

When the greens are cool enough to handle, cut them into approximately 1½-inch lengths and place in a wide shallow bowl. (You should have about 3 cups.)

Add the sliced shallots and the fried garlic or fried garlic–fried shallot mixture, and toss a little. Add the dried shrimp powder, peanuts, and toasted chickpea flour and toss. Add the shallot oil and lime juice and mix well with your hands, kneading the dressing lightly but firmly into the greens. Add the fish sauce or salt, as you wish, and mix well.

Mound the salad on a plate, top with the fried shallots, and serve.

long-bean salad with roasted peanuts

SERVES 4 Yard-long beans are the long pods of the cowpea. They are a wonderfully versatile version of green beans, for they hold their texture when cooked and are beautiful too. Here they're briefly boiled until just tender, cut into lengths, and simply dressed for a classic central Burmese salad. You can cook the beans an hour ahead and they'll keep their good firm texture. (Green beans can be substituted for long beans, but they don't hold as well.) There's a nice crunch from the roasted peanuts and fried shallots.

About ¾ pound long beans
¼ cup Chopped Roasted Peanuts (page 35)
1 tablespoon plus 1 teaspoon fresh lime juice
2 teaspoons fish sauce

2 teaspoons Shallot Oil (page 24)
½ teaspoon salt, or to taste
2 tablespoons Fried Shallots (page 24)

Bring a pot of water, about 4 cups, to a boil. Toss in the beans and cook at a rolling boil for about 5 minutes, until just tender but still firm. Drain and set aside to cool for 5 minutes.

Trim the ends from the beans and cut into 1½- to 2-inch lengths. (You should have about 4 cups loosely packed.) Transfer to a serving platter or bowl and set aside until ready to serve.

Add the peanuts to the beans. Stir the lime juice, fish sauce, and shallot oil together in a small bowl or cup, then pour over the beans and toss. Sprinkle on the salt and toss again. Sprinkle the fried shallots decoratively on top.

shan tofu salad [TOHU THOKE]

SERVES 4 OR 5   There's something wonderfully satisfying about this Shan tofu dish, ideal for a hot day. Perhaps it's the dressing that coats the strips of tofu with flavor: shallot oil and a little soy sauce, vinegar, salt, and fresh herbs, including fine strands of wild lime leaf (also called kaffir lime leaf). Perhaps it's the smooth, firm texture of the tofu. This is comfort food for me.

Make the tofu a day ahead, let it chill and set overnight, and then you're free to mix this up any time. Serve as a salad or an appetizer.

About 1 pound Pale Yellow Shan Tofu (page 126)
6 to 8 fresh wild lime leaves (see Glossary), or substitute 1 cup loosely packed chopped coriander
2 tablespoons Toasted Sesame Seeds (page 32), or to taste

DRESSING
1 teaspoon minced garlic
2 teaspoons soy sauce
2 tablespoons rice vinegar, or to taste
1 tablespoon Shallot Oil (page 24), or to taste
1 teaspoon salt, or to taste

Slice the tofu fairly thin and then cut the slices crosswise into 1- to 2-inch-long pieces. Divide among four or five wide bowls.

If using lime leaves, strip out the tough central vein of each, then stack them, roll up into a tight "cigar," and slice crosswise very thin. Distribute this chiffonade among the bowls of tofu. If using coriander leaves instead, simply sprinkle over the tofu. Sprinkle on the sesame seeds.

Mix together the dressing ingredients in a small bowl, whisking to blend well. Pour about 1 tablespoon of dressing over each serving, then toss gently to coat the tofu with dressing. Serve at room temperature.

Long beans and round green eggplants, in Hpa'an, Karen State.

INTENSELY GREEN RICE PADDIES, water everywhere, and soft gray clouds and mist draped in patches on the horizon: those were my first images of Burma as the small plane came circling in to land in Rangoon thirty years ago. It was July, the heart of the rainy season. When I stepped out of the plane, the air was heavy with moisture. As we came into the city, the trees and landscape were lush, densely green. The golden dome of Shwedagon, the huge hilltop temple complex that towers above Rangoon, gleamed against the dull sky.

The city has grown since then, engulfing the farmland around it; tall buildings sometimes block the view of Shwedagon. But those early images remain vivid in my mind's eye, reminders that although not everyone eats rice every day, and not everyone is a Buddhist, for most people in Burma, rice and Buddhism are part of the fabric of life.

CLOCKWISE FROM TOP: *Rice fields outside Hpa'an in late November. A woman winnows rice at the main market in Kengtung in eastern Shan State. A monk in prayer at Shwedagon.*

chinese kale (or broccoli rabe) with pork cracklings

SERVES 6 I learned this salad from a Shan woman who was born and raised near Inle Lake and now lives in northern Thailand, not far from the Burmese border.

The original recipe used Chinese kale, a broccoli-like green that is widely available in Asian groceries (where it's often labeled *gai lan*, its Cantonese name) and in large supermarkets. Broccoli rabe is a delicious alternative.

The greens are dressed and flavored with roasted peanuts, coarsely ground pork cracklings, and aromatics.

1 pound Chinese kale or broccoli rabe
2 tablespoons peanut oil
¼ cup minced garlic
Scant 2 cups fried pork skin (chicharrones), store-bought or homemade (see Glossary)
½ cup Chopped Roasted Peanuts (page 35)
1 Soybean Disk (page 40), or substitute 1 to 2 tablespoons Toasted Chickpea Flour (page 32) plus 1 teaspoon brown miso

2 mild white onions or 4 shallots, very thinly sliced lengthwise (1½ cups)
2 or 3 small Roma (plum) or other fleshy tomatoes, cut into thin wedges (about 1½ cups)
½ teaspoon cayenne
2 teaspoons salt, or to taste

Bring a large pot of water to a rolling boil. Toss in the greens and cook for several minutes, until starting to soften. Drain thoroughly and set aside to cool.

Heat the oil in a skillet or wok over medium heat. Add the garlic and cook for 2 or 3 minutes, or until a rich golden color. Set the garlic and oil aside.

Pound or process the fried pork skin to coarse lumps and powder in a mortar or food processor (you should have about 1½ cups). Set aside. Pound or process the peanuts briefly to reduce them to a coarse powder, and set aside.

If using the soybean disk, lightly toast it over a flame or in a cast-iron skillet over medium-high heat until aromatic. Pound or process it to a powder.

Slice the greens into ½-inch lengths and place in a large bowl. Add all the remaining ingredients and use your hands to blend them together thoroughly. Taste and adjust for salt if you wish.

CLOCKWISE FROM TOP: *Broccoli Rabe with Pork Cracklings; Banana Flower Salad, Rakhine Style (page 57); Tender Greens Salad with Crispy Fried Shallots (page 49); and some tamarind liquid.*

roasted eggplant salad

SERVES 4 Crunchy and a little hot from the fine slices of raw shallot, smooth textured from the eggplant, this salad has a nice balance of tart lime juice and aromatic shallot oil. It's one of my favorites: I serve it with any and every kind of meal. It's also a great dish for a potluck.

1 pound long Asian eggplants (3 medium)
⅓ cup thinly sliced shallots, soaked in cold
    water for 10 minutes and drained
1 tablespoon Shallot Oil (page 24)
1 tablespoon fresh lime juice

2 teaspoons Fried Shallots (page 24),
    or to taste
1 teaspoon salt, or to taste
About ¼ cup coarsely torn coriander, finely
    chopped mint, or Vietnamese coriander
    (see Glossary)

Preheat the oven to 450°F or preheat a charcoal or gas grill to medium-hot.

Prick the eggplants all over with a fork and place on a baking sheet in the center of the oven, or place on the grill rack about 5 inches above the fire. Bake for about 30 minutes, or until brown and very softened. Or if grilling, turn the eggplants to expose all sides to the heat, until cooked through and very soft, about 20 minutes. Set aside to cool.

Once the eggplants are cool enough to handle, separate the flesh from the skin and stem: you can either cut the eggplants lengthwise in half and scrape out the flesh, or cut off the stems and then peel off the skin. Place the flesh in a bowl (you should have about 1½ cups). Mash with a fork, leaving it a little lumpy.

Add the sliced shallots, shallot oil, and lime juice, then mix thoroughly. Add the fried shallots, salt, and herbs and mix again. Taste and adjust seasoning before serving.

banana flower salad, rakhine style

SERVES 6

*Photograph on
page 55*

Banana flowers are like artichokes, tightly layered leaves with an enticing astringent flavor. They're beautiful too—dark-red to purple tapered cones. They are now often available here in Southeast Asian groceries. For this dish, you need a fairly small one, as fresh as possible, so its color is bright and it's firm to the touch. If you want to double the recipe, use 2 small banana flowers rather than 1 large one.

Unlike the Shan and Thais, who use banana flower raw in salads, people in Rakhine State cook it first. Its slightly bitter taste is very appealing, here balanced and softened by shallot oil and the sweetness of fried shallots. If you taste the cooked chopped banana flower before you add the seasonings, you'll notice an aroma like that of cooked artichoke, and its astringency will hit you. As you add ingredients, the flavor balance shifts in a delicious way.

This is also a great example of the way meals in Burma are composed of dishes that complement one another. Eaten on its own, this salad is intense; eaten as part of a meal, it comes to taste wonderfully necessary. Serve it with a slightly sweet mild dish such as Eggplant Delight (page 120), or as an accompaniment to roast pork or grilled lamb.

1 small banana flower (about ¾ pound)
1 tablespoon Chopped Roasted Peanuts
  (page 35)
1 tablespoon sesame seeds, lightly toasted
1 teaspoon fish sauce

½ teaspoon salt, or to taste
2 tablespoons Shallot Oil (page 24)
3 tablespoons Fried Shallots (page 24),
  or more to taste

Bring a medium pot of water to a vigorous boil. Put in the banana flower, cover, and cook at a strong boil until cooked through, about 15 minutes. Test by piercing it with a knife: if the knife slides easily into the center, it's done. Lift out of the water and set aside to cool for a few minutes.

Peel off 2 or 3 of the outer leaves of the banana flower and discard. Cut the banana flower into 5 or 6 chunks, place in a food processor, and pulse several times, just until you have a coarsely chopped mass. Turn out into a bowl, add the peanuts, sesame seeds, fish sauce, salt, and shallot oil and toss. Taste for salt and adjust if necessary, then add the fried shallots and toss again.

Serve at room temperature.

SHWEDAGON, an enormous temple complex that sits on a hill overlooking downtown Rangoon, is the most important place of worship for Burmese Buddhists. The main pagoda is a huge *chedi* (a bell-shaped Buddhist reliquary) more than 300 feet high, made of solid brick and covered in layers of gold leaf. The Burmese name describes it: *shwe* means "gold," and *dagon* is another word for *chedi* (in fact, some English-language guidebooks render the name as two words: Shwe Dagon). For Burmese and other Buddhists, Shwedagon is full of meaning and feeling. Like a world apart, it soars far above the worries and distractions of daily life.

The approach is made in bare feet, for all shoes and socks must come off at the entryway at the bottom of the hill (there's a shoe-check place). The steep, shadowy stairway is composed of endless cool stone steps under a high, sloping wood ceiling. On each side of the stairs are small shops selling offerings of flowers, candles, and incense.

More than thirty years ago, the first time I went, I was dazed by what I saw when I reached the top of the steps: golden spires; gilded lions with open jaws; glowing white marble; Buddhas large and small, seated and standing, smiling and severe; and everywhere people alone or in groups, walking or kneeling or bowed in prayer,

pouring water, lighting incense, making offerings of flowers, or sounding a gong—*dong!*—that reverberated on and on.

A ragged determined line of women wielding large brooms came walking past me, sweeping rainwater off the tiles and marble with a *swoosh swoosh*. The crows were noisy. I started walking around the central golden *chedi* in the clockwise direction that is customary when circumambulating a Buddhist holy place. Round once, then round again, slowly, each time noticing new details. After a while it began to rain, so I headed back down the steps. And after I got to the bottom, reclaimed my sandals, and emerged out onto the street, I felt I'd returned from another world.

Each time I get to Rangoon I visit Shwedagon, and I always return again just before I leave the city. These visits are an homage to the power of the place, as well as a kind of prayer that I can come back again.

Now that I know my way around a little, I have favorite places in the complex of temples and platforms where I sit awhile watching the crowd and listening to the tinkling of small bells and the boom of gongs, the voices of people as they chat together, the quiet murmurs of those in prayer, the splash of water being poured over Buddha statues, the click of cameras, and the crows, always the crows, cawing loudly.

LEFT: *In late February 2012, for the first time since 1988, there was a temple festival held at Shwedagon. The temples, shrines, and chedis were decorated with tiny colored lights, and the crowds were even bigger than usual. Even with the added glitter, the huge golden dome dominated the scene.* FAR LEFT, FROM TOP: *A long line of women comes through to sweep the marble floor. Monks visiting Shwedagon. Visitors light candles and place them as offerings in front of shrines and statues.*

mandalay grated carrot salad

SERVES 4 Grated carrot salads exist in many culinary traditions, but this one takes the prize. It has a beautiful light balance of flavors and is very refreshing.

I like eating carrot salad with rice, as if it were a cooked dish rather than a side salad. It's a little salty, as rice accompaniments should be, with a bit of warmth from the minced chile.

½ pound carrots, coarsely grated
   (about 2 cups)
1 tablespoon fresh lime juice, or more to taste
1 teaspoon fish sauce
2 teaspoons Dried Shrimp Powder (page 30)
1 teaspoon Toasted Chickpea Flour (page 32)
1 teaspoon minced green cayenne chile, or
   substitute a pinch of Red Chile Powder
   (page 28)

½ teaspoon salt, or to taste
1 tablespoon Chopped Roasted Peanuts
   (page 35)
1 to 2 tablespoons Fried Shallots (page 24)
2 tablespoons chopped coriander or finely
   chopped mint or Vietnamese coriander
   leaves (see Glossary)

Place the grated carrots in a large mortar or a bowl, add the lime juice and fish sauce, and lightly pound or press with the back of a wooden spoon for several minutes to break them down a little.

Transfer to a serving plate or shallow bowl, add the shrimp powder and toasted chickpea flour, and toss thoroughly. Add the chile and salt and toss.

Just before serving, add the peanuts and shallots and toss, then add the chopped herbs and toss again. Taste and adjust flavorings if you wish (I often add an extra squeeze of lime juice) before serving.

OVERLEAF: *During the Shwedagon temple festival in 2012, many of the shrines, pagodas, and temples were outlined in tiny colored lights.*

green mango salad

SERVES 3 In Asia, mangoes, like papayas and jackfruit, are treated as vegetables when they are green or unripe. Here green mango, tart and crisp, is dressed with a little oil and with sweet and pungent flavors—shallots, both raw and fried, and dried shrimp powder—as well as a little chile.

The trick is to find a completely unripe mango or a sour mango; both are sold as "green mango." If the mango is unripe, it will be very hard, so it will need to be tossed with salt to soften it and bring out its flavor before it is dressed with the other ingredients. If it is a sour green mango, it will be an intense green color and not rock-hard; it will also be very sour. In that case, add the sugar—it will make all the difference.

2 small green mangoes
½ teaspoon salt, or to taste
1 teaspoon fish sauce
About 2 tablespoons thinly sliced shallots
1 teaspoon Shallot Oil (page 24)
1 tablespoon Toasted Chickpea Flour
   (page 32)

1 teaspoon Dried Shrimp Powder (page 30)
¼ teaspoon sugar if using sour green mango
1 green cayenne chile, seeded and minced
   (about 1 tablespoon)
1 tablespoon Toasted Sesame Seeds
   (page 32; optional)
About 1 teaspoon Fried Shallots (page 24)

Peel the mangoes and use a coarse grater or a sharp knife to make long, wide strips of mango. (You should have 1½ to 2 cups, loosely packed.)

Place the mango strips in a shallow bowl, add the salt, and toss. Add the remaining ingredients except the fried shallots and toss well. Let stand for 10 minutes before serving.

Just before serving, add the fried shallots and toss, then taste for salt and adjust if necessary.

burmese tea-leaf salad [LAPHET THOKE]

SERVES 6 AS A SNACK

This salad is often called Burma's national dish. *Laphet* is the word for "green tea" and *thoke* means "salad" (it's pronounced "la-pay toe"). It's a dazzling combination of fermented tea leaves, soft-textured and a little acid and astringent, with other tastes and textures: crisp, roasted peanuts and other crunchy beans, toasted sesame seeds, dried shrimp, and fried garlic. It may come to the table already mixed (and including a little chopped tomato) or, more often, be served with all the ingredients in separate piles so that guests can pick up their own combination of flavors and textures each time they reach for a handful. *Laphet thoke* is traditionally served as a final taste at the end of the meal, much like sweetened whole spices may be served at the end of a north Indian meal, or tea or coffee at the end of a Western meal.

Packages of prepared *laphet thoke* ingredients—the tea leaves and all the other flavorings—are sold everywhere in Burma. Burmese who live abroad buy stacks of the packages when they return on visits to take back with them. In other words, finding fermented tea leaves outside Burma and northern Thailand can be a problem. So, although the tea leaves are sometimes available in North America (you can order them online from a New York–based company called Minthila: www.minthila .com), they're often hard to get. This recipe is here as an act of optimism, in the hope that fermented tea leaves will soon become more widely available.

If you are starting with unprocessed fermented tea leaves, then start preparing them several hours or as long as the night before you wish to serve the salad: they need to be soaked in water to remove their strongest tart and bitter edge.

About ¾ cup packed fermented tea leaves, rinsed and coarsely chopped
2 tablespoons Toasted Sesame Seeds, lightly ground (page 32)
2 to 3 tablespoons roasted peanuts (see page 35), whole or coarsely chopped
2 to 3 tablespoons fried split roasted soybeans (see Glossary)
½ cup thin tomato wedges (optional)
2 tablespoons dried shrimp, soaked in water for 10 minutes and drained

1 cup shredded green cabbage or Napa cabbage (optional)
Salt

OPTIONAL DRESSING
1 to 2 tablespoons Garlic Oil (page 25)
1 to 2 tablespoons fresh lime juice
1 teaspoon soy sauce or fish sauce
Pinch of salt

At least 6 hours before you wish to serve the salad, place the tea leaves in lukewarm water and mash with your hands a little. Drain and squeeze out. Repeat, then add cold water and let stand for 1 hour (or as long as overnight). Drain, squeeze thoroughly to remove excess water, and discard any tough bits. Chop finely by hand or in a food processor; set aside.

If serving the salad unmixed, omit the tomato and cabbage. Place small piles of all the ingredients on a platter, or put each ingredient in a small bowl and place the bowls on a platter. Serve the dressing, if using, in a separate small bowl. Put out spoons with each ingredient, or invite guests to use their hands. Invite guests to help themselves as they wish; they can eat two or three of the ingredients together or mix up a combination for themselves on their own plates.

If serving as a mixed salad, combine all the ingredients (except salt) in a bowl. Mix with your hands, separating any clumped tea leaves and the shreds of cabbage to blend everything thoroughly. Add the dressing ingredients and blend thoroughly with your hands. Add salt to taste and adjust other seasonings if you wish.

shan tea-leaf salad

This salad, called *niang ko* in Shan language (and *yam miang* in Thai), is always served mixed together. Traditionally the Shan use fresh tea leaves, immerse them in hot water briefly, then squeeze them out thoroughly, discard any tough patches and leaf veins, and chop them finely. Most of us don't have access to fresh tea leaves, so use either ½ cup packed fermented tea leaves, processing them as instructed above by repeated soakings, or about 1 cup loosely packed dried green tea leaves (these work very well, especially leaves with a good green color). Add the dried tea leaves to hot water, stir, and let soak until very softened, about 10 minutes; then drain, pick through the leaves, and discard any tough bits.

Squeeze out the tea leaves thoroughly, chop finely, and put in a medium bowl. Add about 1 cup finely chopped green cabbage, 1 loosely packed cup mixed chopped coriander and scallion greens, and 2 tablespoons finely chopped ginger (preferably young ginger). Mix together thoroughly and set aside.

Fry ¼ cup sliced garlic in 2 to 3 tablespoons peanut oil until golden. Set aside. Add ¼ cup Chopped Roasted Peanuts (page 35) or whole unsalted roasted peanuts, and 2 to 3 tablespoons toasted sesame seeds; toss. If you started with dried or fresh tea leaves, add about 2 tablespoons freshly squeezed lime juice, to give a sour note. Pour over the reserved garlic and oil. Mix and blend some more, add ½ teaspoon salt, mix again, taste and adjust if needed, and serve.

TO REACH HSIPAW, I rode in a share-taxi with no shock absorbers and unreliable brakes up a sometimes scary winding road from Mandalay. People grew wheat up in the Shan hills, as well as barley—a surprising sight in the tropics. Rows of cauliflower and other temperate-climate vegetables grow in terraced gardens. I would have loved to stop to take a closer look and ask the farmers about their crops, but the share-taxi lumbered on past, leaving me with many questions unanswered. Six hours later we reached Hsipaw.

The next day, I got up well before dawn and headed out to Hsipaw's morning market. The going was slow there, for the market street was crowded. A candle or two lit each small display: a few fresh fish; a stack of small cauliflowers; handfuls of tomatoes, onions, cucumbers, and leafy greens of every kind; curved slices of pumpkin; cooked sweet black sticky rice. Some were on low tables; most were on a piece of cloth or plastic on the ground. A few vendors had small fires going to help warm them in the predawn chill. People threaded their way carefully, occasionally pausing and crouching to take a closer look at the food on offer. A line of monks walked through on their morning alms round and the crowd parted to let them pass.

As the sky lightened, sometime after six, one by one the vendors pinched out their candles and packed up. They carried everything off the street and (as the authorities had decreed) moved to a nearby open area by the river, where item by item they unpacked and set up for a second time. During my stay in Hsipaw, I returned daily to the market in the dark. And every morning, as the sun came up over the river, the market was gilded with radiant light, transformed.

Hsipaw market scenes. **TOP AND FAR LEFT:** *Vendors crouch or sit on low stools by their produce in the pre-dawn candlelight.* **MIDDLE:** *A butcher's stall first thing in the morning.* **LEFT:** *Fresh fish at the market.*

shrimp salad

SERVES 4 TO 6   This shrimp salad makes an enticing appetizer. The shrimp are briefly fried and then dressed with minced chiles, chopped scallions, and a blend of fish sauce and lime juice. Cucumber gives a refreshing crunch.

2 tablespoons peanut oil or Shallot Oil
   (page 24)
About 1 pound medium to large shrimp, peeled,
   deveined, and rinsed
3 scallions, halved lengthwise and thinly sliced
½ medium English cucumber
2 tablespoons chopped coriander

1 green or red cayenne chile, minced, or
   ¼ to ½ teaspoon Red Chile Powder
   (page 28)
1 teaspoon fish sauce
About 2 tablespoons fresh lime juice
Salt (optional)

Place a wok or large skillet over medium-high heat. Add the oil, then toss in the shrimp and stir-fry just until they turn pink, a minute or two.

Transfer the shrimp to a cutting board. Slice on the diagonal and place in a shallow bowl. Add the scallions.

Cut the cucumber into 1½-inch lengths and slice each length into julienne (you should have a scant cup). Add the cucumber, coriander, and chile to the shrimp and toss lightly. Add the fish sauce and lime juice and toss to mix well. Taste and add a little salt if you wish, then toss and serve immediately.

shrimp and winged bean salad

You can substitute 10 to 12 winged beans (see Glossary) for the cucumber. Briefly cook them in a little boiling water until barely tender, 3 to 4 minutes; drain, trim off the tough ends, and cut into ½-inch-thick slices on the diagonal.

fish cake salad with shaved cabbage

SERVES 4   This is great hot-weather food, served as an appetizer at a Western meal or as part of a rice meal. The crispy greens are a pleasing contrast to the smooth bite of the fish cake slices. You can make the fish cakes up to a day ahead, then slice them and assemble the salad at the last minute.

DRESSING
1 teaspoon fish sauce
1 teaspoon Shallot Oil (page 24)
1 tablespoon fresh lime juice
¼ teaspoon salt, or to taste

Fish Cakes (page 133)
**About 1 cup grated or shaved Napa cabbage or
    Savoy cabbage**

1 green cayenne chile, minced
**1 teaspoon Toasted Chickpea Flour
    (page 32)**
1 tablespoon Fried Shallots (page 24)
About 1 tablespoon chopped coriander or mint

Whisk together the dressing ingredients and set aside.

Slice each fish cake into 2 to 4 strips and place in a bowl. Add the cabbage. Whisk the dressing once more and pour over the fish cakes. Toss gently to distribute the dressing. Sprinkle on the chile and chickpea flour and toss again. Top with the fried shallots and chopped herbs and toss to mix. Taste and adjust the seasonings, if necessary, before serving.

poached fish salad with shallots and herbs

SERVES 4 AS A LIGHT LUNCH,
6 AS AN APPETIZER This recipe starts with fresh fish fillets, but you can instead use leftover fish, poached or baked or grilled, as people in Burma do. Use any fish you like, from trout or salmon to haddock, tilapia, or sea bass.

The salad makes an easy appetizer or a refreshing main course on a hot day. Serve with plain rice or good bread, along with a simple stir-fry such as Lima Beans with Galangal (page 110) or Smoky Napa Stir-Fry (page 115).

About 1½ cups water
1 stalk lemongrass, trimmed and smashed
1 teaspoon salt
About 1 pound fish fillets, rinsed

DRESSING
¾ cup thinly sliced shallots, soaked in cold
    water for 10 minutes and drained

2 tablespoons fresh lime juice
2 teaspoons Shallot Oil (page 24)
2 tablespoons Fried Shallots (page 24)
½ to 1 teaspoon salt
1 to 2 teaspoons minced green cayenne chile
¼ cup chopped coriander, or mint, or
    Vietnamese coriander (see Glossary)

Pour the water into a small pot with the lemongrass, bring to a boil, and add the salt. Add the fish and bring the water back to a boil, then cover, lower the heat, and poach at a strong simmer just until the flesh is opaque throughout, about 5 minutes. Remove the fish from the water and set aside on a plate to cool. Reserve the poaching water for another purpose or discard.

When the fish is cool enough to handle, shred loosely into bite-sized pieces and place in a shallow bowl. Add the shallots, lime juice, shallot oil, fried shallots, ½ teaspoon salt, and the green chile and mix together well. Taste and add a little more salt if you wish. Top with the chopped fresh herbs and toss again briefly. Serve at room temperature.

chicken salad, burma style

**SERVES 2 AS A LIGHT LUNCH,
4 AS AN APPETIZER** Almost any leftover cooked ingredient can be made into salad, and often is, say my Burmese friends. If you have leftover cooked chicken, as I often do after making chicken broth from whole legs or roasting a chicken, transform it into this refreshing salad. Serve as a light main course for lunch, or as an appetizer.

About 2 cups large bite-sized pieces cooked
   chicken (cut or pull the chicken into pieces)
⅓ to ½ cup thinly sliced shallots, soaked in
   cold water for 10 minutes and drained
2 tablespoons fresh lime juice
2 teaspoons Shallot Oil (page 24)
1 teaspoon salt, or to taste

2 teaspoons minced green cayenne chile,
   or to taste
1 tablespoon Toasted Chickpea Flour
   (page 32; optional)
1 to 2 tablespoons Fried Shallots (page 24)
Scant ½ cup chopped coriander, or mint, or
   Vietnamese coriander (see Glossary)

Place the chicken in a shallow serving bowl. Add the shallots and toss.

Mix together the lime juice, shallot oil, salt, and green chile in a small bowl or cup. Pour over the salad and, using your hands, mix thoroughly. If you have the time, let stand for 10 minutes.

Just before serving, add the toasted chickpea flour, if you wish, the fried shallots and herbs, and mix well. Taste and adjust the seasonings.

SOUPS

BURMESE HAVE A STRONG AND WONDERFULLY varied soup tradition. In North America soup now seems to be an afterthought, rarely made at home or ordered in a restaurant. But in Burma soups are an essential part of the main meal of the day, flavorful and appealing broths that are sipped from time to time during the meal instead of water. (For noodle soups, another category altogether, see the Noodles chapter, page 247.)

Everyday soups are clean-flavored broths that usually have a few vegetables floating in them and are lightly soured with lime juice or tamarind. All of them work well as a soup course in a Western meal. They include Classic Sour Soup (page 90) and Ambrosial Chicken Broth with Shallots and Lime Juice (page 77).

The more substantial soups are like French potage, thick and warming on a cold day. Some, such as Mimi's Bean Soup with Tender Leaves (page 98) and Silky Shan Soup (page 94), are made with legumes and no meat, yet are deeply satisfying. The heartiest soups, those with a little meat, are from non-Bamar peoples: Hearty Pork and Vegetable Soup (from the Karen, page 88) and Kachin Rice Powder Soup with Chicken and Ginger (page 91).

basic chicken broth

MAKES 6 TO 8 CUPS It's a pity to waste any of the flavor from meat or bones. That's why broths are the cook's best friend. And of all the broths, chicken broth is arguably the easiest to make and the most versatile. Many butchers sell chicken carcasses that have had the breasts and legs cut off but still have plenty of meat and flavor in them. You can also use whole pieces of chicken.

I always add aromatics—ginger, shallots, garlic—but sometimes omit one or another of them. I don't season the broth until I am going to serve it, when I add salt and perhaps a dash of fish sauce, for extra depth of flavor.

3 pounds chicken necks and wings, 1 large chicken carcass plus 1 pound wings, or 2 pounds chicken legs or breasts, rinsed
About 10 cups water

3 slices ginger
3 shallots, halved, or substitute 4 scallions, trimmed

Place the chicken in a large pot and add 10 cups water. Bring to a boil over high heat, and toss in the ginger and shallots or scallions. Partially cover the pot, reduce the heat to maintain a low boil, and cook for 1 hour. If the chicken is not completely immersed in the water, turn it from time to time; add another cup of water after 20 minutes if the level of water has dropped a great deal.

If using legs and breasts: Remove the chicken and strain the broth. Set the meat and broth aside to cool. When it is cool, pull the meat off the bones and slice or chop into bite-sized pieces. Use to make Chicken Salad, Burma Style (page 72) or for another purpose.

If using necks and wings or a chicken carcass: Lower the heat and simmer for another 30 minutes, turning the meat and bones several times. Let cool, covered, for 20 minutes or so. Strain the broth and discard the solids.

Transfer the broth to a ceramic or glass container, cover, and refrigerate. Once cool, the broth can be skimmed of fat if you wish. It can be stored in well-sealed containers in the refrigerator for 3 days or in the freezer for up to a month.

Sunrise and morning mist over the Doktawaddy River in Hsipaw, Shan State.

ambrosial chicken broth
with shallots and lime juice

SERVES 4 TO 6   I came across this soup for the first time in Mrauk U (see page 107), a basic chicken broth that's transformed by the addition of fresh shallots and lime juice. If you have chicken broth on hand, the soup is ready in less than 15 minutes. The shallots, which are first soaked in water to remove their sharp edge and then simmered briefly, give the broth texture and a slightly sweet, fresh note.

6 cups Basic Chicken Broth (opposite) or store-bought chicken broth
1 cup thinly sliced shallots, soaked in cold water for 10 minutes and drained

About ¼ cup fresh lime juice
Salt
¼ cup minced coriander (optional)

Heat the broth to nearly boiling in a saucepan. Add the shallots and simmer for 2 to 3 minutes. Remove from the heat and stir in the lime juice. If your broth is not seasoned, you will want to add about 2 teaspoons salt; add salt gradually and taste as you go.

Serve hot, sprinkled with the coriander, if you wish.

lemongrass chicken soup with lime leaves

SERVES 4 TO 6 This is one of those great last-minute soups. The flavor of the lemongrass infuses into the broth in about 20 minutes. The lime leaves, cut into fine slivers, are added at the very end. Serve as part of a Burmese-style rice meal or as a simple but elegant soup course in a Western meal.

6 cups Basic Chicken Broth (page 76) or
    store-bought chicken broth
2 stalks lemongrass
1 teaspoon freshly ground black pepper

Salt and/or fish sauce
About 8 fresh lime leaves, deveined and
    scissor-cut into fine slivers, or substitute
    about ¼ cup chopped coriander leaves

Pour the broth into a large pot and set it over medium heat. Trim the tough root end off the lemongrass, smash with the flat side of a cleaver or heavy knife, make several lengthwise cuts in each stalk, and add to the broth. Bring to a boil, then reduce the heat and simmer gently for 20 minutes to infuse the broth with the lemongrass.

Add the pepper. Taste and add salt as well as a little fish sauce if you wish (seasoning will depend on the broth you are using). Scatter the lime leaf slivers or coriander over the soup and stir in.

CHICKEN SOUP WITH NOODLES: *At a small stand near the Bothataung Temple in Rangoon, a woman sells a hearty noodle version of this soup. The broth is served in a small bowl on the side, to accompany a large bowl of rice noodles mixed with strands of Shan tofu (see page 126) and dressed with shallot oil, fish sauce, crushed roasted peanuts, dried red chile powder, and chopped coriander. You take a mouthful or two of the noodles, then have a sip of soup.*

cho cho's bean thread soup

SERVES 4   Cho Cho lives in Taung Be, a small village near Old Bagan by the Irrawaddy River. Foreigners and tourists from other parts of Burma come by the busload to marvel at the hundreds of old temples in the Bagan area. But not far away from the much photographed ancient sites in Taung Be and other off-the-beaten-track hamlets, village life still goes on.

I met Cho Cho through her nephew in Rangoon. He had suggested that I could learn some traditional Burmese village dishes from her. That's how I found myself one day in her airy kitchen, watching her cook, and photographing. It was a real pleasure, for Cho Cho has a calm beauty and an unhurried grace. Her movements were deft and economical, and when we sat down to a traditional midday rice meal, her food was spectacular. This simple broth with transparent bean thread noodles floating in it was one of the dishes she served.

Like many cooks in Burma and other parts of Southeast Asia, Cho Cho uses MSG to give depth of flavor, especially in dishes where there's no shrimp paste (*ngapi*). She used about 1 teaspoon MSG, for which I substitute extra fish sauce (see "Umami," page 31).

¼ **pound bean threads (see Glossary)**
¾ **cup large dried shrimp (see Note)**
2 cups warm water
3 to 4 garlic cloves, minced
  (a generous 1 tablespoon)
Scant ¼ cup peanut oil
Scant ½ teaspoon turmeric
¾ **cup sliced shallots**

½ **to 1 teaspoon Red Chile Powder (page 28)**
  or ½ teaspoon cayenne
3 cups water
1 teaspoon salt, or to taste
1 to 2 tablespoons fish sauce
½ **teaspoon freshly ground black pepper,**
  or to taste

Soak the bean threads in cold water for 10 minutes. Drain, cut into approximately 6-inch lengths, and set aside.

Meanwhile, soak the dried shrimp in the warm water for 20 minutes. Drain, reserving the water, and set both shrimp and water aside.

If you have a mortar, pound the minced garlic to a paste.

Heat the oil in a large pot over medium heat. Toss in the turmeric and shallots and cook until the shallots are translucent and softened, about 5 minutes. Add the garlic, chile or cayenne, and reserved shrimp and stir to blend. Cook for several minutes, then add the reserved shrimp water and the 3 cups water, raise the heat, and bring to a boil. Cook at a medium boil for 5 minutes.

If you are serving immediately: Add the bean threads, salt, and fish sauce and cook at a gentle boil just until the noodles are tender, about 5 minutes.

If you are serving later: Remove the soup from the heat and set aside for up to 2 hours, covered. Just before serving, bring to a boil, add the bean threads, salt, and fish sauce, and cook until just tender.

Stir in the black pepper just before serving.

A NOTE ON DRIED SHRIMP: *Dried shrimp come in many sizes and colors, from tiny and the palest pink to about 1 inch long and dark red. Because the shrimp are the primary flavoring in this soup, it's important to buy the best quality you can find—in other words, large dark-pink to red shrimp. They will have a much better flavor and texture than the tiny pale ones that are on sale in most Asian groceries.*

Cho Cho cooking in her kitchen.

SOON AFTER I LANDED at the tiny airport in Sittwe, on Burma's west coast, I was accosted by a tout, a rare experience in Burma. He presented himself as the person I needed to guide me while I was in the area: he'd get me a boat for Mrauk U, he'd show me where to eat, he'd show me around. "No thanks," I said, but he persisted like a drunk in a bar. I dodged him and caught a motorcycle rickshaw into town.

Sittwe was sleepy and felt vaguely colonial. There were fruit bats near the clock tower, a couple of small hotels and guesthouses, a few shops, and a fish market by the river. At my guesthouse, the friendly, laid-back owner advised me to head straight up the Kaladan River to Mrauk U the next morning: "You'll take a lot of days to visit the ruins and you can always come down a day ahead if you want to spend more time here in Sittwe," he explained. I talked to a quiet friend of his who said he'd arrange for a boat at the river that would take me to Mrauk U, a seven-hour journey. He said I could leave before dawn. And no, he wouldn't be coming with me, he would just make the arrangements.

It was still dark when I left the guesthouse next morning for the jetty. The sky was lightening as I walked there: people and objects started to take shape, and the river water gleamed in the early light. The quiet man was waiting at the river. He showed me the boat, said, "You pay the boatman," gave me a little wave, and then walked away.

The boatman started the engine. The kid helping him loosened the mooring rope, and just then the pushy guy from the airport stepped onto the boat. "I've been looking for you," he said. "Thank you but no," I said. "I'd like to be alone. Thank you!" Something in the firmness of my voice must finally have got through to him. He stepped back onto the dock and we pulled away.

As we moved slowly through the pale silver of the water, past the darkened riverbanks and the occasional small boat, all thoughts of him—all thoughts of any kind—fell away. We entered a timeless vast space of wide, wide river and endless open sky, the colors pale and gradually warming in the early light. We were dwarfed by the vastness, a small skiff chugging up a wide expanse of water toward a brilliant horizon.

Heading up the Kaladan River from Sittwe, in the first hour after dawn.

fragrant fish broth

MAKES ABOUT 5 CUPS; SERVES 4 This perfect fish broth has depth and nuance, everything in balance. It is great to have a stash of it in the freezer to serve as a simple broth at any time, or to use in making the central Burmese essential Classic Sour Soup (page 90) or other soups in this chapter.

I often use fish fillets for this broth. A more traditional choice is fish heads. Don't use salmon; its flavor is too strong and distinctive.

2 tablespoons peanut oil or vegetable oil
⅛ teaspoon turmeric
¼ cup minced shallots
1 tablespoon minced garlic
2 tablespoons Dried Shrimp Powder
 (page 30)

About ½ pound fish fillets or pieces
 (see the headnote), rinsed
Scant 1 teaspoon shrimp paste
 (*ngapi*; see Glossary)
About 6 cups water
1 teaspoon salt

Heat the oil in a wide heavy pot over medium-high heat. Add the turmeric and stir, then add the shallots and garlic and cook, stirring occasionally, until softened, about 3 minutes. Stir in the dried shrimp powder and lower the heat to medium. Add the fish and cook, stirring occasionally, until all sides have been exposed to the heat.

Dissolve the shrimp paste in about 2 tablespoons water in a small bowl, then add to the pot, together with a scant 6 cups water. Raise the heat and bring to a boil, then add the salt, lower the heat to maintain a low boil, and cook, partially covered, for 15 minutes.

Strain the broth and discard the solids.

Serve as a simple clear broth, or use to make other soups in this chapter. The broth will keep in a well-sealed container for 3 days in the refrigerator or up to 1 month in the freezer.

dawei fish soup

SERVES 4 OR 5 Dawei, until recently known as Tavoy, is an attractive town halfway down Burma's tail-of-the-kite south coast. The fish in its markets gleam with freshness and are wonderfully varied. The women in Kana Market, Dawei's main wet market, watched me taking photos and more photos, laughing when they saw how amazed I was by the beauty of the fish they were selling.

The fish dishes for which Dawei is famous may originally have been Mon dishes, since this stretch of the Tenasserim coast was part of a Mon kingdom long ago (see Burma over Time, page 306). It's also been a crossroads kind of place for centuries. Chinese merchants, Burmese from other parts of the country, and Muslim descendants of traders from across the Bay of Bengal all still do business here.

I learned about this soup from a generous woman in Dawei known for her home cooking. The basic flavor paste features the distinctive local flavorings: along with ginger and shallots, there's galangal, a resiny and distinctive cousin of ginger, as well as lemongrass in quantities you don't see elsewhere in Burma.

You can serve it as a broth, or instead include bean threads and some chopped Napa cabbage for a more substantial soup. I like to pair it with Perfumed Coconut Rice (page 237) and a simple vegetable curry.

3 pounds fish heads and bones from ocean fish such as kingfish, sea bream, or snapper (not salmon), thoroughly rinsed
About 7 cups water
1 cup sliced shallots
1 teaspoon turmeric
¼ cup very thinly sliced lemongrass
3 tablespoons sliced ginger
2 tablespoons sliced galangal (see Glossary)

2 teaspoons salt, plus additional to taste
4 green cayenne chiles, or to taste
2 ounces bean threads (see Glossary; optional)
1½ cups chopped Napa cabbage (optional)
½ pound cleaned squid, chopped into bite-sized pieces (optional)
¾ cup loosely packed coriander leaves and fine stems, coarsely chopped
Juice of 1 lime, or to taste

Place the fish heads in a pot with 6 cups of the water. Add the shallots and turmeric and bring to a boil, then lower the heat to maintain a strong simmer.

Meanwhile combine the lemongrass, ginger, and galangal in a mortar or small processor, add 1 teaspoon of the salt, and pound or process to a paste.

[Continued]

Blend the paste into another cup of water, then add to the pot together with the remaining 1 teaspoon salt. Toss in the green chiles. Bring the broth back to the boil, partially cover, and lower the heat to maintain a strong simmer. Cook for about an hour. Remove from the heat, taste for seasoning, and adjust as necessary. Strain the broth through a fine strainer into another pot and discard the solids. Set back over the heat. You may find you want to add a little extra water.

If serving immediately: Bring to a gentle boil. Add the bean threads or Napa cabbage or both, if using, and simmer briefly. If using squid, rinse off, then add to the soup and simmer until tender. Taste and adjust the seasonings if you wish. Add most of the coriander and stir, then remove from the heat, stir in the lime juice, and serve topped with a sprinkling of the remaining coriander.

If serving later: Set the broth aside until about 10 minutes before you wish to serve it (refrigerate if the wait will be longer than 2 hours). Then bring the broth back to a gentle boil and proceed as above.

A fisherman near Mrauk U with his net.

fish soup with lemongrass and chiles

SERVES 4   A treat for the cook because of its ease of preparation, and for guests because of its sparkling flavors, this is a great soup to serve on a hot day. The broth is aromatic with lemongrass and ginger, and it gets an extra lift from the condiments and toppings that each guest adds while eating: a little heat from minced green chile, crunch and freshness from shallots and coriander leaves, and the tang of lime juice to pull it all together.

Fragrant Fish Broth (page 84)
½ cup water
2 stalks lemongrass, trimmed and smashed
2 slices ginger
¼ cup thinly sliced shallots, soaked in water for 10 minutes and drained

3 green cayenne chiles, seeded and minced
¼ cup loosely packed chopped coriander
2 limes, cut into wedges

Combine the broth and water in a wide heavy pot, add the lemongrass and ginger, and bring to a boil over medium-high heat. Lower the heat to maintain a medium boil, partially cover, and cook for about 15 minutes to infuse the soup wth flavor.

Meanwhile squeeze any excess water out of the sliced shallots and put out on a serving plate, together with the chiles, coriander, and lime wedges.

Just before serving, remove the lemongrass and ginger slices from the soup and discard. Serve the soup, and invite your guests to sprinkle on some shallots, chiles, and coriander leaves, as they please, and to squeeze on fresh lime juice.

hearty pork and vegetable soup

SERVES 4 OR 5   I had this warming Karen version of sour soup in a village not far from Moulmein, the port at the mouth of the Salween River. Rather than being fish-broth-based, as many sour soups are, it is made with pork and freshly cooked greens. The shrimp paste (*ngapi*) is very subtle and blends into the other flavors seamlessly.

Serve as a main dish over rice, perhaps with some roasted root vegetables or a crisp salad on the side. Leftovers are exceptionally good the next day.

½ pound pork shoulder or other boneless pork, such as tenderloin
¼ teaspoon turmeric
Salt
2 tablespoons peanut oil or vegetable oil
½ cup sliced shallots
1 tablespoon minced ginger
1 stalk lemongrass, trimmed and smashed (optional)
½ teaspoon fermented shrimp paste (*ngapi*; see Glossary)

5 cups light vegetable broth, chicken broth, or water
2 tablespoons tamarind pulp (see Glossary), cut into chunks
1 cup hot water
About 4 cups loosely packed coarsely chopped bok choi, Napa cabbage, or Taiwan bok choi, or substitute 3 cups loosely packed chopped Swiss chard or romaine lettuce

Thinly slice the pork, then cut into small (approximately 1-inch) pieces and place in a bowl. (You should have about 1 packed cup.) Add ⅛ teaspoon of the turmeric and ½ teaspoon salt and turn and mix to distribute the seasonings; set aside.

Heat the oil in a wide heavy pot over medium-high heat. Toss in the remaining ⅛ teaspoon turmeric, and when it sizzles, add the shallots, ginger, and lemongrass (if using), lower the heat to medium, and cook, stirring frequently, until the shallots are softened and translucent, about 5 minutes. Add the sliced pork and cook, stirring frequently, until all surfaces have changed color.

Meanwhile, place the shrimp paste in a small bowl, add about ¼ cup of the broth or water, and stir to dissolve the shrimp paste completely. Add to the pot together with the remaining broth or water and bring to a boil, then reduce the heat and simmer for about 10 minutes.

While the broth thickens, place the tamarind pulp in a small bowl with the hot water. Mash it with a fork to help dissolve it, then set aside for several minutes to soak.

Rub the tamarind with your fingers to help it dissolve further, then place a sieve over a wide bowl and pour the tamarind water through, pressing and mashing the pulp against the sieve to extract as much liquid as possible. Discard the pulp.

Add the tamarind liquid to the broth, bring to a boil, and add the chopped greens. Cook at a medium boil for a few minutes, until the greens are just tender. Add salt to taste (if the broth you started with was unsalted or you used water, you will need about 2 teaspoons salt).

Serve hot or at room temperature.

classic sour soup

SERVES 4 Sour soup is an essential part of a noontime rice meal in central Burma. There's a wide variety of these soups. They're most often made with a fish stock as a base and, as here, lightly soured with tamarind or lime juice. Occasional sips as you eat refresh the palate.

I love the way this soup can be subtly transformed by adding different greens and vegetables. I've eaten sour soup with petals from pumpkin flowers floating in the broth, a beautiful variation. You could use zucchini blossoms, or even nasturtiums. In Mandalay, there's a short time in February just before hot season when the tall kapok trees (*lapin* in Burmese) are in bloom, and cooks add their velvety faded-red flowers to a sour soup flavored with onions, ginger, fermented soybeans, and a touch of tomato.

2 tablespoons tamarind pulp (see Glossary), cut into chunks
1 cup hot water
Fragrant Fish Broth (page 84)

About 2 loosely packed cups coarsely chopped bok choi, Taiwan bok choi, or Napa cabbage, or tender young bean sprouts, or daikon cut into 1-inch chunks, or a combination

Place the tamarind pulp in a small bowl with the hot water. Mash it with a fork to help it dissolve, then set aside for several minutes to soak. Rub the tamarind with your fingers to help it dissolve further.

Place a sieve over a wide bowl and pour the tamarind water through, pressing the pulp against the sieve to extract as much liquid as possible. Discard the pulp.

Pour the broth into a wide pot over medium heat and bring to a boil. Add the tamarind liquid and stir in, then add the vegetable(s) and cook at a low boil until tender. Serve hot or at room temperature.

kachin rice powder soup with chicken and ginger

SERVES 4 The cooks at Myit Sone, a Kachin restaurant in Rangoon, taught me this wonderful version of chicken-rice soup. Instead of starting with whole rice, as most chicken-rice soups do, the Kachin use toasted rice powder. The powder, a common ingredient in Kachin dishes, is a pantry staple you can easily make yourself. It has a seductive toasted-grain aroma, and it gives the soup a thickened texture that's a real pleasure. The Karen have a similar porridge-like soup, *khao beue,* made of toasted rice simmered in a pork broth.

This recipe calls for soy sauce as well as salt; long ago, the Kachin would not have had soy sauce, but years of trade across the border between Kachin State and Yunnan Province in China mean that soy sauce is now a part of many Kachin cooks' pantries.

Serve with a vegetable alongside, such as Lima Beans with Galangal (page 110), and a condiment such as Kachin Salsa (page 200) or Fresh Red Chile Chutney (page 203). This is also a good warming winter soup to serve with cheese and bread. For a punchier version, toss in 1 teaspoon Red Chile Powder (page 28).

5 cups water
1 cup Toasted Rice Powder (page 224)
2 tablespoons ginger cut into matchsticks
½ pound boneless chicken or about ¾ pound
    bone-in chicken, cut into bite-sized pieces

2 tablespoons soy sauce, or to taste
2 teaspoons salt, or to taste
½ cup coarsely chopped Vietnamese coriander
    (see Glossary) or coriander (optional)

Pour 2 cups of the water into a large pot and place over medium heat. Add the rice powder and stir thoroughly to blend it into the water. Add the remaining 3 cups water and the ginger and bring to a boil. Add the chicken, soy sauce, and salt and bring back to a boil, then cover and lower the heat to maintain a simmer. Cook for 20 minutes or so, until the chicken is tender and the flavors have had time to blend.

If the soup is thicker than you want, add more hot water and stir in. Taste and adjust the seasonings if necessary.

Serve plain, or top it with chopped fresh herbs, as you please.

ONE DAY IN DAWEI, in southern Burma, I returned from an excursion out of town to find my small quiet hotel bustling with people. A tall foreigner standing outside explained that they were all in town for "the hospital opening." The Sitagu Foundation had financed a hospital for Dawei. (The foreigner was a Belgian doctor who donates his services to the foundation for several weeks a year.)

As we were chatting, some other men from the foundation came over and invited me to join them for supper; "we can go hear the Sayadaw after," they said. I didn't understand what they meant but was happy to go along.

Over our meal they told me about the Sayadaw ("Sayadaw" is a title for a learned senior monk). The Sitagu Sayadaw has been a monk since he was a small boy. Now in his early seventies, he is a lifelong student of the dharma. But he's a kind of muscular Buddhist, believing that people need to take an active role to help relieve suffering and meet the needs of communities in want—which is why he established the Sitagu Foundation. He raises money for the foundation at home and abroad and mobilizes people to help build the hospitals and schools the group pays for. My supper companions told me that his vision and his practical approach have gained him followers all over the world.

Every evening the Sayadaw gives a dharma talk, a talk about Buddhism. It was about eight thirty by the time we left supper and drove a few miles to a dry rice field at the edge of town, near the new hospital. A generator powered the lighting on the raised platform on which the Sayadaw was sitting, talking into a microphone. His tone was personal, confidential. On the sloping ground before him a crowd of more than 500 sat listening. The lights from the stage illuminated their faces, leaving other details in darkness. The sky was full of stars.

As I sat on the ground listening and watching, I could understand only a few words of the Burmese, but I could feel the warm attentiveness of the crowd. The Sayadaw's voice was resonant and assured. Occasionally he did a question-and-response kind of thing with them—or he'd get them laughing. One of the people with the foundation told me the gist: It was about *karuna*, a fundamental Buddhist concept that best translates as "compassion," the desire to remove harm and suffering.

Next morning was the hospital opening, with banners, flowers, and speeches. Then the Sayadaw was shown around the wards. His cheerful, intelligent energy and personal charisma were remarkable. He animated the patients just by being there, asking questions, noticing everything, it seemed. And then he was gone, off to the small Dawei airport with his entourage to catch a plane to Rangoon. He had another dharma talk to give that evening.

The Sitagu Sayadaw.

silky shan soup [TOHU BYAWK]

SERVES 4 OR 5   At morning markets in Shan areas of Burma and northern Thailand, there is always at least one vendor selling this thick, smooth, pale yellow soup for breakfast, hot and enticing, often poured over fine rice vermicelli. Alongside they sell Shan tofu (see page 126), either in large chunks to take home or cut up and dressed as a salad (see Shan Tofu Salad, page 51).

You don't have to restrict yourself to breakfast, however: serve this vegetarian soup at any meal. On its own or over tender noodles, topped with chopped coriander or other fresh herbs, it's comfort food par excellence.

1½ cups chickpea flour
2½ teaspoons salt
8 cups water, or more as needed
¾ pound fresh rice vermicelli or soba noodles or ½ pound dried rice noodles (see Glossary; optional)
½ cup chopped coriander

OPTIONAL TOPPINGS AND CONDIMENTS
About ½ cup Chopped Roasted Peanuts (page 35)
¼ cup Shallot Oil (page 24) or Garlic Oil (page 25)
¼ cup Palm Sugar Water (recipe follows)
2 tablespoons Red Chile Oil (page 25)
¼ cup Tart-Sweet Chile-Garlic Sauce (page 36)
1 cup or more chopped blanched pea tendrils
A handful of tender lettuce greens

Combine the chickpea flour and salt in a medium bowl and add 2 cups of the water. Whisk well to blend and to get rid of any lumps (if you are having difficulty getting it perfectly smooth, press it through a sieve). Set aside for the moment.

Bring the remaining 6 cups water to a boil in a wide heavy pot, then lower the heat to medium-high. Whisk the chickpea mixture one more time, then, using a wooden spoon, stir continuously as you slowly add it to the boiling water; the liquid will foam at first. Lower the heat to medium and continue to cook, stirring to ensure that the mixture does not stick to the bottom of the pot. After about 5 minutes the mixture will be smooth and silky, with a sheen to it, and thickened. Reduce the heat to low and continue stirring for another couple of minutes. (If you are not going to serve it immediately, cover tightly to prevent a skin forming and set aside. When you want to reheat it, add a little water to loosen it, since it will thicken as it cools, and heat over medium heat. Whisk a little as it heats to prevent lumps from forming.)

[Continued]

Silky Shan Soup, served with rice noodles and toppings.

If serving noodles bring a pot of water to a boil and toss in the noodles: fresh ones will cook in 1 or 2 minutes; dried ones will take about 5 minutes. Lift the noodles out of the water and set aside.

Put out any or all of the suggested toppings and condiments, as you choose.

Serve the soup sprinkled with the coriander. Or, if serving the soup over noodles, place some noodles in each bowl, ladle the hot soup over, and sprinkle on the coriander.

Invite your guests to help themselves to the array of toppings and condiments, then stir it all together and eat with pleasure.

NOTE: *If you have soup left over, pour it into a bowl and refrigerate. In a few hours, it will set into Shan tofu; see page 126.*

palm sugar water

MAKES ABOUT 1 CUP

This almost-black liquid is a basic seasoning seen on many street-food vendors' carts and it gives a slightly sweet and smoky aftertaste to many street dishes, especially those of Shan origin. Make sure you buy darker-colored palm sugar; the darker sugar has a smokier taste and less sweetness.

Pour 1 cup water into a small heavy saucepan and set over medium-high heat. Add ¾ cup chopped palm sugar (¼ pound or so) and stir with a wooden spoon to help it dissolve as the water heats. Bring to a boil and then simmer for about 10 minutes. Let cool, and store in a clean glass jar, well labeled, in a cupboard or pantry.

chickpea soup with lemongrass and ginger

SERVES 4 Chickpeas are often eaten for breakfast in Burma. They're also used to make soothing soups like this one: cooked until tender, then flavored with a little hot oil and aromatics. Serve as a hearty winter soup with rice or bread and a vegetable side.

1 cup small brown or large white dried chickpeas, soaked for 8 hours in water to cover and drained, or 2 cups canned chickpeas, drained and rinsed, or 2½ cups cooked chickpeas
2½ to 5 cups water, or as needed
1 stalk lemongrass, trimmed and smashed
2 slices ginger

2 tablespoons peanut oil or Shallot Oil (page 24)
⅛ teaspoon turmeric
¼ cup minced shallots
1 teaspoon salt, or to taste
2 to 3 tablespoons minced coriander
1 lime, cut into wedges

If using dried chickpeas: Put the chickpeas in a pot with 5 cups water, cover, and bring to a vigorous boil. Lower the heat slightly, maintaining a strong boil, and cook, partly covered, until the chickpeas are softened, 1 to 1½ hours, adding extra water if necessary to prevent them from sticking.

If using canned or cooked chickpeas: Place the chickpeas in a pot with 3 cups water, if canned, or 2½ cups, if home-cooked. Bring to a gentle boil and cook for 5 to 10 minutes, until soft.

Mash the chickpeas, mashing some completely and leaving others just a little broken, or pulse several times in a food processor. Add the lemongrass and ginger slices to the chickpeas, along with more water if necessary to give a soupy texture (you should have about 5 cups of soup). Bring to a boil, then reduce the heat and simmer for 20 minutes.

Meanwhile, heat the oil in a small skillet. Add the turmeric and shallots and sauté until the shallots are softened and translucent. Add the shallots to the soup, with the salt, and cook for another 5 minutes. Taste and adjust the seasoning if necessary. Serve hot or at room temperature, topped by the minced coriander, and put out the lime wedges so guests can squeeze on lime juice if they wish.

tomato-chickpea soup

Add 2 large ripe tomatoes, finely chopped (or 1½ cups crushed canned tomatoes), to the sautéing shallots. Cook for about 5 minutes, stirring frequently, then add to the broth and continue with the recipe. You won't need the lime wedges.

mimi's bean soup with tender leaves

SERVES 4 OR 5　A friend named Mimi introduced me to this beautiful soup. She uses large butterfly beans (*bei leikpya* in Burmese), which are pale green beans tinged with pink that look like exotic limas. You can substitute fresh or frozen lima beans. The beans are cooked in water with lots of shallots to make a mild, slightly sweet soup. Near the end, handfuls of fresh greens or leaves are added.

In Mimi's garden in Rangoon, we gathered the delicate tips of a cucumber-like vine and other tender leaves. In Burma the leaves are added as much for their medicinal properties as for their flavor. Their beauty is another good reason for adding them; this is a very attractive soup to serve to guests.

Use a mixture (at least two or three different kinds) of coarsely chopped greens. Depending on the time of year, and the climate you live in, possible choices include pea tendrils, sawtooth herb, sorrel leaves, nasturtium leaves, tender endive, or other tender leaves. The soup is light on the tongue, a great foil for fried dishes.

1 cup shelled fresh butterfly beans, or substitute fresh or frozen limas
4 cups water
1½ cups minced shallots
¼ teaspoon turmeric
About 2 teaspoons fish sauce or soy sauce

1 to 2 teaspoons salt, to taste
2 cups loosely packed greens, such as coarsely chopped sorrel, sawtooth herb, nasturtium leaves, pea tendrils, and/or others of your choice

Place the beans in a medium pot, add the water and shallots, and bring to a boil over medium-high heat. Add the turmeric, lower the heat to maintain a strong simmer, and cook until the beans are tender, adding more hot water if needed. If using precooked frozen beans, they'll be ready very quickly; otherwise, timing will vary with the freshness and size of your beans.

If you wish, process the beans and broth to a puree before proceeding; return to the pot.

Add the fish sauce or soy sauce and salt to taste. Bring to a gentle boil, stir in the greens, and serve.

Put out a chili sauce, if you wish, for guests who like to spice things up.

Mimi's Bean Soup with Tender Leaves, topped with a dash of chile sauce.

MOSTLY VEGETABLES

IN THE SUBTROPICAL CLIMATE of central and southern Burma, fresh vegetables are available year-round and they play a huge role at the table. Every rice meal includes a plate of fresh or steamed vegetables as well as a spiced vegetable dish or two. The possibilities are endless. Fresh beans, from limas to yard-long beans, are included in mixed vegetable dishes such as the intriguing Kachin Vegetable Medley (page 117) or stir-fried (see Lima Beans with Galangal, page 110, for example). In another stir-fry, Napa cabbage is flavored with a little oyster sauce (see page 115)

Eggplant may be grilled and then flavored, as it is in Eggplant Delight (page 120), or simmered in a shallot-ginger flavor base (enriched with tiny dried fish) to make Traveler's Eggplant Curry (page 104). Tomatoes make a sauce for cooking meaty vegetables such as mushrooms (Mushroom and Tomato Curry, page 111) or for eggs (Golden Egg Curry, page 122). The easy and wonderfully versatile Shan tofu is here, both smooth and deep-fried (see pages 126–28), and so are crunchy chayote fritters (see page 125), which make delicious appetizers.

Temperate-climate vegetables like potatoes, pumpkin, and broccoli rabe also have a place at the table, especially in the cooler months. Broccoli Rabe with a Hint of Pork (page 108) is one example; another is the warming and delicious Tamarind-Pumpkin Curry (page 103).

okra-shallot stir-fry

SERVES 4 Okra is widely available in Burma, a reminder that the nation borders on Bangladesh and India, where okra is a common and much appreciated vegetable.

This is a quick pan-fry of chopped okra and shallots. Because it's cut small, the okra gets crispy at the edges and is quickly cooked. The shallots give a hint of sweet and balance while the ginger and cayenne add a bit of warmth. I like to serve this as a side with beef stew or a hearty soup.

½ pound okra
3 tablespoons peanut oil
⅛ teaspoon turmeric
1 cup thinly sliced shallots

1 tablespoon minced ginger
1 teaspoon minced green cayenne chile
1 teaspoon fish sauce
¾ teaspoon salt, or to taste

Cut the stems off the okra, and the tips too, if they are tough. Cut the okra into ¼-inch-wide slices. (You will have about 3 cups.) Set aside.

Place a wok or wide heavy skillet over medium-high heat. Add the oil, and then after a few moments, the turmeric. Stir for a moment, add the shallots, and sauté, stirring occasionally, until they are translucent and starting to brown in spots, about 5 minutes. Add the ginger, stir, and cook for several minutes until softened.

Raise the heat to high and add the okra. Cook, stirring frequently, for several minutes, then add the green chile, fish sauce, and salt. Continue to cook, stirring occasionally, until the okra is tender and has some brown spots.

Turn out into a shallow bowl and serve hot or at room temperature.

tamarind-pumpkin curry

SERVES 4 The sweetness of pumpkin or squash in this attractive dish is balanced by a touch of sour tamarind. This is a good foil for spicy dishes such as Kachin Pounded Beef with Herbs (page 178) or Chile-Oil Fish (page 152). Serve hot or at room temperature. Leftovers are delicious.

1½ pounds pumpkin, or kabocha,
   acorn, or other hard winter squash
About 2 teaspoons tamarind pulp
   (see Glossary), coarsely chopped
½ cup hot water
1 tablespoon oil
Pinch of turmeric
1 tablespoon minced shallot
1 teaspoon minced garlic
½ teaspoon minced ginger

2 tablespoons Dried Shrimp Powder
   (page 30)
¼ to ½ teaspoon Red Chile Powder
   (page 28), or ¼ teaspoon cayenne,
   or to taste
1 tablespoon fish sauce, or to taste
¾ cup water
Salt (optional)
About ¼ cup chopped coriander,
   or 2 to 3 tablespoons minced mint

Cut the pumpkin or squash into approximately 1-inch cubes (you should have about 3 cups). Peel them and set aside.

Put the tamarind pulp in the hot water. Mash it with a fork to dissolve it. Let stand for 10 minutes, then press the liquid through a sieve into a bowl. Discard the pulp.

Heat the oil in a heavy skillet or saucepan or a wok over medium heat. Add the turmeric and stir, then add the shallot, garlic, and ginger and cook, stirring frequently, until the shallot is softened and translucent, 3 to 4 minutes. Add the shrimp powder and cook for about a minute, until softened. Add the chile powder or cayenne, pumpkin cubes, tamarind liquid, fish sauce, and the ¾ cup water, raise the heat, cover, and bring to a boil. Lower the heat to maintain a strong simmer and cook until the pumpkin or squash cubes have softened, 5 to 8 minutes (timing will depend on the kind of pumpkin or squash). Remove the lid and simmer for another minute so the sauce cooks down a little.

Taste the sauce and adjust the seasonings if you wish by adding a dash more fish sauce or a little salt. Top with the coriander or mint and serve.

sweet potato curry

To use sweet potato in place of pumpkin, peel about 1½ pounds sweet potatoes and cut into bite-sized cubes. It will take a little longer to cook.

traveler's eggplant curry

This curry was one of the dishes on offer at a roadside eatery in the mountains of Shan State. It was a real find, with mild heat and a little reddish oil floating on the top, a sign that the dish had simmered long enough. It's delicious over rice and makes great leftovers. Pair it with a green salad, for a contrast of textures and flavors.

Please do *not* taste the curry partway through cooking, since the dried anchovies' taste is dominant until the curry is thoroughly cooked. At that point, the anchovies just give a lovely depth of flavor. Dried shrimp powder makes a good substitute.

About 3 tablespoons dried anchovies (see Glossary), or substitute a generous 2 tablespoons Dried Shrimp Powder (page 30)
3 tablespoons peanut oil
⅛ teaspoon turmeric
½ cup minced shallots
1 teaspoon minced ginger

½ cup minced or crushed tomato
About 1 pound Asian eggplants (3 medium) cut into ¾-inch cubes (about 4 cups)
1 cup water
1 teaspoon salt, or to taste
½ to 1 teaspoon Red Chile Oil (page 25) or store-bought

Coarsely chop the dried anchovies (see Note). Place in a small bowl with about ½ cup warm water and set aside to soak.

Place a large heavy saucepan over medium heat and add the peanut oil and turmeric. When the turmeric fizzes, toss in the shallots. Cook, stirring occasionally, for about 4 minutes, until the shallots are well softened. Add the ginger and tomato and cook for another 3 or 4 minutes until the ginger is softened. Add the eggplant and stir and turn it for several minutes to expose all surfaces to the flavored oil.

Drain the anchovies and add them, along with the 1 cup water. Raise the heat and bring to a boil. Lower the heat to maintain a strong simmer and cook for 5 minutes. Add the salt and chile oil to taste; if using dried shrimp powder, add it now. Continue to simmer, half-covered, for another 30 minutes. The oil will rise to the surface of the cooking liquid and the eggplant will be tender and succulent.

Taste for salt and adjust if you wish.

NOTE: *As the dish cooks, the anchovies melt into the eggplant, all but the small silvery heads. If you wish, cut off and discard the heads before chopping the anchovies.*

I TRAVELED SEVEN HOURS up the Kaladan River to Mrauk U to see the astonishing monuments and temples built during its heyday. Mrauk U was the cosmopolitan capital of a wealthy kingdom that flourished from the fifteenth century until the early nineteenth century. These days, it's an "extended village," with small markets, a little tourism, and not much action. There's electricity (from a generator) for a few hours every day. Everyone uses candles or kerosene lanterns. The outside world feels far away.

Mrauk U is an accumulation of hamlets built around lots of steep hills, most of them topped by *chedis*. There aren't many roads, just narrow dirt lanes. People get around on foot or by bicycle. It's easy to feel disoriented among all the hills and bumps in the landscape, but when I climbed a hilltop with a sketch map in my hand, I began to situate myself. To the south I could see the waterways that I'd traveled in on. All around me were hills and ridges topped by *chedis* and monuments. Smoke from cooking fires drifted among the palm trees. And to the north, a road led through rice fields golden with stubble.

One day I headed out through those fields to see where the road would take me. Traveling at bicycle speed (one-speed-bicycle speed) I could notice details: the rooflines of the houses, the shapes of the trees, the smells in the air.

After a week in Mrauk U, I traveled by boat back down the river to Sittwe on the coast. The sound of the boat motor seemed loud, much louder than on my way up. Sittwe—which had seemed a small town on my way in—felt like a city after the peace of Mrauk U. I caught a plane late that afternoon and by nightfall I was walking along a crowded sidewalk in Rangoon, headed for an internet café.

I found the landscape of Mrauk U hauntingly lovely. In the midst of grand monuments and chedis, the timeless patterns of rural village life continue: unhurried conversations between old friends, the slow creak of an oxcart . . .

broccoli rabe with a hint of pork

SERVES 4   Like many Shan dishes, this combines vegetables and meat: the bitter flavor of broccoli rabe and the slight sweetness of pork complement each other well. The recipe calls for fermented soybeans (you can substitute miso paste); because the soybeans or miso vary in saltiness, hold back on salt until the dish has come together.

This is a quick dish for a weeknight supper, light on meat and yet satisfying. Serve as one of several dishes with rice or as a light lunch; it's also a good complement to Silky Shan Soup (page 94) or a minestrone.

1 pound broccoli rabe	3 or 4 dried red chiles
¼ pound pork shoulder or boneless pork tenderloin, thinly sliced	A generous tablespoon of Fermented Soybean Paste (page 39) or store-bought, or substitute
2 tablespoons peanut oil	1½ teaspoons brown miso paste
1 tablespoon thinly sliced garlic	1 to 1½ cups water
1 teaspoon minced lemongrass	½ teaspoon salt, or to taste

Chop the tough ends off the broccoli rabe and discard. Cut the greens into 2-inch lengths. Wash thoroughly in cold water, drain, and set aside.

Cut the pork slices crosswise into approximately 1-inch lengths; set aside.

Place a wok or wide heavy pot over medium-high heat. Add the oil, and when it is hot, toss in the sliced garlic. Cook, stirring, for about 30 seconds, then add the lemongrass and chiles and stir. Raise the heat to high, toss in the pork, and stir and turn to break up any clumps and ensure that all surfaces get exposed to the hot oil. Once the meat has changed color, a minute or two, add the chopped greens, and stir and turn to mix well.

Mix the soybean or miso paste into 1 cup water and add, together with the salt. Bring to a vigorous boil, cover, lower the heat slightly to maintain the boil, and cook for 3 to 4 minutes, until the broccoli rabe is just tender. Add another ½ cup or more water if you want more liquid. Taste for salt and adjust if necessary. Serve hot or at room temperature, with rice or noodles.

vegetarian shan greens
Substitute ½ pound portobellos or button mushrooms, sliced, for the pork. Add once the chiles have gone in, and stir-fry until they soften and begin to give up their juices, about 5 minutes, before adding the greens.

lima beans with galangal

SERVES 4 TO 6 In Burma the cook starts not with dried beans but with fresh butter beans or limas. Those are hard to come by in North America, so I usually substitute frozen limas or edamame (soybeans), both available in well-stocked supermarkets and Asian groceries.

Here, the bright green, beautiful beans are cooked in hot oil flavored with a little garlic and slices of galangal. If you cannot find galangal, substitute ginger; the flavor will be different but still pleasing, and with a warm tingle to it. Serve the beans hot or at room temperature.

1 pound (about 2 cups) fresh or frozen lima
  beans or shelled soybeans (edamame)
2 tablespoons peanut oil
1 clove garlic, smashed

3 slices or 1 generous tablespoon coarsely
  chopped galangal (see Glossary)
¼ cup hot water
1 teaspoon salt

Place the fresh or frozen beans in a large sieve and rinse briefly with cold water to wash off any ice or dirt. Set aside.

Place a medium saucepan over medium-high heat and add the oil. Lower the heat to medium, toss in the garlic and galangal, and cook for 2 to 3 minutes, until softened and fragrant. Raise the heat to high, add the beans, and cook for 2 to 3 minutes, stirring constantly to expose them all to the hot oil. Add the hot water and salt and continue to cook, stirring frequently, until the beans are just tender to the bite, another 5 minutes or so (timing will depend on the beans). Turn out and serve.

garden peas with galangal

Freshly shelled garden peas are delicious cooked this way, their slight sweetness balanced by the resinous flavor of the galangal. Use a little less water to cook them. And the cooking time is shorter, just a minute or two, especially if the peas are young and tender.

mushroom and tomato curry

SERVES 2 AS A MAIN COURSE, 4 AS A SIDE

The stretch of road between Myitkyina and Bhamo, in Kachin State, has a particularly wonderful set of roadside restaurant stalls (see photograph, page xi), as does the Hpa'an-to-Rangoon road. They put out about twenty curries for customers to choose from. When a bus arrives, the businesses compete with one another for customers, then rush to get everyone fed. Whatever curries you choose come with rice and soup as well as steamed vegetables and condiments. It's an amazing performance.

It was at one such roadside stall that I came across this full-flavored mushroom and tomato curry. It makes a good vegetarian main course (substitute soy sauce for the fish sauce) or a substantial vegetable side and is wonderful served nontraditionally over noodles or pasta.

3 tablespoons peanut oil
¼ teaspoon turmeric
1 cup thinly sliced shallots
About 2 teaspoons minced garlic
2 cups chopped oyster, portobello, or king mushrooms (about ½ pound)

1½ cups chopped ripe tomatoes (about ½ pound)
½ teaspoon Red Chile Powder (page 28; optional)
1 teaspoon Shallot Oil (page 24)
1 teaspoon fish sauce
½ teaspoon salt, or to taste

Heat the oil in a wok or a wide pot over medium-high heat. Add the turmeric and stir until it dissolves, then add the shallots and cook over medium to medium-high heat until they soften without browning, about 4 minutes. Add the garlic and cook for a minute or two, then raise the heat to high and toss in the mushrooms. Stir-fry, pressing the mushrooms against the hot pan until they soften and give off a little liquid, 4 to 6 minutes.

Add the tomatoes and, if using, the chile powder and bring to a boil, then lower the heat and simmer until the tomatoes have completely broken down and the mushrooms are cooked through and tender, 5 to 7 minutes.

Add the shallot oil, fish sauce, and salt and stir. Cook for another 30 seconds or so, then turn out into a shallow bowl and serve hot or at room temperature.

mandalay mushroom-tomato curry with green chiles

Add 3 green cayenne chiles, coarsely chopped, when you add the tomatoes. The chiles give heat and another layer of flavor.

peas for many occasions

Cooked dried peas (chickpeas, cowpeas, black-eyed peas, and more) are so versatile. They can top fried rice, and in Burma they are often served on *nan-piar*—unleavened wheat flatbreads that are close cousins of South Asian naan (see Tender Flatbreads, page 244). They're also one of the toppings for Street-Side Rice Crepes, Myitkyina Style (page 240).

Use whichever legume pleases you. I love having a cache of cooked peas in the freezer. All I need to do is reheat them in a little broth or water and season them, and they are ready to be used as a topping, perhaps with the addition of chopped fresh herbs or a squeeze of lime juice. They can also go into a soup to give it more substance. When using them as a topping, mash them a little to prevent them rolling off the bread or crepe.

1 cup dried cowpeas, black-eyed peas, or
   chickpeas, soaked overnight in water
   to cover
4 cups water or as needed
1 large shallot, coarsely chopped,
   plus ¼ cup sliced shallot
1 slice ginger, left whole or minced (optional)

2 tablespoons peanut oil
¼ teaspoon turmeric
¾ teaspoon salt, or to taste
2 teaspoons fish sauce, or to taste
2 to 3 tablespoons chopped coriander or
   other fresh herbs (optional)
Juice of 1 lime (optional)

Drain the peas and place in a medium pot with the water, chopped shallot, and ginger, if using. Bring to a vigorous boil, then cover, lower the heat, and simmer until the peas are tender, 1½ to 2 hours; timing depends on the age of the peas. Add more hot water if it runs low.

About 10 minutes before the peas are done, heat the oil in a heavy skillet over medium-high heat, add the turmeric and sliced shallot, and cook until the shallot is translucent, 3 to 4 minutes. Add to the peas and season to taste with the salt and fish sauce. (If freezing for later use, do not season the peas until you reheat them.) If you wish, top with chopped herbs or some lime juice.

NOTE ON DOUBLING THE RECIPE: *I often make a double quantity, then divide the cooked peas and freeze them in two or three smaller batches. To cook 2 cups peas, use 7 cups water, 2 or 3 chopped shallots, and double the ginger (if using).*

Mya Mya in her kitchen in Pakkoku.

MYA MYA WAS BORN over seventy years ago in Myitkyina, of mixed Kachin, Shan, and Bamar parents. She married a Bamar man from Pakkoku and she's been living in that central Burmese town, ever since, for nearly fifty years. As we walked to the market together, many people greeted her on the street. She nodded back politely, but said to me, "You know, even after all these years, they still call me the tribal woman because my mother was Kachin."

Mya Mya's husband died recently; she's carrying on their small guesthouse business day by day. Her daughter, Ko Ko, and four grandchildren live with her in the old house overlooking the river. Mya Mya has style: she pulls her hair back in a bun and wears soft pinks and mauves that flatter her skin. Her earrings are small Burmese rubies set in gold. She's beautiful to watch as she goes about her day.

I spent almost all my time in Pakkoku hanging out in Mya Mya's kitchen. Her daughter-in-law was visiting from Rangoon with her daughter, so there were a lot of people to feed, and lots of hands to do the work too. Everything happened in and around the kitchen, a cluttered high-ceilinged room that opened onto the backyard. The daughter-in-law chopped and cooked in one corner while Ko Ko's children sat on the floor in front of small mirrors carefully applying *thanaka* paste (see page 169) before heading to class. I'd chat with Mya Mya while Ko Ko's oldest daughter agonized over which outfit to wear to a friend's wedding.

By the time Ko Ko took me to the Bagan-bound boat on her motorcycle a couple of days later, I felt I'd become part of the family. Before leaving I signed their new guestbook and had a look at all the old ones. There were entries from the last thirty years, written by people from Korea, Spain, the USA, and elsewhere, travelers who had found a temporary home and welcome shelter in this small place on the Irrawaddy.

new potatoes with spiced shallot oil

SERVES 4 TO 6 In temperate and northern climates, we take the year-round availability of potatoes for granted. But in Rakhine State on Burma's west coast, there's a very limited growing season for potatoes, from February until early May—in other words, from a month before the start of the hot season until the rains begin.

Potatoes are eaten only in season there, and when they are small. In this dish they are dressed with shallot oil that is, in typical Rakhine fashion, made hot with a little chile. There's an enticing contrasting tartness that comes in Burma from hibiscus flowers. To get the same effect, I use sorrel leaves (especially in summer, when sorrel grows in my garden, in season with the new potato crop), which have a fresh lemony tang, or I get a tart edge from chopped tomatillos or green tomatoes. If you have none of these, a generous squeeze of lime or lemon juice gives the same balance.

**About 2 pounds very small new potatoes
(1- to 1½-inch diameter) or small fingerling
potatoes
3 to 4 tablespoons Shallot Oil (page 24)
1 green or red cayenne chile, or substitute
1 serrano chile, seeded and minced**

**½ cup thinly sliced sorrel leaves, or
minced tomatillo or green tomato
(see the headnote)
1 teaspoon salt, or to taste**

Place the potatoes in a pot of cold water to barely cover and bring to a boil, then lower the heat and cook at a low boil until just cooked through. Drain, place back in the pot, cover, and set aside for 10 minutes.

Heat the oil in a small skillet over medium-high heat. Add the chile, and as soon as the oil starts to bubble around it, remove from the heat and set aside.

If the skin on the potatoes is at all tough, strip it off; otherwise, leave it on. Place the potatoes in a wide bowl, pour the chile oil over, add the sorrel or tomatillos or tomato, and toss. Add the salt and toss. Taste for salt, and adjust if you wish.

new potatoes with greens
You can wilt about 1½ cups chopped dandelion greens or fenugreek leaves in the oil alongside the chile, then add to the potatoes.

smoky napa stir-fry

SERVES 4 Another light take on green vegetables. The oyster sauce, available in Asian grocery stores and well-stocked groceries, gives a smoky undernote to the dish. Try to find fresh young Napa cabbage for extra crispness.

About ¾ pound Napa cabbage
½ cup hot water
1 scant tablespoon oyster sauce
2 tablespoons peanut oil
⅛ teaspoon turmeric

2 dried red chiles
1 medium shallot, minced
1 teaspoon minced ginger
¼ teaspoon salt, or to taste

Cut the cabbage crosswise into ¼-inch slices, then slice them crosswise to make bite-sized pieces (you should have 4 loosely packed cups). Place in a bowl of cold water to wash thoroughly, then lift out, drain, and set aside.

Pour the hot water into a small bowl, add the oyster sauce, and stir well. Set aside.

Place a medium or large wok or large deep skillet over high heat. Add the oil, then lower the heat to medium-high and stir in the turmeric. Add the chiles, shallot, and ginger and stir-fry for about 30 seconds, until the shallot starts to soften.

Raise the heat to high, toss in the chopped greens and salt, and stir-fry, tossing and pressing the greens against the hot sides of the pan. When they have wilted and softened, 2 to 3 minutes, add the oyster sauce mixture. Bring to a boil, turn and stir for another 15 seconds or so to distribute flavors and finish cooking the greens, and turn out into a wide shallow bowl.

Serve hot or at room temperature.

simmered cabbage, shan style [GALAAM OOP]

SERVES 4 AS A MAIN COURSE The Shan name of this dish indicates the cooking method (*oop*) used for cooking the cabbage (*galaam*). The *oop* method of cooking involves a slow simmer of ingredients under a tightly sealed lid, with very little water and little or no oil. It's a classic Shan cooking method, one that is also used by the Tai Koen of eastern Shan State and northern Thailand. Here depth of flavor comes from soybean disks (miso paste is a fine substitute) and from the interplay of the roasted peanuts with the tomatoes and cabbage. The dish comes together in less than thirty minutes of simmering.

¼ cup peanut oil or vegetable oil

1½ teaspoons Red Chile Powder (page 28), or to taste

1 teaspoon turmeric

1 cup thinly sliced shallots

2 teaspoons powdered toasted Soybean Disks (see Cooking with *Tua Nao*, page 41), or 1 teaspoon medium brown miso paste (see Glossary)

1 tablespoon salt, or to taste

1 small green cabbage or Savoy cabbage, finely shredded (about 4 cups) and washed

1 cup thin wedges of Roma (plum) or other fleshy tomatoes

⅓ cup Chopped Roasted Peanuts (page 35)

Place a wok or a wide heavy pot over medium heat and add the oil. Toss in the chile powder, turmeric, shallots, and the *tua nao* powder, if using (do *not* add the miso now), and salt, and stir-fry for several minutes, until the shallots are starting to soften and become translucent.

Add the cabbage and tomatoes and stir well, then cover, lower the heat to medium-low, and cook for about 10 minutes, until the cabbage is partly wilted. Add the peanuts and the miso, if using, stir well, cover again, and continue to cook for another 10 to 15 minutes, until the cabbage is a softened mass.

Taste and adjust the salt if necessary, then serve hot or at room temperature.

simmered cabbage with pork (or beef)

If you'd like a heartier version of this dish, include a little pork or beef; you can then omit the *tua nao* or miso. Use ½ pound boneless pork shoulder, thinly sliced, or ground pork or ground beef. Once you have cooked the aromatics, add the meat and stir-fry until it has changed color, then add the cabbage and proceed as above. You'll need to add a little more salt.

kachin vegetable medley

SERVES 2 OR 3 AS A MAIN COURSE, 4 AS A SIDE DISH

This mixed vegetable dish is tender and succulent, with a subtle toasted flavor from toasted rice powder. It's traditionally made by steaming the vegetables and rice powder in a leaf-wrapped package. This adaptation uses a pot with a tight-fitting lid and a small amount of oil to prevent sticking. The vegetables slow-cook in their own steam, very like the Shan method of cooking called *oop* (see Simmered Cabbage, Shan Style, opposite).

The combination of vegetables here is a place to start but you can, for instance, substitute another leafy green for the bok choi. The important thing is to use vegetables that will soften easily in the steam, which means no carrots or other hard root vegetables. Every version of this dish that I have tasted includes a bitter element—I use radicchio or dandelion greens or a combination—as well as a balancing hint of sweetness and heat from ginger and a little red chile. With one chile, the heat is barely perceptible; two give more warmth.

Serve with roast chicken or roast beef or as a vegetarian main course.

3 tablespoons Toasted Rice Powder (page 224)
2 tablespoons Chopped Roasted Peanuts (page 35), ground even finer
About 2 tablespoons peanut oil
½ cup water
1 cup yard-long beans, cut into 1-inch lengths, or substitute sliced green beans
½ to 1 cup coarsely chopped small bok choi leaves
3 tablespoons minced ginger
1 cup chopped radicchio or dandelion greens, or a mixture

1 or 2 red cayenne chiles, seeded and finely sliced
½ cup sliced oyster or button mushrooms or other tender mushrooms
½ cup small okra or tender broccolini cut into ½-inch lengths, or substitute some small zucchini, sliced
¼ cup coarsely chopped Vietnamese coriander (see Glossary)
¼ cup chopped sawtooth herb (see Glossary) or sorrel
¾ teaspoon salt, or to taste

Place a wide heavy pot with a tight-fitting lid over medium heat. Add the rice powder, peanuts, oil, and water and mix, then add all the remaining ingredients and stir and turn to mix them well. Cover tightly, lower the heat to medium-low, and cook until the vegetables are tender, 10 to 15 minutes (take a peek after about 5 minutes and give a thorough stir to make sure things aren't sticking; if they are, add another couple tablespoons of water and lower the heat a little more, then cover again).

Turn out into a bowl and serve.

CHIN STATE borders on the Indian states of Manipur, Mizoram, and Nagaland and is home to Chin people from a number of related cultures, all of whom speak Tibeto-Burman languages that are related to Burmese. The Chin are famous for their beautiful fine textiles, which are locally distinctive markers of identity.

I've never been to Chin State, for it's still closed to independent travelers, but I'm told the countryside is beautiful, mountainous, and fertile. A few years ago I was able to visit several Chin villages south of the state border, in Rakhine, traveling upriver by boat from Mrauk U. In those villages people were growing fruit of all kinds and had rice fields and vegetable gardens.

Thanks to generous Chin people living in Rangoon, I've been able to taste some traditional northern Chin food and to learn a little of the food

traditions of the Chin. Here is what I've learned: In northern Chin the most important grain is corn rather than rice (although rice and sticky rice are also eaten). Millet seems to have been the original staple, since the word for millet is *mim* and the term for corn is *vai mim* or "foreign millet." Millet is cooked using the absorption method, in a measured amount of water that gets absorbed as the millet cooks. The main protein is dried fish from the rivers and lakes, or in some regions tiny frogs, all cooked with onions and vegetables, and with hibiscus and other leaves that give the food a tart edge.

Cooks in Chin State have many mushrooms to work with, and plenty of vegetable greens, both cultivated and wild-gathered. Flavorings are fairly simple: apart from onions, Chin people use chiles rather than pepper, and salt rather than fish sauce. In central and southern Chin State, a sesame-salt blend made of toasted sesame seeds that are pounded in a mortar until there's a sheen of oil, then mixed with a little salt, is sprinkled on rice as part of everyday eating. Northern Chin grind toasted sesame more lightly and use the sesame-salt combination only with sticky rice.

Most dishes are boiled and simmered; any frying is done in goat butter or rendered fat, not in vegetable oil. The main meal among the northern Chin is a soupy porridge like polenta, made of corn, and eaten with a fermented bean sauce that is used as a flavoring. The bean sauce is an acquired taste for outsiders, as many fermented foods are, but to those who grow up with it, of course it tastes of home and is delicious. The loose corn polenta is served boiling hot and eaten with a beautiful dried-gourd spoon or scoop. Diners use their scoops

to toss the soup a little to cool it, a graceful technique that, I've discovered, takes practice. Green vegetables are part of every meal.

Recently I spent some time in a town called Kalaymyo, just twenty miles from the border of Chin State. The Chin Hills rise tantalizingly just west of town, but foreign travelers are still not permitted to go there. A Chin restaurant in town had "mython" on the menu, a new meat to me. The mython is a species of large cow that the Chin eat on special occasions. A poster on the restaurant's wall showed a mython grazing: the large stocky creature with horns looked like a *gaur*, a mountain cow found in India. The people I asked in Kalaymyo could not agree whether they're the same creature or perhaps just close relatives. It makes you wonder what other mysteries there are in Chin State. . . .

OPPOSITE: *A cart with a crowd of youngsters soliciting donations travels across a bridge near Myitkyina in Kachin State.* **ABOVE:** *A Chin woman with a beautifully tattooed face.*

eggplant delight

SERVES 4 Another easy pleasure I discovered in Mrauk U, this eggplant puree, like many classic eggplant dishes, begins by grilling whole eggplants. The smoky-tasting, tender grilled eggplant flesh is then mixed with an egg and a little seasoning and briefly cooked again to a smooth, silky puree. It makes a great side with rice, slightly sweet (from the egg), and it's also an appealing accompaniment for fish or grilled beef. Leftovers are delicious.

The recipe is so simple that it is tempting to make it more complicated. Please don't.

3 medium Asian or 1 large Mediterranean
   eggplant (about 1 pound)
1 medium or large egg
1½ tablespoons Shallot Oil (page 24) or peanut
   oil
⅛ teaspoon turmeric

1 dried red chile
1 small shallot, minced
¾ teaspoon salt, or to taste
About 2 tablespoons torn coriander or
   finely chopped mint (optional)
1 lime, cut into wedges (optional)

Heat a charcoal or gas grill to medium-hot, or preheat the oven to 450°F.

Prick the eggplant(s) all over with a fork. Grill about 5 inches from the flame, turning to expose all sides to the heat, or place on a baking sheet and bake, until very soft, about 20 minutes. Set aside to cool for 10 minutes.

Cut the eggplants lengthwise in half, then use a large metal spoon to scrape the flesh out of the skin; or you may find it easier to peel the skin off the flesh. Place the flesh in a bowl (you should have about 1½ densely packed cups), add the egg, and use a nonreactive fork to blend it into a puree.

Place a wok or a heavy skillet over medium-high heat. Add the oil and swirl it a little. Add the turmeric, then toss in the chile and shallot. Cook for 10 to 15 seconds, then add the eggplant mixture and stir constantly with a wooden spoon, moving the puree around and around in the pan so that it cooks evenly without sticking and stays soft and smooth, for about 1 minute. Add the salt and stir again, then turn out into a shallow bowl. Take out the dried red chile.

Top the eggplant with the coriander or mint and squeeze on some lime juice, if you wish. Serve warm or at room temperature.

easy coriander-tomato omelet

One afternoon while I was staying in Pakkoku (see "'Tribal Woman,'" page 113), the daughter-in-law whipped up several omelets as a midafternoon snack for the family.

This version of her omelet is loaded with flavor from the tomatoes and aromatics that cook ahead in the pan, and from the fresh coriander that is stirred into the eggs.

Serve with bread or Fried Rice with Shallots (page 226). Put out a plate of chopped cucumbers or some salad greens if you wish. Either Tart-Sweet Chile-Garlic Sauce (page 36) or Tamarind Sauce (page 205) makes a great condiment.

**3 extra-large or 4 medium eggs,
  preferably free-range**
1 to 2 tablespoons water
¾ teaspoon salt, or to taste
**¼ cup loosely packed coarsely chopped
  coriander**

1 to 2 tablespoons peanut oil or vegetable oil
⅛ teaspoon turmeric
Scant ¼ cup thinly sliced shallots
1 generous tablespoon minced garlic
¼ cup thin tomato wedges

Break the eggs into a bowl, add the water and salt, and whisk until foaming. Add the coriander and whisk again, then set aside.

Place a large wok or a cast-iron or other heavy skillet over medium-high heat. Add the oil, and then the turmeric, and swirl the oil gently. Toss in the shallots and stir-fry over medium heat for about a minute. Add the garlic and tomatoes and cook until the tomatoes are softened, about 3 minutes.

Whisk the eggs briefly again, then pour the egg mixture into the pan and tilt the pan a little to help the eggs flow across the hot surface. Lower the heat to medium and cook for a minute or so, then lift an edge of the omelet and tilt the pan so that the liquid egg mixture pours over the edge and onto the hot pan. Repeat at several other places around the edges. Cover with a lid and cook for about a minute, then flip over, so that the top surface is cooking directly on the hot pan; it will cook through in less than a minute. Turn out onto a plate and serve.

easy coriander-tomato omelet for four

If you have only a small pan, make 2 batches of the recipe. If you have a large pan, use 6 extra-large eggs, 3 or 4 tablespoons water, 1½ teaspoons salt, ½ cup chopped coriander, 2 to 3 tablespoons oil, ⅛ teaspoon turmeric, ½ cup sliced shallots, ¼ cup minced garlic, and ½ cup tomato wedges. Cooking times at each stage will be longer.

golden egg curry

SERVES 4 Burmese egg curry is a beautiful way of presenting eggs. They're first boiled, then peeled and fried in medium-hot oil. The smooth whites blister and firm up into an attractive golden crust. Only then are the eggs cut in half and added to a sauce—here, a light tomato-based sauce that's mildly chile hot.

Serve with rice or bread, a crisp salad, and a condiment like Crispy Shallot and Dried Shrimp Relish (page 210) or Tart-Sweet Chile-Garlic Sauce (page 36).

4 large or extra-large eggs, preferably free-range

⅓ cup peanut oil or unroasted sesame oil (see Glossary)

⅛ teaspoon turmeric

2 small shallots, minced

2 teaspoons minced garlic

¼ teaspoon Red Chile Powder (page 28), or to taste

2 medium tomatoes (about ½ pound), finely chopped

2 teaspoons fish sauce

½ teaspoon salt, or to taste

2 or 3 green cayenne chiles, seeded and sliced lengthwise into 3 or 4 strips each

Place the eggs in a saucepan, add cold water to cover, bring to a boil, and cook at a medium boil for 8 minutes. Drain the eggs and cool in cold water. When the eggs are cool enough to handle, peel them.

Heat the oil in a wide heavy skillet over medium-high heat. Add the turmeric and stir to dissolve it. When the oil is hot enough to sizzle when a drop of water is dropped into it, add the peeled eggs and fry until golden and a little blistered all over: cook on each side in turn, then try to balance the eggs on their ends to cook the tips. Frying the eggs is a fun little task, quickly done, and it makes them very attractive. With a slotted spoon, lift the eggs out of the hot oil and onto a plate. Cut them lengthwise in half and set aside.

Pour off all but 2 to 3 tablespoons of the oil (the oil can be used again for stir-frying). Heat the oil remaining in the pan over medium heat, add the shallots and garlic, and fry briefly, until translucent. Add the chile powder and tomatoes and, stirring frequently to prevent sticking, cook at a strong simmer until the tomatoes have broken down into a softened mass, about 10 minutes.

Stir in the fish sauce and salt, then taste and adjust the seasoning if you wish. Raise the heat to medium-high, add the chile strips, and stir. Place the eggs cut side down in the sauce and cook until the oil sizzles, about 3 minutes. Serve hot or at room temperature.

paneer in tomato sauce

SERVES 4 TO 6 AS
A MAIN COURSE This interesting cross between a sauce and a curry has echoes of the Indian subcontinent but is distinctively Burmese. Paneer is a fresh firm cheese that does not melt when heated; it's available in South Asian groceries (see Glossary for more). You can also, nontraditionally, substitute pressed tofu for the paneer. The taste is a little different, but the result is very similar.

Made with paneer and soy sauce or miso, this dish is vegetarian; with tofu, it becomes vegan. Serve it over rice, pasta, or rice noodles. To reduce the heat, cut back the amount of chile powder and/or strip the seeds out of the cayenne chile.

5½ cups roughly chopped ripe tomatoes or 5 cups canned crushed tomatoes
Generous ¼ cup peanut oil
½ teaspoon turmeric
½ cup chopped shallots
2 tablespoons minced or pounded garlic
1 to 2 teaspoons Red Chile Powder (page 28), to taste
1 teaspoon shrimp paste (*ngapi*; see Glossary), or substitute 1 tablespoon fish sauce or soy sauce or 1 teaspoon brown miso

About 1 pound firm paneer (see the headnote), or substitute pressed tofu
4 to 5 green cayenne chiles, cut into ½-inch-wide slices
2 teaspoons salt, or to taste
1 cup minced scallion greens
Scant 1 cup minced coriander leaves and stems

Place the tomatoes in a food processor and puree. Set aside.

Heat the oil in a wide pot or a large wok over medium heat. Add the turmeric and shallots and cook, stirring occasionally, until the shallots are softened, about 4 minutes. Add the garlic, chile powder, and shrimp paste, if using, and stir to mix well. Add the tomato puree and fish sauce, soy sauce, or miso, if using, and bring to a boil, then lower the heat and simmer for 10 minutes.

Meanwhile, slice the paneer or tofu into ¼-inch-thick slices about 1 inch long and ½ inch wide. Add the paneer or tofu, chiles, and salt to the pan and simmer for 10 minutes. A couple of minutes before the dish is ready, stir in the scallion greens. Taste for salt, and adjust by adding salt or fish sauce, as you wish.

Turn out into a serving bowl, add the coriander, and stir; serve hot or at room temperature.

deep-fried chayote fingers

SERVES 4   In Burma, this fried treat is made most often with bottle gourd, but chayote is more available in North America, so that's what I use. Chayote is a pear-shaped gourd that originated in central America (see Glossary). Substitute zucchini if you wish.

These are easy to make and a real crowd-pleaser, crispy and tender at once, with a hint of ginger. Be sure to get your condiment sauces ready before you start cooking, because like any deep-fried snack, these are best eaten hot.

Serve as a snack or appetizer or to accompany mohinga (see pages 256–61).

About ½ pound chayote (1 medium),
   bottle gourd, or zucchini

BATTER
½ cup rice flour
⅛ teaspoon turmeric
½ teaspoon salt
Scant ½ cup lukewarm water
1 tablespoon minced ginger

Peanut oil for deep-frying

DIPPING SAUCE POSSIBILITIES
Tamarind Sauce (page 205)
Tart-Sweet Chile-Garlic Sauce (page 36)
Fresh Red Chile Chutney (page 203)

If using chayote or gourd, peel it lengthwise, cut into quarters, and scoop out the seed. Thinly slice lengthwise. If using zucchini, cut into 2- to 3-inch lengths and slice into matchsticks. Set aside on a plate.

Combine the rice flour, turmeric, and salt in a bowl. Add the water and whisk to blend to a smooth batter. Add the ginger and stir. Set aside for 10 minutes. Meanwhile, set out tongs, a spider, or a slotted spoon by the stove. Put out several more plates to receive the cooked vegetables.

Heat 2 inches of the oil in a deep fryer or a stable wok over medium to medium-high heat. Test the temperature by dropping a small spoonful of batter into the oil: it should sink and then rise, without burning.

Stir the batter. Pick up a clump of 2 or 3 slices of chayote; drag them through the batter to coat and then slide into the oil. Once the batter starts cooking, it will hold the slices together in a bundle. Repeat with 3 or 4 more bundles, without crowding. Cook for 7 or 8 minutes, until golden all over, using tongs to move the bundles around so they cook evenly. When they're done, lift them out of the oil, and transfer to a plate. Repeat with the remaining vegetable slices and batter.

pale yellow shan tofu

MAKES ABOUT
2½ POUNDS

Photograph on
page 129

The smooth, pale yellow "tofu" that the Shan make with chickpea flour is one of the great unsung treasures of Southeast Asia, beautiful to look at and a pleasure to eat in many forms. It's also another reminder of how much of the Shan repertoire is ideal for vegetarians.

Unlike "regular" (soybean) tofu, Shan tofu is easy to make at home, and it has a much better flavor. Chickpea flour is widely available in health food stores and in Ethiopian and South Asian groceries (it's sometimes labeled "besan," its Hindi name). The flour is stirred into water and cooked gently, then the mixture is set aside to firm up for a few hours and, *voilà*, it's done!

Apart from the ease of making it, Shan tofu is a cook's friend because of its versatility. You can chop it up and serve it in a salad (see page 51); slice it into long strands and use it as a noodle base for a soup or sauce of any kind; cut it into thin pieces and deep-fry it for a delicious snack (see Deep-Fried Shan Tofu, page 128); or serve it as a satisfying soup (see Silky Shan Soup, page 94) before it cools and firms.

2 cups chickpea flour
2½ teaspoons salt

6 cups water
Peanut oil or vegetable oil

Place the chickpea flour and salt in a medium bowl and add 2 cups of the water. Whisk to blend well; you want to get rid of all lumps. (If you are having difficulty getting it perfectly smooth, press it through a sieve into another bowl.) Set aside for a moment.

Lightly oil two 8-inch ceramic or glass pie plates or shallow bowls at least 1½ inches deep (or pans of similar volumes—7- or 8-inch square cake pans, for example).

Bring the remaining 4 cups water to a boil in a wide, shallow, heavy pot, then lower the heat to medium-high. Whisk the chickpea mixture one more time, then use a wooden spoon to stir continuously as you slowly add it to the boiling water. The liquid will foam a little at first. Lower the heat to medium and continue stirring to ensure that the mixture does not stick to the bottom of the pot. After about 5 minutes, the mixture will be smooth, with a silky sheen to it, and will have thickened. Immediately pour it into the prepared plates or pans.

Let stand for a few minutes to cool slightly, then place in the refrigerator to firm up and set. After 1 hour, it will be firm enough to serve as tofu, but if you are planning to slice it for deep-frying, or to make a salad, it's better to let it chill for at least 4 hours, or even as long as overnight if you wish.

When ready to proceed, turn the tofu out onto a board. It should be smooth, dense, and firm, not sticky, so that it can be thinly sliced without breaking; if it is still soft, place it back in the refrigerator to firm up. Use a sharp chef's knife to slice it.

TOFU STRIPS: *Some Shan cooks use a kind of cheese slicer to make long shavings of the tofu, rather like noodles. If your tofu is very firm, use a sharp cheese slicer to make thin strips for tofu salad or for "noodles" to go under soup or in sauces.*

turmeric-yellow shan tofu

In central Burma, Bamar cooks tend to add turmeric, which makes for a more yellow tofu (they do the same with Silky Shan Soup; see page 94). Just add ¼ teaspoon turmeric to the chickpea flour and salt.

deep-fried shan tofu

SERVES 4 TO 6 Shan tofu makes a great deep-fried snack. Let the tofu set firmly overnight, then cut it into shapes. If you cut it thin, the fried pieces will be crisp; thicker pieces will have a tender interior and a crisp outer crust. Serve with one or more dipping sauces, or use as a topping for noodle soups.

Pale Yellow Shan Tofu (page 126),
   chilled overnight
Peanut oil for deep-frying

OPTIONAL DIPPING SAUCES
Tamarind Sauce (page 205)
Tart-Sweet Chile-Garlic Sauce (page 36)
Kachin Salsa (page 200)

Slice the tofu into ⅛-inch-thick strips about 2 inches long, or into triangles, or slice it into ¼-inch-thick pieces (see the headnote). If your tofu is in a rectangular pan, slices are easier. If it is in a round pan, cut it into quarters, then slice each of them into triangular slices thin or thick as you please.

Pour 1½ to 2 inches of peanut oil into a deep fryer, stable wok, or wide shallow pot, and heat over high heat. When the oil reaches 360°F (if you don't have a thermometer, stand a wooden chopstick or wooden spoon handle in the oil—if the oil bubbles up along the wood, it is at temperature). One at a time, slide the strips or triangles of tofu into the oil near the side of the pan; try to make sure that they are not overlapping. Working in batches, use a slotted spoon or a spider to separate any that are sticking together. Lower the heat to medium-high and keep moving the pieces around so they brown evenly; turn them over occasionally. After about 5 minutes, they should have changed color a little. Use tongs or a spider to lift them out of the hot oil, pausing to shake them a little and let excess oil drain off, and transfer to a paper-towel-lined plate. Repeat with the remaining tofu.

Serve hot or warm, on their own or with one or more dipping sauces.

Versatile Shan tofu in two forms: in the back, Pale Yellow Shan Tofu (page 126); and in front, Deep-Fried Shan Tofu.

FISH AND SEAFOOD

WITH BURMA'S THOUSAND miles of coastline, you might imagine that people there prefer ocean fish, but freshwater fish are the favorites, carp and catfish in particular.

Like home cooks everywhere, Burmese cooks are creative and resourceful: fish is fried, or steamed with aromatics, or simmered in curry. Dried anchovies are quickly fried with ginger and chiles to make an easy snack food (see page 132). Boneless fish is mashed to make fried fish cakes (see page 133) or dressed almost like a salad (Fluffy Lemongrass Fish, page 138). And then there's curry—fish, shrimp, or crayfish simmered in aromatic flavorings, usually with a little tomato (see page 136). The Kachin have a seductive herb-laden steamed fish curry (see page 142). And the Tai Koen in the eastern part of Shan State combine catfish with lemongrass and herbs (see page 150). You'll also find fish and seafood dishes in Salads and in Soups.

Use fish that are available where you are, and try to choose fish that are not endangered but are being raised or caught sustainably. Get into the habit of asking where the fish at your local grocery or fishmonger come from. Consult an online resource such as http://www.foodandwaterwatch.org/fish/seafood/guide to find out which fish are "low risk." The situation keeps changing, so it's always a good idea to check.

crispy anchovies with chiles and ginger

SERVES 4 TO 6 I love having a supply of fried anchovies on hand. I put them out as a snack or at mealtime as a little side condiment. They keep well for several weeks if stored, once completely cooled, in a well-sealed glass jar.

Dried anchovies, 1½ to 2 inches long and silvery, are widely available in Asian markets, usually in plastic bags. There's a little chile heat here as well as warmth from fried ginger and garlic.

**2 cups (about 2 ounces) loosely packed
    dried anchovies**
5 or 6 dried red chiles

2 to 3 cups peanut oil for deep-frying
1 tablespoon thinly sliced garlic
2 teaspoons fine matchsticks ginger

Rinse the anchovies, pat dry, and set aside to air-dry.

Break the chiles in half, discard the seeds and stems, and place in a bowl with hot water to cover. Let soak for 10 minutes to soften, then drain, mince, and set aside.

Pour the oil into a stable wok or a deep fryer or deep pot; you want the oil to be about 2 inches deep, to cover the anchovies. (If you want to use less oil, fry the anchovies in 2 batches.) Heat the oil to 350°F—use a thermometer or else the following test: hold a wooden chopstick or the handle of a wooden spoon vertically in the pan, touching the bottom; if oil bubbles up along the wood, then it is at temperature. Add the anchovies and fry for about a minute, until crisped up and just starting to turn color, then transfer to a paper-towel-lined plate.

If you used a wok, pour off all but a scant tablespoon of the oil and heat over medium-high heat. If you used another arrangement, place a wok or heavy skillet over medium-high heat and add a scant tablespoon (a little more if using a skillet) of the anchovy-frying oil. Toss in the garlic and ginger and stir-fry briefly, until the garlic starts to turn golden; then add the chiles and stir-fry for another 10 seconds or so. Add the anchovies and stir for about 30 seconds.

Transfer to a bowl. Serve hot or at room temperature.

fish cakes and fish balls

SERVES 4 TO 6 AS AN APPETIZER Fish cakes are made of boneless fish that is blended with aromatics, shaped into patties, and fried. It's an easy process, especially with a food processor rather than the traditional mortar and pestle. Fish cakes can be served as an appetizer, or else sliced and dressed for a salad (Fish Cake Salad with Shaved Cabbage, page 70). The paste can also be shaped into small round fish balls, which once boiled are perfect as appetizers or as an addition to noodle soups.

To serve cakes or balls as an appetizer, set out on tender lettuce leaves and drizzle with Tart-Sweet Chile-Garlic Sauce (page 36).

About ½ pound tilapia or other white fish fillets, rinsed and coarsely chopped
About 2 tablespoons minced shallots
2 teaspoons minced garlic

1 teaspoon minced ginger
Scant ½ teaspoon salt
Peanut oil for shallow-frying

Combine the fish, shallots, garlic, ginger, and salt in a food processor and process to a smooth, even paste.

Put a lightly oiled large plate on your work surface. *For fish cakes:* Scoop up a scant 1 tablespoon fish paste at a time, shape it into a smooth ball between your palms, flatten it to a disk about 1½ inches in diameter, and set on the plate. You should have 15 to 18 patties. *For fish balls:* scoop up a generous 1 teaspoon of the paste, roll it lightly between moist palms to shape a ball, and set on the plate; repeat with the remaining paste.

To fry fish cakes: Heat a large heavy skillet over medium-high heat. Pour in about ¼ inch of peanut oil. When the oil is hot, slide in the patties one by one. Cook in batches; stop adding them when the pan gets crowded. Cook until the underside is golden, 3 to 4 minutes, using a spatula to prevent the cakes from sticking to the pan. Turn them over and cook until golden on the underside. Hold a spider or sieve ready in your other hand as you use the spatula to lift out each disk, and place it in the sieve or spider, letting excess oil drain off, then transfer to a plate to cool and firm up. Repeat with the remaining fish cakes.

To cook fish balls: Drop the balls into a pot of boiling broth or water. Once cooked through, in 2 to 3 minutes, they can be used in noodle dishes or frozen for later use.

MYITKYINA, the capital of Kachin State, sits high on the west bank of the Irrawaddy, with a view of the mountains. It's not as beautiful as you might expect from that description, because the place was so heavily bombed during the Second World War that only a couple of old buildings remain from earlier times. A travel agent in Rangoon had warned me as he sold me my plane ticket that I'd be disappointed in Myitkyina: "There's nothing of interest left to look at there." And yet . . .

Myitkyina is a crossroads: the Chinese border is about a hundred miles to the east, and India lies to the west. During the war the Japanese advanced up the Irrawaddy Valley, chasing the British army before them, and the British then retreated through the mountains into India. Once the Japanese occupied the town, the Burmese Frontier Forces (BFF) waged battle from the hills. It seems like ancient history in some ways, but reminders of that time are everywhere.

At the YMCA one day, I met a Kachin man named Nkula who had served in the BFF. Now in his early eighties, he'd joined the British army as a teenager just before Rangoon fell to the Japanese. He then found himself hiding in the hills fighting a guerilla war against the Japanese for over two years, under the command of a British officer. And now, he told me, there are only seven veterans of the Kachin BFF still alive. In his quiet way he was proud of his war service. No, he'd not received any pension from the British—none of them had. After we talked I watched him as he straddled his motorcycle, lean and lithe and not showing his age at all. And then with a courteous wave, he was off down the road, heading home.

A few days later I got a ride in a jeep from an outgoing man in his fifties with a generous black moustache. I asked him where his father was from. "From Pakistan, the Punjab, but then it was British India," he said cheerfully. "He came here to Myitkyina with the British during the war. They seconded him to the Americans to work as a driver when they were building the Burma Road." Once the Allies retook northern Burma, they focused on building this road, a supply route to link India to China; it was finished as the war ended. "My father died just last year," he continued. "He was ninety-six. You see this jeep? This is the same jeep he drove during the war." He patted it with affection.

There may not be many old buildings in Myitkyina, but there's lots of history.

CLOCKWISE FROM TOP: *Two men labor up the steps from the river carrying loaded baskets of tomatoes to the Myitkyina market. A mother and baby at the market steps. One of the last survivors of the Kachin insurgency force that fought the Japanese in World War II.*

shrimp curry

Tomato is a classic foil for shrimp. Here the combination makes an appealing curry with plenty of sauce for drizzling on rice. Pair it with Smoky Napa Stir-Fry (page 115) or a salad of cooked greens.

The green cayenne chiles give a nice little underlying heat; if you want more intensity, add a sprinkling of Red Chile Powder (page 28).

If you find yourself with leftovers, add a little water, taste, and adjust the seasoning, then chill to serve as a delicious cold soup.

Generous 1 pound shrimp, peeled and deveined
¼ cup minced shallots
½ teaspoon minced garlic
3 tablespoons peanut oil
⅛ teaspoon turmeric
1½ cups chopped ripe tomatoes or canned crushed tomatoes

¾ cup water
2 teaspoons fish sauce
2 green cayenne chiles, seeded and minced, or to taste
½ teaspoon salt, or to taste
About ¼ cup coriander leaves (optional)
1 lime, cut into wedges (optional)

Rinse the shrimp and set aside. If you have a mortar, pound the minced shallots and garlic to a paste.

Heat the oil in a wok or a wide heavy skillet over medium-high heat. Add the turmeric and stir, then toss in the shallots and garlic, lower the heat to medium, and cook, stirring frequently, until softened and translucent, about 2 minutes. Add the tomatoes and cook for several minutes at a medium boil, stirring occasionally, until the tomatoes are well softened and the oil has risen to the surface.

Add the water and fish sauce, bring to a medium boil, and add the shrimp. Cook for several minutes, or until the shrimp start to turn pink, then toss in the minced chiles and salt, stir briefly, and remove from the heat. Taste and adjust the seasoning if necessary.

Turn out into a bowl, top with the coriander leaves, if using, and put out lime wedges, if you wish. Serve hot or at room temperature.

crayfish curry

For a crayfish version of this curry, use 1½ pounds crayfish in their shells and increase the fish sauce to 1 tablespoon and the green chiles to 4.

fluffy lemongrass fish

This dish is ideal for those who don't like dealing with fish bones. It comes to the table aromatic with lemongrass and ginger. Be sure not to taste for seasoning until after you have added the lime juice; it brings all the flavors together. Serve as a main course, with a salad or a vegetable side, or as an appetizer.

One 1¾- to 2-pound whole snapper or other
    firm-textured fish, such as lake perch or
    trout, cleaned, scaled, and head cut off, or
    1½ pounds halibut steaks
¼ teaspoon turmeric
½ teaspoon salt, or to taste
2 tablespoons minced shallots
1 teaspoon minced garlic

2 teaspoons minced ginger
2 stalks lemongrass, trimmed and minced
¼ cup peanut oil
2 teaspoons fish sauce
1 to 2 tablespoons Fried Shallots (page 24)
1 tablespoon fresh lime juice, or to taste
1 or 2 limes, cut into wedges

Rinse the fish. Put about ¾ inch water in a 10- to 12-inch heavy skillet and place over medium-high heat. Add ⅛ teaspoon of the turmeric and ½ teaspoon salt and slide the fish into the water. Bring to a boil, then lower the heat to maintain a gentle boil. Turn the fish over after 3 minutes (2 minutes if using steaks) and cook for another 1 to 2 minutes, or until it is just barely cooked through. Flake with a fork to test for doneness; the flesh should be opaque.

Remove the fish to a platter and let cool for a few minutes. (Set the broth aside for another purpose.) Lift the flesh off the bones and pull it into smaller flakes or pieces; discard the skin and bones.

If you have a mortar, pound the shallots, garlic, ginger, and lemongrass to a paste; set aside. Alternatively, put them in a miniprocessor and process.

Place a wide heavy skillet or a wok over medium heat. Add the oil, then stir in the remaining ⅛ teaspoon turmeric. Add the shallots, garlic, ginger, and lemongrass and cook, stirring frequently, until softened, about 5 minutes. Add the fish and stir to break it into smaller pieces and to combine it with the oil and flavorings, then add the fish sauce and stir. Cook for several minutes, until the fish is lightly touched with gold.

Transfer to a shallow serving bowl, add the fried shallots, and toss. Add the lime juice and toss again, then taste; add a little salt if you wish. Put out the lime wedges so guests can squeeze on extra lime juice.

river fish celebration

SERVES 4 OR 5 Far upriver from the coast of Rakhine State lies Mrauk U, a sleepy tourist destination of villages and Buddhist ruins (see page 107). On my last night there, the main dish for supper at the guesthouse where I was staying was a whole fish—I can't tell you the kind—cooked this way. It's a remarkable expression of the Rakhine palate, with chiles, galangal as well as ginger, and a little bitterness from cooked coriander.

You'll need a pan that is large enough to hold the whole fish (snapper or trout is a good choice), one with a tight-fitting lid to seal the steam in.

Serve with rice or boiled new potatoes. Start with a light soup (Ambrosial Chicken Broth with Shallots and Lime Juice, page 77, is a good option), and serve a mild vegetable dish such as Eggplant Delight (page 120) alongside.

AROMATIC RUB
2 garlic cloves, minced
1 medium shallot, minced
1 tablespoon minced ginger
1 tablespoon minced galangal
   (see Glossary)
½ lime, including skin, minced
½ teaspoon salt
¼ teaspoon turmeric

1¼ to 1½ pounds cleaned whole firm-fleshed
   fish, such as snapper or trout, rinsed and
   dried
3 tablespoons peanut oil
½ cup thinly sliced shallots
2 garlic cloves, minced
2 red cayenne chiles, minced, or 4 dried
   red chiles, broken in half
8 to 10 coriander stalks
About ¼ cup hot water

Combine all the rub ingredients in a mortar or mini processor, and pound or process to a coarse paste. Rub the fish all over with the paste and set aside for 15 minutes.

Place a wide shallow wok or a heavy skillet that is big enough to hold the fish over high heat. Add the oil, heat for a minute, then lower the heat to medium. Add the shallots and cook, stirring frequently, until translucent, about 5 minutes. Add the garlic and cook for another minute.

Toss in the chiles and raise the heat to high. Add half the coriander, place the fish in the pan, cover tightly, and lower the heat to medium-high. Cook for about 4 minutes, then add the hot water. Bring to a boil, turn the fish over, add the remaining coriander, cover, and cook for another 3 minutes, or until the fish is just cooked through (the flesh should be opaque and should flake when pulled with a fork).

Serve from the pan or transfer to a platter and serve.

OVERLEAF: *River Fish Celebration, served in the pan.*

kachin carp curry with herbs

SERVES 4 There are two verions of this dish, which I learned from the cooks at Myit Sone, a Kachin restaurant in Rangoon. On the stovetop, the fish is rubbed with a ginger-garlic-chile paste, poached briefly, and then combined with chopped herbs and cooked a few minutes longer. For the traditional version, which requires wrapping the fish in banana leaves, I use foil that is lined with lettuce leaves.

I've made this with carp, which is delicious and traditional, as well as with tilapia and with pickerel, which both work very well.

The chiles in the flavor paste provide a sharp hit of chile heat; for less, reduce to one chile, or use a milder chile, such as a banana chile.

This makes a knockout light lunch or supper with rice or bread and a salad (Long-Bean Salad with Roasted Peanuts, page 50, for example, or a green salad). Or, more traditionally, serve it hot or at room temperature as part of a rice meal. Fresh Red Chile Chutney (page 203) makes a good condiment sauce.

FLAVOR PASTE
1 tablespoon minced garlic
1 tablespoon minced ginger
2 green cayenne chiles, minced
¾ teaspoon salt

1½ pounds carp, skinned and cleaned of bones, cut into 1-inch pieces, or about 1 pound tilapia, pickerel, or other firm fillets, cut into 1-inch pieces
½ cup water (if making a stovetop curry)
2 tablespoons fresh lime juice
1 cup packed coarsely chopped Vietnamese coriander (see Glossary)

1 cup loosely packed coarsely chopped sawtooth herb (see Glossary)
Scant ½ cup chopped scallion greens
2 green cayenne chiles (if making a stovetop curry)
1 tablespoon peanut oil (if making a stovetop curry)
2 teaspoons soy sauce, or substitute ¾ teaspoon salt, or to taste
8 large tender lettuce leaves (if steaming the fish in packages)
Salt to taste
2 limes, cut into wedges (optional)

To make the flavor paste: Combine the garlic, ginger, chiles and salt in a mortar or in a small processor and pound or process to a paste. Place the fish in a bowl, add the paste, and stir and toss to coat the fish with the paste.

To make a stovetop curry: Place a large wok over medium heat. Add the fish, with all of its flavor paste, the water, and lime juice. Cover, bring to a vigorous boil, and then cook uncovered until the fish is nearly opaque and cooked throughout, about 2 minutes. Add the coriander and sawtooth herb and stir, then add the scallion greens and chiles. Stir, and cook for another minute. Stir in the oil. Taste and add soy sauce or salt if you wish, stir, and turn out onto a platter or individual plates.

[Continued]

Alternatively, to make a more traditional wrapped steamed curry: Preheat a charcoal or gas grill to medium heat, or place a steamer over a pot of water and bring to a boil. Cut eight 8-inch squares of aluminum foil.

Add the lime juice, herbs, and scallion greens to the fish and stir to distribute. Divide the fish mixture into 4 equal portions. Place 2 lettuce leaves on one piece of foil. Pile one-quarter of the fish mixture onto the leaves. Fold over two opposite sides of the foil square, overlapping them and making a double fold to seal, then fold over the other two sides, making a double fold again. Place the package seam side down on another piece of foil and repeat the wrapping technique. Repeat to make 3 more packages.

Place the foil packets 5 or 6 inches from the coals or flame, or put in the steamer and cover. Cook over low to medium heat, turning them frequently, until done, 20 to 30 minutes. (Open one package to check for doneness: the fish should be opaque and the aromatics should be tender.) If steaming, maintain a strong boil and steam until done, about 20 minutes.

Unfold each package and turn the leaf-wrapped fish out onto individual plates.

To serve either version: Serve with lime wedges, if desired.

EVOLVING KACHIN COOKING TECHNIQUES: *The Kachin of northern Burma traditionally rely on grilling, steaming (in leaf-wrapped packages), or boiling to cook their food. Until recently, they had little access to cooking oils because they lived in the mountains and high valleys of Kachin State. These days, many Kachin have migrated to lower-lying towns and villages in their home state and in other parts of the country. There they have less access to wild-gathered leaves, but oil is more available. This recipe, which uses a dash of peanut oil to great effect, is an example of how Kachin cooking techniques have adapted.*

fish stew with aromatics

SERVES 6 TO 8 This cross between a stew and a soup, called *gaeng pla* by the Shan, has a layered depth of flavor that makes it a real keeper. Starting with a paste of ginger, lemongrass, garlic, and shallots that perfumes the water the fish cooks in, the stew gets a balancing acid note from fresh tomato and a little heat from green chiles.

Use whatever fish you prefer, from freshwater options such as trout, tilapia, or pickerel to barramundi, snapper, haddock, or even salmon.

Serve the stew as a main course over rice or, nontraditionally, over couscous or new potatoes. Accompany with a simple vegetable stir-fry and a salad.

¼ cup thinly sliced lemongrass
2 tablespoons sliced turmeric root
   (see Glossary), or substitute
   1 tablespoon ground turmeric
2 tablespoons salt
½ cup coarsely chopped shallots
¼ cup coarsely chopped garlic
¼ cup sliced ginger
2 tablespoons minced coriander roots
   (see Glossary), or roots and stems
½ cup sliced green cayenne chiles
8 cups water

1 cup tomato wedges
2 tablespoons chopped or crumbled
   toasted Soybean Disk (see Cooking
   with *Tua Nao*, page 41), or substitute
   2 teaspoons brown miso paste
3 to 3½ pounds cleaned whole fish
   (see the headnote), cut into steaks
   about ¾ inch thick and rinsed
Scant 2 tablespoons minced scallions
2 cups loosely packed Thai basil leaves,
   or a mix of basil and coriander leaves

Combine the lemongrass, turmeric, and a pinch of salt in a large mortar or food processor and pound or process to a coarse paste; set aside. Using the mortar or food processor, make a coarse paste of the shallots, garlic, ginger, coriander, chiles, and a pinch of salt. Combine the two pastes and mix well.

Bring the water to a boil in a wide pot. Add the spice paste, along with the tomatoes, crumbled soybean disk (do *not* add miso paste now), and the remaining salt, bring to a boil, and boil hard for 10 minutes.

If using miso paste, scoop out a little broth and use it to dissolve the paste, then add back to the pot. Add the fish, including the heads if available, cover, and cook at a medium boil until the fish is cooked through, about 10 minutes. Add the scallions and stir, then add the basil (and coriander) leaves, stir, and remove from the heat.

Serve hot or at room temperature.

WHEN I FIRST traveled to Burma, in the early 1980s, foreigners were given a one-week visa, and nothing more. They were allowed to visit Rangoon and a triangle of places in the middle of the country: Bagan, Mandalay, and Inle Lake. Some people hit all three, taking short plane hops to manage the feat. I opted for sinking into one place and so flew straight up to the lake.

Only three other guests were staying at my small guesthouse in Yaunghwe, the old Shan capital next to the lake: a young doctor from Rangoon, her brother, and his wife. The brother worked for the Burmese Broadcasting Corporation doing radio news. The siblings both spoke beautiful English. It was not only a pleasure to listen to, but also a great bit of luck, for we could have easy conversations about anything and everything.

Many years later, at a hospital opening in Dawei (see "Meeting Monk," page 93), I was introduced to a fine-looking man from Inle Lake, dressed in a beautiful Shan-style suit. He looked vaguely familiar. I told him that I'd visited Inle Lake the first time I came to Burma. "Where did you stay?" he asked. "In a small, friendly guesthouse called the Inle Inn," I replied. He responded, "Then you stayed with me!"

These days Inle Lake is a favorite tourist destination. Accommodations range from family-run guesthouses to exquisite hotels. But even with the growth in tourism the lake remains beautiful—and mysterious too. The Intha people live in villages that float on wooden stilts in the lake, and they grow tomatoes on floating islands. Lively village markets are full of fresh food. All the local people—Shan and Pa-O as well as Intha—welcome visitors warmly.

Portraits from Inle Lake. **OPPOSITE, CLOCKWISE FROM TOP:** *A march of chedis along the shore of a second lake south of Inle. A floating pagoda at the south end of the lake. Two small monklets play at a rural market by the lake. Pa-O women at the same market at the far end of the southern lake.* **OVERLEAF:** *A fisherman with his net in the shallow waters of Inle Lake, with the Shan Hills in the background. The lake is rich in nutrients, home to many fish, and boasts floating islands where the Intha people grow tons of tomatoes for shipping to Rangoon.*

herbed catfish laap [LAAP PLA]

SERVES 4 OR 5 From the old Tai Koen capital Chiang Tung, also known as Kengtung, in the mountains of eastern Shan State comes this wonderful take on fish.

Laap dishes are made of chopped fish or meat dressed with aromatics. Here the fish is poached whole in a little broth flavored with lemongrass and galangal, then flaked off the bone and finely chopped. The cooking broth is combined with a flavor paste of grilled aromatics to make a dressing for the fish. The list of ingredients is long because of the variety of herbs that are added just before serving. If you are missing one or two kinds of herbs, don't worry, just increase the quantity of the others.

Serve the delicious traditional way, with Sticky Rice (page 232) and a plate of steamed and raw vegetables (see page 217).

One 2-pound cleaned catfish
  (or 2 smaller ones), well rinsed, or
  another firm-fleshed freshwater fish,
  such as pike, pickerel, or trout
4 shallots
5 garlic cloves
5 dried red chiles
1 Soybean Disk (page 40), or substitute
  1½ teaspoons brown miso paste
2 cups water
2 stalks lemongrass, trimmed and smashed
1 teaspoon shrimp paste (*ngapi*; see Glossary)
3 slices galangal (see Glossary)

1 teaspoon turmeric
¾ teaspoon salt, or to taste
Peanut oil
2 tablespoons minced lemongrass
2 tablespoons Toasted Rice Powder (page 224)
2 to 3 tablespoons tender coriander leaves
2 to 3 tablespoons minced scallion greens
1 tablespoon minced mint
1 tablespoon chopped Vietnamese coriander
  (see Glossary)
1 tablespoon chopped tender green tips of
  sawtooth herb (see Glossary)

If using catfish, preheat a gas or charcoal grill, or heat a large wok or pot over medium-high heat. Lightly brown the catfish skin by exposing it to the flame or hot surface just long enough that the skin sears and browns. Remove from the heat and rinse the catfish, rubbing it clean. If not using catfish, then just rinse the fish.

If you haven't heated a grill, heat a cast-iron or other heavy skillet over medium-high heat. If using the grill, thread the shallots, garlic, and chiles onto skewers (this will make it easier to turn them and control the cooking process). Put the shallots, garlic, and chiles on the grill or in the skillet and cook, turning occasionally, to soften them. Be careful that you cook the chiles just until they are softened, not burned black, which would make them bitter. The shallots and garlic will take longer; cook them until they are softened with some black patches on their skins. Set aside to cool for a moment. Add the soybean disk to the grill, wok, or skillet and toast for 30 seconds to 1 minute, until pale but not scorched.

Meanwhile, combine the water, lemongrass stalks, shrimp paste, galangal, and turmeric in a large pot and bring to a boil. Add the fish and cook at a strong boil for about 10 minutes, turning it to ensure that all parts of it get cooked through. Lift the fish out and set aside in a large bowl to cool. Strain the cooking liquid and set aside in a bowl. (You will have about ¾ cup.)

Remove and discard the stems from the chiles, and remove the skins and any blackened patches from the shallots and garlic. Combine the chiles, shallots, and garlic in a food processor or large mortar and process or pound to a paste. Add the grilled soybean disk or the miso and salt and process or pound briefly to blend. (You should have about ½ cup paste.)

Stir the paste into the reserved cooking liquid to make the dressing and set aside.

Lift the fish flesh off the bones and transfer to a cutting board. Finely chop to reduce it to a smooth texture. Place in a wide shallow bowl and pour on the dressing. Mix well and set aside.

Put 1 to 2 tablespoons of oil in a wok or skillet and heat over medium-high heat. Add the minced lemongrass and stir-fry until crisp, 30 seconds to 1 minute. Lift the lemongrass out and set aside. Add the fish skeleton to the hot oil and fry until crisp and brown, 2 to 3 minutes. Lift out and transfer to a mortar or food processor. Add the fried lemongrass and pound or process to a powder.

Just before serving, add the powdered fish bones and lemongrass, toasted rice powder, and herbs, and mix well. Taste for salt, and adjust if necessary. Serve at room temperature.

chile-oil fish

SERVES 4 In Sittwe, the capital of Rakhine State, there's a family-run restaurant off the main street that features home-style cooking. The butterfish I ate there was delectable, bathed in a hot sauce and served with a small side condiment of green chiles—they were pounded with salt and a little shrimp paste, to give a fresh chile hit on top of the chile oil's heat.

Since butterfish is now listed as endangered, I make this dish and its Rangoon variation with black cod (rich and delicious) or with salmon. Check an online list and use whatever fish you can find that is rich in oils and nonendangered. The dish has an intense and lingering chile heat. Those who want to proceed cautiously can start by using only 1 or 2 teaspoons chile oil; this also allows you to adjust for variations in the heat of different chile oils.

Serve with plain rice or over couscous or wild rice to soak up the sauce. In winter, roasted celery root slices or pan-roasted potatoes are a great accompaniment; in summer, pair with crisp salad greens or a Burmese salad such as Intensely Green Spinach and Tomato Salad with Peanuts (page 44).

About 1½ pounds fish fillets—black cod, salmon, or other rich fish
¼ teaspoon turmeric
Salt
½ cup minced shallots
1 tablespoon minced garlic
1 tablespoon minced ginger
2 tablespoons peanut oil

1 tablespoon Red Chile Oil (page 25), or to taste
1 teaspoon shrimp paste (*ngapi*; see Glossary), or substitute 2 teaspoons fish sauce
1 teaspoon Red Chile Powder (page 28)
Green Chile Paste (recipe follows)

Rinse the fish and cut into 1- to 2-inch pieces, pulling out and discarding any bones. Place in a bowl, add the turmeric and ½ teaspoon salt, and turn and mix to coat the fish. Set aside for 10 to 15 minutes.

Meanwhile, if you have a mortar, pound the shallots to a paste with a pinch of salt; set aside. Pound the garlic and ginger to a paste with a pinch of salt; set aside.

Heat the peanut and chile oils in a wok or wide shallow pot over medium heat. Add the shallots and cook for several minutes, until softened and starting to turn golden. Add the garlic and ginger, the shrimp paste, if using (not the fish sauce), and the chile powder and stir to dissolve the shrimp paste in the hot oil. Cook, stirring, until the shallots and garlic are softened, another couple of minutes.

Add the fish and the fish sauce, if using, and cook for 2 minutes. Stir gently to turn the fish and cook for another minute or two, until the fish is just opaque throughout. Taste and adjust the seasonings if necessary, using salt or fish sauce.

Serve hot or at room temperature with the chile paste.

green chile paste

MAKES ABOUT
3/4 CUP

8 green cayenne chiles
¼ cup hot water

⅛ teaspoon salt

Crush the chiles in a mortar, or use the side of a cleaver or chef's knife to crush them on a cutting board. Slice each one crosswise into 3 or 4 pieces. Place in a bowl with the water and salt and set aside to soak until ready to serve.

fish with tart greens

A friend and I ate another memorable butterfish dish, this one at a restaurant in Rangoon called Aung Thu Daw. It was milder, without chile oil or green chile paste. Instead, the fish was cooked with tart local greens, a great pairing. I substitute sorrel or sawtooth herb (see Glossary) for the tart local greens used in the original.

Omit the chile oil and green chile paste, and increase the peanut oil to 3 tablespoons. When the shallots and garlic are softened, toss in 3 cups coarsely chopped sorrel or sawtooth herb and stir-fry for a couple of minutes, just until wilted. Then add the fish and proceed as above.

CHICKEN

THERE'S USUALLY A CHICKEN or two around when a family wants to feast. Maybe that's why there are so many good chicken dishes in Burma. This chapter gives just a glimpse of the variety. There's a chile-hot Rakhine minced chicken (see page 166) and a mild chicken curry from central Burma (see page 156). From Shan State comes a chicken stew with potatoes (see page 170) and from the Kachin tradition there's a succulent steamed curry (see page 159).

There are also two takes on fried chicken, one a street-side classic (see page 174) and the other a simple home-cooked version with an interesting technique (see page 175).

Many of these recipes call for chicken cut into small pieces, on the bone. The advantage of small pieces is that there is more surface area for the marinade and sauce to cling to, and the cooking time is shorter. If you have a good cleaver or chicken shears, you can chop the bird up yourself, or ask your butcher do it (see A Note on Chopped Chicken, page 157). You may also prefer to leave the pieces larger.

Village cooks insist that "village chickens"—that is, free-range long-legged chickens—have much more flavor. Those birds tend to look scrawny to us. Free-range chickens in North America are more sheltered than their Burmese village cousins, but they still have better flavor than battery-raised chickens, so do try to find free-range birds.

village boys' chicken

SERVES 6 The story behind the name of this easy curry is that it's the kind of dish that village boys who have stolen a neighbor's chicken would cook up for themselves. I learned it from a generous-hearted friend in Rangoon, as well as a similar version from Cho Cho (see page 80) in her village near Bagan.

In Burma this is usually made with calabash, a kind of gourd that is peeled and cut into bite-sized cubes. I like to use chayote, which is now available in North American groceries, but you can use winter melon or potato if you prefer. With four dried red chiles, the sauce in this curry has a kick; for less heat, remove the chile seeds.

I like to serve this with broccoli rabe or baby bok choi, lightly dressed with a vinaigrette. Another possibility when tomatoes are in season is a simple salad of chopped tomatoes. Or serve it hot over rice.

One 2½- to 3-pound chicken, preferably free-range, chopped into small pieces (see Note), liver reserved, or substitute 2½ pounds legs and breasts, chopped into pieces

SPICE RUB
½ teaspoon salt
¼ teaspoon turmeric
¼ teaspoon black pepper
1 tablespoon peanut oil

1 tablespoon minced garlic

1 tablespoon minced ginger
3 or 4 dried red chiles, soaked in warm water for 10 minutes and drained
¼ cup peanut oil
½ cup minced shallots
1 stalk lemongrass, trimmed, smashed, and cut into 2-inch lengths
About 3 cups water
4 cups bite-sized cubes chayote or winter melon
Fish sauce or soy sauce (optional)

Rinse the chicken pieces thoroughly with cold water, then pat dry. Place in a wide bowl, add the rub ingredients, and turn and mix so the chicken is well coated. Set aside for 10 minutes, loosely covered.

Meanwhile, if you have a mortar, pound the garlic and ginger together to make a paste; set aside. Remove the stems from the soaked chiles, and discard the seeds if you wish (they give extra heat). Chop the chiles and pound to a coarse paste in the mortar, or finely mince; set aside.

Heat the oil in a wide skillet or a wok over medium heat. Add the shallots and cook, stirring occasionally, until translucent. Add the garlic and ginger and cook for 30 seconds, then add the chiles and lemongrass and stir. Add the chicken pieces, along with the liver if you have it, stir, and cook briefly. Remove the liver after 2 minutes or so, when it is just cooked; set aside. Continue cooking and stirring until most of the surfaces of the chicken pieces have changed color, then add about 2 cups of water (you want it half an inch deep or so), cover, and bring to a boil. Lower the heat and simmer for 10 to 15 minutes.

If the water level seems too low, add another ½ cup or more and bring back to a boil. Add the chayote or melon cubes and cook at a medium boil until tender and the chicken is cooked through, about 10 minutes.

Taste for salt, and add fish sauce or soy sauce, if needed. If you have the liver, add it just before serving.

A NOTE ON CHOPPED CHICKEN: *I prefer that the chicken be chopped into small pieces, about 10 pieces to the pound. That translates into the following: Chop each drumstick into 2 pieces, the thighs into 3; split the breasts and cut each half-breast into 4 pieces; and chop the wings into 2 pieces. If you are lucky enough to have a good butcher, ask him or her to chop a whole chicken into small pieces, otherwise, use kitchen shears or a sharp cleaver to cut it up. Rinse off the chopped chicken thoroughly to get rid of stray shards of bone, then pat dry.*

A pair of young monks clowns around on the steps of their monastery in Kengtung.

curried chicken livers

SERVES 4 After a morning's explorations in Mandalay, I stopped for lunch at a hole-in-the-wall on a side street. I ended up lingering over my meal, for the day was hot and the food a pleasure, especially this curry.

The sauce is smooth and creamy, the chicken livers, in bite-sized pieces, creamy too. It's a great combination with rice or new potatoes and a vegetable side or a salad.

**1 pound chicken livers,
preferably from organic birds**
¼ cup peanut oil
¼ teaspoon turmeric
1 cup minced shallots
1 tablespoon crushed or minced ginger

½ cup crushed or minced ripe tomato
½ cup hot water
2 teaspoons fish sauce
1 teaspoon salt
¼ to ½ teaspoon Red Chile Powder (page 28)

Rinse the chicken livers and trim off any fat and off-colored parts. Cut into small pieces, about ½ to ¾ inch across, and set aside.

Place a heavy wok or skillet over medium heat. Add the oil, and when it is hot add the turmeric and stir, then add the shallots. Cook, stirring occasionally, until the shallots are softened and translucent, about 5 minutes. Add the ginger and tomato and simmer for 3 or 4 minutes, stirring occasionally.

Push the sauce out to the sides of the pan, raise the heat to high, and add the chicken livers. Cook, stirring and pressing the livers against the pan to expose all surfaces to the heat, for about 1 minute, or just until all surfaces have changed color. Pull the sauce back into the center of the pan, add the water, and bring to a boil. Add the fish sauce, salt, and chile powder and lower the heat to maintain a simmer. The livers will be just cooked through but still tender in another minute or two and the sauce will have thickened. Remove from the heat and serve.

kachin chicken curry

This dish can be cooked in a bowl set in a steamer or in a tightly covered pot. The chicken is chopped into small pieces, on the bone. It cooks more quickly than it would in large pieces, and more surface area is exposed to the flavor paste and the broth.

The chicken is rubbed with a flavor paste of garlic, ginger, ground coriander, turmeric, and dried red chiles. It steams in its own juices, emerging tender and succulent.

About 1½ pounds chicken parts, chopped into about 15 pieces (see A Note on Chopped Chicken, page 157)
1 tablespoon minced garlic
1 tablespoon minced ginger
1 teaspoon salt
2 to 4 dried red chiles, seeded and minced

Scant 1 teaspoon ground coriander seed
¼ teaspoon turmeric
1 tablespoon water, or as needed
1 tablespoon peanut oil or vegetable oil, if slow-cooking
2 tablespoons minced scallion greens or chopped coriander (optional)

Rinse the chicken pieces, remove most of the skin, and set aside. Place the chicken in a wide bowl.

Pound together the garlic, ginger, salt, chiles, coriander, and turmeric in a mortar to make a paste. *Alternatively,* mash the garlic and ginger with the side of a knife. Place in a small bowl, add the salt, chiles, coriander, and turmeric, and use the back of a spoon to blend them.

Stir the water into the paste, and add it to the chicken. Turn and mix the chicken and paste until the pieces are well coated. Set aside while you organize your cooking method.

If steaming the chicken: You need a shallow bowl that will fit into your steamer basket when the lid is on and that is large enough to hold all the chicken. You also need a pot that is just about the same diameter as your steamer, so that no steam escapes.

Pour about 3 inches water into the pot and set the steamer basket in the pot. Transfer the chicken and flavorings and the reserved skin to the wide shallow bowl and place in the steamer. Put on the steamer lid, then heat the water over high heat. When it comes to a strong boil, turn the heat down slightly. Steam the chicken until cooked through, 1¼ to 1½ hours. Check on it after 45 minutes: be careful as

you lift off the lid not to burn yourself on the steam, then stir the chicken so that pieces that are underneath will be exposed to the hot steam. Cover again and resume steaming.

Check one of the largest pieces of chicken for doneness after an hour or so. Also check that the pot has enough water and is not running dry. When all the chicken is cooked through, remove the steamer from the pot, again taking care not to burn yourself on the steam.

If slow-cooking the chicken: Add 2 tablespoons more water and the oil to the chicken. Place in a wide heavy pot with a tight-fitting lid, add the reserved skin, and stir to mix well. Place over medium-low heat, with the lid on, and bring to a simmer. Reduce the heat to low and cook for 1 hour, or until all the chicken is cooked through. The chicken will be bathed in a light sauce and will be tender and succulent.

To serve: Remove the skin and discard. Serve hot or at room temperature, topped, if you like, with a sprinkling of scallion greens or coriander.

TO DOUBLE THE RECIPE: *Double all the amounts and cook in two bowls set in stacked steamers; if using the sealed-pot method, use a 10- to 12-inch heavy pot, so the chicken is not stacked too deep. The cooking time will be a little longer.*

The steamed version of Kachin Chicken Curry is presented here with Fried Rice with Shallots (page 226) and Fresh Red Chile Chutney (page 203). Notice that the chicken is in larger pieces here than those called for. My notes from Myitkyina include a comment about this slow-cooked dish from the Kachin repertoire: "Delish, sucking flavor off the bone."

chicken in tart garlic sauce

SERVES 3 OR 4 I had this at a Shan restaurant in Hsipaw and fell in love with it. The sauce that bathes the chicken is tangy with a little lime juice and aromatic with garlic and ginger. Fresh green cayenne chiles give noticeable heat.

You can make this with boneless chicken or chicken on the bone. Serve with new potatoes or rice.

2 tablespoons minced garlic
1 tablespoon minced ginger
About 1 teaspoon salt
3 tablespoons peanut oil
4 or 5 green cayenne chiles, each slit
    lengthwise several times

1 pound boneless chicken, cut into
    approximately ½-inch pieces, rinsed, or
    about 1½ pounds chicken legs and/or
    breasts, cut into small pieces (see A Note on
    Chopped Chicken, page 157) and rinsed well
1 cup water
2 tablespoons fresh lime juice
¼ cup minced scallion greens or coriander
    leaves (optional)

If you have a mortar, pound the garlic and ginger together to a paste with a pinch of salt.

Heat the oil in a heavy pot or a wok over medium heat. Add the garlic and ginger and cook, stirring frequently, for several minutes until softened. Add the chiles and cook a minute longer, then raise the heat to high. Add the chicken pieces and cook, turning and stirring to expose all surfaces to the hot oil, about 4 minutes. Add the water and bring to a boil. Add 1 teaspoon salt and stir, then lower the heat to maintain a simmer and cook for another 5 minutes, or until the chicken is cooked through (chicken on the bone will take a little longer). Remove from the heat and add the lime juice.

Sprinkle on the scallion greens or cilantro, if you wish. Serve hot or at room temperature.

easy grilled chicken

SERVES 6   In Burma chicken is most often served as a curry rather than grilled. But traditional Burmese flavorings make a great marinade for grilled chicken, and the result is delectable. Allow an hour for it to marinate.

Serve with Sticky Rice (page 232) or with flatbreads. Put out Tart-Sweet Chile-Garlic Sauce (page 36) or Tamarind Sauce (page 205) with it. Another option is Kachin Salsa (page 200), especially since you can grill the vegetables for it while you are grilling the chicken. A salad or a stir-fried green vegetable rounds the meal out nicely.

2½ to 3 pounds chicken breasts and/or legs, chopped into small pieces (see A Note on Chopped Chicken, page 157)

MARINADE
½ teaspoon salt
¼ teaspoon turmeric
½ teaspoon Red Chile Powder (page 28) or cayenne
About 1 tablespoon minced garlic
1 tablespoon minced ginger
2 tablespoons fish sauce

Rinse off the chicken and pat dry; set aside in a bowl.

Combine the salt, turmeric, chile powder, garlic, and ginger in a mortar or a bowl and pound with a pestle or mash with the back of a spoon to blend together. Stir in the fish sauce.

Add the marinade to the chicken pieces and rub it in well with your hands. Set aside to marinate for 30 minutes.

Meanwhile, preheat a charcoal or gas grill to medium heat.

Grill the chicken, turning the pieces frequently to expose all sides to the heat and prevent scorching, until cooked to the bone, about 20 minutes.

OVERLEAF: *Easy Grilled Chicken served with Tart-Sweet Chile-Garlic Sauce (page 36) accompanied by Sticky Rice (page 232) made with a blend of white and black rice, and by Succulent Grapefruit Salad (page 45). The chicken has been left in larger pieces here, rather than being cut small.*

minced chicken with galangal and tomato

SERVES 4 Every evening in Mrauk U I had the luxury of eating at a small guesthouse on the edge of town, where the innkeeper's wife, Shwe Nwe, served a multidish supper. The food was so varied and so fresh tasting that I think of those dinners as some kind of eating-Eden experience. Best of all, I was able to go to the kitchen daily and learn as I watched Shwe Nwe cook.

This dish has become a favorite in my family. Like many dishes from Rakhine State, it has a marked chile heat, a little hit of galangal, and a balanced complexity. Serve over rice or as a delectable nontraditional sauce for pasta. Accompany with a chopped cucumber salad or lightly dressed greens.

1 pound boneless chicken or ground chicken
3 tablespoons peanut oil
¼ teaspoon turmeric
1 cup minced shallots
1 tablespoon minced galangal (see Glossary)
2 cups chopped ripe tomatoes or canned crushed tomatoes
1 teaspoon shrimp paste (*ngapi*; see Glossary), or substitute 1 tablespoon fish sauce

1 teaspoon salt, or to taste
2 teaspoons Red Chile Oil (page 25) or store-bought, or to taste, or 2 teaspoons Shallot Oil (page 24) plus ½ to 1 teaspoon Red Chile Powder (page 28) or cayenne
¼ cup chopped coriander (optional)

If using boneless chicken, thinly slice it, then chop with one or two cleavers until it is reduced to a coarsely ground texture, about 5 minutes. Or coarsely chop, place in a food processor, and pulse several times to grind it. Set aside.

Place a wok or wide heavy pot over medium heat and add the oil. Add the turmeric and stir, then toss in the shallots and cook, stirring frequently, until softened, about 5 minutes. Add the galangal and cook for another couple of minutes. Add the tomatoes and stir to blend, then cook for a minute.

Add the chicken and cook, stirring to break up lumps and blend the chicken into the sauce, until all the chicken has changed color. Add the shrimp paste and stir well. Add the salt and stir, then stir in the chile oil. Cook over medium heat for another 5 minutes or so, to give the flavors time to blend. The oil will rise to the surface.

Serve hot or at room temperature, topped with a sprinkling of chopped coriander if you wish.

aromatic chicken from the shan hills [KHUA HAENG]

SERVES 6   What always strikes me about the recipes from the Shan repertoire is how economical they are for the cook. Often there's only one pot needed, and the techniques involved extract the maximum flavor from the ingredients in a short time.

For this dish, there's no marinade, no waiting around, just a quick first frying of the chicken with flavorings, and then the addition of aromatics for the last fifteen minutes or so as it cooks to tender succulence. Serve with rice or over noodles, with some greens, say Tender Greens Salad with Crispy Fried Shallots (page 49) or Lima Beans with Galangal (page 110).

⅔ cup chopped garlic
½ cup sliced ginger
2 dried red chiles, stemmed
About 1 tablespoon salt
¼ cup peanut oil or vegetable oil
One 3- to 3½-pound chicken, chopped into small pieces (see A Note on Chopped Chicken, page 157) and rinsed

1 cup sliced white or yellow onion
1 tablespoon turmeric
3 stalks lemongrass, trimmed, smashed, and sliced into 1-inch lengths
2 Roma (plum) or other fleshy tomatoes, cut into small wedges (about 8 per tomato)
⅓ cup very fresh tender young lime leaves
½ cup coriander leaves, finely chopped

If you have a mortar, pound the garlic, ginger, and chiles together with a little salt to make a coarse paste; if not, mince them. Set aside.

Heat the oil in a large pot or wok over medium-high heat. Add the chicken and turn the pieces in the hot oil for about 3 minutes. Add the onion, 2 teaspoons of the salt, the turmeric, lemongrass, garlic, ginger, chiles, and tomatoes and stir and cook for 2 minutes. Lower the heat to medium, cover, and simmer for 5 minutes.

Add the lime leaves and another ½ teaspoon salt, stir, and simmer for 10 minutes, or until the chicken is tender and cooked through. Taste and adjust the salt if you wish.

Add the coriander, stir in, and serve.

THANAKA IS A LIGHTLY aromatic pale-yellow paste made of the wood of the *thanaka* tree (*Murraya thanaka*). There's a special flat stone mortar called a *kyauk pyin* (pronounced "chok-pyin") on which you grind the wood; once you have some ground, you add a little water to make a paste. Every morning in households all over Burma, women grind *thanaka* and apply the paste to their faces, necks, and arms, and to their children's skin too. They say the paste protects the skin from the sun and helps make it soft and paler (in Burma, as in India, pale skin is prized).

Most people believe that the best *thanaka* comes from Shwebo, a town not far from Pakkoku, where the Chindwin River flows into the Irrawaddy. At country fairs and temple festivals there are rows of booths with small logs for sale, all advertised as genuine Shwebo *thanaka*. But nowadays there's an easier option: small plastic pots of prepared *thanaka*. You just take some paste from the pot and add a little water.

Then comes the fun. It can go on just like a cream, almost invisible and lightly scented with sandalwood, or you can make a design. Women and children, and sometimes young men, have yellow circles and lines of *thanaka* on their faces, applied with care and worn with pride. It's a look that often startles first-time visitors to the country.

In the Chin villages I visited in northern Rakhine, the older women's faces are decorated, not with *thanaka* but with delicate and beautiful tattoos. The tattoos are all the same pattern, but the pattern expresses itself differently on each woman. It's like a spiderweb of fine blue lines that follow the contours of the face, emphasizing the bone structure, circling the eyes and mouth (see photograph, page 119). The women's skin looks soft and smooth, somehow more beautiful because of the design etched onto it. Unlike the *thanaka* patterns, which a person can change from day to day at will, these are there for life, identifying a woman as southern Chin, confirming her place in her universe.

LEFT: *A young girl in Mrauk U has a fun* thanaka *design on her face.* FAR LEFT, FROM TOP: Thanaka *logs on sale at a food market in Rangoon. A woman in Hpa'an has a thick layer of* thanaka *on her face, perhaps because she's trying to keep her skin extra pale as she works in the sun. A market woman in Rangoon.*

chicken aloo [GAENG GAI SAI ALOO]

SERVES 4   The potato is a staple in the Shan hills, where it's known as *aloo*, the Hindi and Urdu word for potato. The same word is used for potato in Burmese. (The potato, of course, is native to the Americas, and it traveled to Asia sometime after 1500.) Interestingly, the word for potato in neighboring Thailand is not a variant of *aloo*, but *man farang*, which translates, literally, as "foreign tuber."

I ate this welcoming stew sitting outside under the stars at the farm of a good friend, with white rice, a blanched greens salad (see page 49), and a Shan-style tea-leaf salad (see page 65). I like to serve it on cold winter nights with roasted root vegetables and plain rice.

1 small (2½-pound) whole chicken, chopped into 1½-inch pieces, or about 2 pounds chicken legs and/or breasts, chopped (see A Note on Chopped Chicken, page 157), rinsed
1 cup small shallots
1 tablespoon salt, or to taste
About 4 medium Roma (plum) or other fleshy tomatoes, cut into thin wedges (1½ to 2 cups)
1 teaspoon turmeric

½ teaspoon cayenne
1 tablespoon toasted and ground Soybean Disk (page 40 and see Cooking with *Tua Nao*, page 41), or substitute 1 teaspoon brown miso paste
2 stalks lemongrass, trimmed and smashed
¼ cup peanut oil or vegetable oil
5 cups water
3½ to 4 cups 1-inch cubes peeled potatoes
½ cup chopped coriander leaves and stems
½ cup minced scallion greens

Place the chicken, shallots, salt, tomatoes, turmeric, cayenne, *tua nao* powder or miso, and lemongrass in a large heavy casserole, drizzle on the oil, and place over medium heat. Stir and turn to mix and to distribute the oil, then cover and cook for 2 to 3 minutes. Stir and turn to expose more surfaces to the hot pot, cover, and cook for a few more minutes.

Add the water, raise the heat, and bring to a boil, then lower the heat to maintain a medium boil and cook, covered, for 10 minutes. Add the potatoes and boil, half-covered, until they are tender, 10 to 15 minutes. Taste and add salt if needed.

Sprinkle on the chopped coriander and scallion greens, stir, and serve.

IT'S A LIVELY MARKET TOWN, Hpa'an, set in a beautiful Chinese-painting-like landscape of limestone hills and rice fields. The markets are full of produce and prepared foods of all kinds; the streets are busy, lined with tea shops, tailor shops, little restaurants and eateries, and more. The Salween River flows past the town, which is the capital of Karen (now Kayen) State, wide and smooth and beautiful.

The boat from Moulmein, an old ferry, makes the trip up the Salween every afternoon, arriving in Hpa'an at sunset, when the sky and river are aglow. The trip is peaceful, for the river now has very little traffic, apart from local fishermen in small boats.

The more important artery for Hpa'an these days is the road. Rangoon is about five hours' drive to the north-west, and less than seventy miles due east as the crow flies lies the Thai border, across a chain of steep mountains. No wonder Hpa'an is prosperous, since all the traffic to and from the border passes through town.

My first night there, I went out with a friend to eat at a small restaurant. There were six or seven curries to choose from, and side dishes aplenty, to have with our rice and Mandalay beer. Next evening when I returned to the same eatery with a couple of other travelers, there was very little choice of food and the restaurant was empty. It seemed odd, the difference, so I asked the owner of my guesthouse about it later that night.

"Oh, it's the one-way road," he said. "The last fifty kilometers of road toward the border are winding and dangerous going through the mountains, so they made the road one way, on alternat-ing days. Today was eastbound, so drivers headed out to the Thai border. Tomorrow is westbound. Tomorrow night you'll see, the restaurants will be busy because of all the incoming traffic." Aha! The ebb and flow of life in Hpa'an.

*Scenes from the wonderful market in Hpa'an, capital of Karen State. **CLOCKWISE FROM BOTTOM:** The loaded cycle rickshaw is carrying bananas on the stem and a stack of greens. The painted hats of Karen women contribute another layer of beauty to the market. Papaya slices for sale. A woman chooses her watermelon.*

deep-fried street-stall chicken

SERVES 6 This is great street fare, especially when eaten with a tart dipping sauce, but you don't have to go to Burma to enjoy it. Deep-frying chicken is easy at home when the chicken is cut into small pieces.

You will have to fry the chicken in batches unless you have a large deep-fryer. I usually deep-fry in my large wok, but you can also use a wide pot.

Serve as an appetizer with one or more of the sauces suggested below, or as a main with rice, a green salad, and a vegetable curry.

One 3-pound chicken, or 2 to 2½ pounds breasts, legs, and wings, chopped into small pieces (see A Note on Chopped Chicken, page 157)
2 teaspoons kosher salt or sea salt
¼ teaspoon turmeric
3 to 4 tablespoons fish sauce
Peanut oil for deep-frying

DIPPING SAUCE OPTIONS
Tart-Sweet Chile-Garlic Sauce (page 36)
Tamarind Sauce (page 205)
Fresh Red Chile Chutney (page 203)

Trim off any loose skin and any excess fat from the chicken. Rinse it, pat dry, and place in a large bowl. Sprinkle on the salt and turmeric and rub them into the chicken, then pour on the fish sauce and turn and stir to ensure all the chicken is coated with flavor. Cover and marinate in the refrigerator for 2 to 3 hours.

When ready to proceed, put several paper-towel-lined plates by your stovetop. Have a spider or slotted spoon and a pair of tongs handy. Pour 2 to 3 inches of oil into a large stable wok, deep cast-iron skillet, or wide heavy pot and heat to 350°F. Check the temperature of the oil with a thermometer or by holding a wooden chopstick or the handle of a wooden spoon upright in the oil, and touching the bottom of the pan. If the oil bubbles up along the wood, it is at temperature.

Slide 2 pieces of chicken into the hot oil, taking care not to splash yourself with oil, then another couple, and then, after a pause (to let the oil heat back up), another one or two; the chicken pieces should be in one layer. Move the chicken pieces around and turn them over occasionally. They will gradually change color, turning a pale gold and then a deeper red-brown. Cook until they are a rich red-brown, then lift them out, pausing to let excess oil drip off, and place them on a paper-towel-lined plate to drain. Repeat with the remaining chicken.

home-style fried chicken

SERVES 2 TO 4 This is another dish from Cho Cho, a marvelous cook I visited near Bagan (see page 80). She fried some drumsticks and thighs in a wok set over a wood fire, using this simple method, which guarantees that the chicken will be cooked through with no risk of burning the skin.

The chicken is first steamed briefly, then shallow-fried. Cho Cho fried the pieces whole; I like to steam them whole and then chop them smaller for frying, to get more crispy fried surfaces.

Serve with a dipping sauce as an appetizer or as part of a meal with a fresh salad or green vegetable. I usually make Sticky Rice (page 232) when I am serving fried or grilled chicken; it's great with the dipping sauces and other accompaniments.

2 chicken drumsticks and 2 thighs, rinsed
1 teaspoon salt
About ½ cup water
Peanut oil for shallow-frying

ACCOMPANIMENTS
Tart-Sweet Chile-Garlic Sauce (page 36)
Shallot-Lime Chutney (page 219; optional)

Put the pieces of chicken in a wok or a deep cast-iron or other heavy frying pan and place over high heat. Sprinkle the salt onto the chicken pieces, then pour the water down the side of the wok and cover as tightly as possible. When the water has come to a vigorous boil, lower the heat slightly, maintaining the boil, and cook until the pan is nearly dry, about 5 minutes. Pour off any remaining liquid, reserving for another purpose. and wipe out the pan.

Use a cleaver (or chicken shears) to chop each drumstick and thigh into 2 or 3 pieces. Put the chicken back in the wok, place the wok over medium-high heat, and pour about ⅓ cup oil down the side of the wok. Fry the chicken, turning the pieces frequently to expose all sides to the hot oil, until the skin is crisp and golden and the meat is cooked through, 7 to 10 minutes. Serve hot.

BEEF AND PORK

WITH FISH, GREENS, AND RICE readily available, beef and pork play the role of extras at the Burmese table. In central Burma they are served as intense curries that come as one of many dishes in a rice meal. In outlying areas they are more often cooked together with vegetables, as in the Shan dish Three-Layer Pork with Mustard Greens and Tofu (page 190).

I've included two central Burmese beef curries here (see pages 184 and 185), as well as a spiced take on beef and potatoes (see page 181). There's also an intriguing beef dish from the Kachin (see page 178), in which spices and herbs are pounded into tender chunks of cooked beef.

The Shan repertoire of beef and pork dishes makes up the rest of the chapter. On page 188, slices of pork are stir-fried and then briefly simmered in a smoky sauce with a hint of sweetness. Sweet-Tart Pork Belly Stew (page 189) is a warming dish perfumed with lemongrass.

Two of the recipes here can be made with either beef or pork. One is spice-rubbed, air-dried, and then fried (Spice-Rubbed Jerky, page 196)—a real crowd-pleaser with intense flavor that originates in methods used by people in the mountains to cure their meat. The others, Lemongrass-Ginger Sliders (page 192), is a succulent take on ground meat, taking the slider to new heights.

kachin pounded beef with herbs

SERVES 4 This is one of the most unusual and delicious dishes I have ever come across. The beef is first cooked in a little water, then briefly fried to firm it up, and finally is lightly pounded to blend the herbed flavor paste into it. It sounds complicated, but it's easy. The flavor paste includes Sichuan peppercorns, a reminder that China and Kachin State share a long border, and that there's been trade across it for centuries. In Myitkyina, people told me that they refer to Sichuan pepper as Kachin pepper.

The result is meltingly tender beef. It's great served with drinks, seductively warming and deeply flavored.

About 1 cup water
1 to 1¼ pounds stewing beef or boneless beef shoulder, trimmed of fat and cut into approximately 1-inch cubes
1 teaspoon ground Sichuan pepper
1 scant tablespoon peanut oil or vegetable oil

FLAVOR PASTE
1 tablespoon chopped ginger
2 teaspoons chopped garlic
2 dried red chiles, stemmed
1 teaspoon lightly toasted Sichuan peppercorns
1½ teaspoons salt
½ cup loosely packed Vietnamese coriander (see Glossary), coarsely torn or chopped, or substitute coriander leaves

Pour ½ inch of water into a wok or wide pot, add the beef and Sichuan pepper, and bring to a boil. Cook at a low boil until the meat is tender, 20 to 30 minutes, decreasing the heat gradually as the water evaporates. There should be very little liquid left. Remove from the heat.

Place a heavy skillet or a wok over medium heat, add the oil, and tilt the pan to coat the cooking surface. Add the meat and cook, turning occasionally, until all surfaces have changed color a little, about 6 minutes. Set aside.

If you have a large mortar, combine the ginger, garlic, dried chiles, Sichuan peppercorns, and salt and pound and grind to a paste. Add the coriander and pound to incorporate it. Add the meat and pound to blend the flavor paste thoroughly into the meat. (If your mortar is too small to accommodate all the meat at once, remove half the paste and then work with half the meat and half the flavor paste at a time.) The meat will soften and break down but should not be completely pulverized.

Alternatively, mince the ginger and garlic very fine and set aside in a small bowl. Use a spice grinder or coffee grinder to reduce the dried chiles and Sichuan peppercorns to a powder. Stir the powder into the garlic and ginger, then add the salt

and use the back of the spoon to blend them together. Chop the coriander fine and blend into the flavor paste. Place the meat in a wide bowl, add the flavor paste, and use a wooden mallet or a wide wooden spatula to press and pound the flavoring into the meat.

Serve at room temperature.

A NOTE ON LEFTOVERS: *I've eaten this fresh from the mortar and pestle and as leftovers the next day. As often happens, the leftovers have an even greater depth of flavor than the freshly made dish.*

The main food market in Myitkyina sits on a high riverbank by the Irrawaddy. This woman arrived by boat with a load of produce that others were carrying up the steep flight of stairs from the water—the huge squash was enough of a cargo for her!

saucy spiced meat and potatoes

SERVES 3 OR 4 This simple dish of cubes of potato simmered in an aromatic ground beef sauce lends itself to experimentation. I sometimes add mushrooms, for example, to the simmering sauce. Or I make the dish with lamb or goat instead, using cubes of eggplant in place of or in addition to the potato.

The initial spicing of cumin, coriander, shallot, and ginger is reminiscent of northern India. Black pepper is not traditional, but I find it a great addition.

Serve as a simple one-dish meal, on its own or over rice, with a vegetable side or a salad.

About 1 pound lean ground beef
1 teaspoon salt, or to taste
⅛ teaspoon turmeric
½ teaspoon ground cumin
½ teaspoon ground coriander
2 tablespoons peanut oil
¼ cup minced shallots
1 tablespoon minced ginger

3 medium potatoes (about 1 pound),
** peeled and cut into 1-inch cubes**
1 to 2 cups water
1 cup finely chopped tomatoes
½ teaspoon Red Chile Powder (page 28),
** or to taste**
¼ teaspoon freshly ground black pepper
** (optional)**

Mix the meat with the salt, turmeric, cumin, and coriander in a bowl. If you have time, set aside for an hour, covered, in a cool place to let the flavors blend.

Place a skillet or wok over medium heat. Add the oil, and when it is hot, toss in the shallots and ginger and cook until the shallots are translucent and softened, about 4 minutes. Add the potatoes and cook for 3 or 4 minutes, until lightly browned; then raise the heat to high, add 1 cup water, cover, and bring to a boil. Lower the heat and simmer until the potatoes are nearly cooked, about 10 minutes.

Add the meat mixture and stir to break up any lumps and to incorporate it. If the water has boiled away, add another ½ cup so there's enough liquid to make a meat sauce texture. Stir in the tomatoes and chile powder and simmer, uncovered, until all the meat has changed color and the potatoes are tender; add a little more water while everything cooks if you'd like more sauce. Add the black pepper, if using, then taste and adjust the seasoning with salt if needed.

rakhine chile-hot meat and potatoes
Add 1 tablespoon minced galangal (see Glossary) to the spice mixture, and add 3 green cayenne chiles, slit lengthwise, when you add the water to the potatoes.

NEVER MIND!

WHEN THE ELECTRICITY cuts out, the bus you're in breaks down, or any one of many other things goes wrong, the way to deal with it Burmese style is to stay cool and to say with a smile, to yourself or to others, *"Ya-ba-day"* ("Never mind"). It's a phrase to have on hand at all times, a reminder that things could be worse and that we'll all be fine, despite the inconvenience/hardship/frustration of the moment. The thing *not* to do is show annoyance or frustration.

Cultivating a calm frame of mind is a lot easier if you're a traveler than if you're living in a place where, for example, the electricity is unreliable. How do you get that shirt ironed and then get to work on time if things have come to a standstill for some reason? How do you deal with the possibility that the police could arrest you for your political views? The answer is that you learn to cultivate a certain equanimity. It's the one thing you can control. And one way of doing that is to learn to laugh a "never mind" at an unexpected difficulty, or at the painfulness of your situation, rather than getting upset or angry.

Two places in Burma that have taught me a lot are the internet café and the tea shop. When I'm on the computer in an internet café, I tend to get cranky if connections are slow or there's a problem accessing my e-mail. But those problems are constant in Burma, and I've learned to let it go. My models for that are the young guys who work at these cafés—they manage to stay cool even with the endless technical glitches that come with old equipment and unreliable electricity. They're an ongoing reminder about *ya-ba-day.*

The tea shop lesson also has to do with a certain detachment, but it's more subtle. In the early morning, people stop at tea shops for a bite to eat, then head out quickly to work or other obligations. Later in the day, things are more relaxed: people meet for a tea and conversation, maybe a snack too.

Everyone in the tea shop keeps an attentive eye on the street and on the comings and goings in the shop. They notice who's there, who's new and strange. Life anywhere can have its unexpected events, but when the military is all-powerful and the government is totalitarian, as it was for years in Burma, things feel extra-fragile. As Burma opens up and life gets easier, maybe people in tea shops won't need to be so alert. But in the meantime their attentiveness to the vibe helps everyone stay calm, so they can meet whatever comes next with dignity.

CLOCKWISE FROM TOP LEFT: *A Pa-O woman at a rural market south of Inle Lake; Pa-O women wear scarves or towels as turbans, as well as distinctive narrow black jackets and tunics. A bus breakdown, this time for a flat tire. The driver of a scooter taxi takes a nap. In the Mandalay market, crowded local truck-buses serve as public transport out of town.*

warming beef curry with tomato

In this beef curry—a real pleasure on a cold day—tomato helps tenderize the meat while also adding an acid note to the sauce. The meat is marinated, seared briefly, and then simmered in plenty of water for two hours, until extremely tender.
Serve with rice, a salad, and a simple vegetable dish.

1 pound stewing beef, cut into ¾-inch pieces
½ teaspoon salt, or to taste
⅛ teaspoon turmeric
1 small-medium ripe tomato, finely chopped, or substitute ¼ cup canned chopped tomatoes
1 teaspoon minced ginger

2 tablespoons minced shallots
1 teaspoon Red Chile Powder (page 28), or to taste
3 tablespoons peanut oil
4 cups water

Place the meat in a large bowl, add the salt and turmeric, and mix well. Add the tomato, ginger, shallots, chile powder, and 1 tablespoon of the oil and stir and mix so the meat is coated with the flavorings. Cover and set aside to marinate for at least 30 minutes, or as long as 2 hours (refrigerate if the wait will be more than 1 hour).

Place a large wok or a wide heavy pot over medium-high heat and add the remaining 2 tablespoons oil. Toss in the beef with the marinade, and cook, stirring frequently, until all the meat has changed color. Add the water and bring to a boil, then lower the heat to maintain a gentle simmer and let cook, half-covered, for 2 hours, or until the meat is meltingly tender and the oil is floating on the surface of the sauce. (Add more water if the liquid is running low.)

Taste for salt, and adjust if necessary. Serve hot or at room temperature.

simplest beef curry with whole shallots

SERVES 4 This inviting take on beef curry, adapted from Ma Thanegi's book *An Introduction to Myanmar Cuisine,* is also delectable as leftovers the next day. Be sure to allow for 90 minutes of cooking time so that the meat is meltingly tender.

Serve with rice and a vegetable with a tart or bitter edge, such as stir-fried dandelion greens or radicchio or broccoli rabe, to complement the sweetness of the shallots.

1 pound stewing beef, cut into ¾-inch pieces
½ teaspoon salt
⅛ teaspoon turmeric
1 tablespoon minced garlic
1 tablespoon minced ginger
2 tablespoons peanut oil

3 cups water
2 teaspoons fish sauce
2 tablespoons Fried Shallots (page 24)
8 small shallots (about 1 cup)
½ teaspoon Red Chile Powder (page 28)

Place the beef in a wide bowl, add the salt and turmeric, and mix with your hands, rubbing the flavors into the meat. Let marinate, covered, in the refrigerator for at least 1 hour, or as long as 4 hours.

If you have a mortar, pound the garlic and ginger to a paste; set aside.

Place a wok or heavy skillet over medium heat. Add the oil, then toss in the garlic and ginger and cook until softened, 2 or 3 minutes. Raise the heat to medium-high, add the meat, and cook for several minutes, stirring and pressing the meat against the hot surface of the pan. Add the water and fish sauce and bring to a boil, then partially cover and simmer for 1 hour. Most of the water will evaporate; add more water if the pan is running dry. (The dish can be made ahead to this point, allowed to cool, and refrigerated for as long as 24 hours; add ½ cup water and bring back to a simmer before proceeding.)

Add the fried shallots and stir in, then add the whole shallots and chile powder and cook for another 20 minutes or so, until the shallots are soft and the meat is very tender.

Serve hot or at room temperature.

IN MYITKYINA I stayed at the YMCA, a small hostel right near the train station. Well, "train station" is a bit misleading— I should say, near the platform where trains stop in Myitkyina when they pull in from their journeys. Myitkyina is the end of the line: trains take nearly four days to travel the 600 miles from Rangoon, passing through Mandalay at the halfway mark and then heading on north. They always arrive late. They turn around in Myitkyina on a long loop of track, and then head back south, slowly, the old tracks making anything more than an amble impossible. Because the train tracks are right across from the Y, every once in a while, day and night, there's a whistle and a heavy rumbling as a train lumbers past.

Apart from the nightly train awakenings, the Y was a great place to stay and an ideal place to hang out. I got to see the daily comings and goings as kids and adults came for English-language lessons, more kids for karate classes, families for weddings and other parties. It was never hard to find someone to chat with, a boon for me because I always had questions about things I'd seen in the course of my wanderings around town.

Every day I went to the huge riverside market in the early morning and then to a nearby street market in the late afternoon, photographing and tasting as much as I could—listening, looking, and trying to understand the human landscape. Language can be a great way to learn who is around. In the Myitkyina markets I heard Yunnanese and Mandarin, Shan, Burmese, and Kachin (always a safe guess here), as well as various South Asian languages.

When I went on a long bicycle ride through the southern end of town, I came upon small weaving factories, where women sitting at noisy electric looms were turning out cotton *lungyi* (sarongs). Nearby was a more peaceful workshop with three or four women at old-style looms handweaving intricately patterned silk *lungyi*. On the other end of town I found the university, the museum, and the huge field where the Kachin New Year ceremonies and dances take place each January. Every day I filled in more details of my personal map of Myitkyina: temples, mosques, churches, new large houses and charming smaller ones, markets, and shops.

One day, while exploring a neighborhood, I smelled hot mustard oil, something I associate with Bengali and Nepali cooking. Back at the Y, I asked Lam, the young Kachin guy who manned the desk, "Are there Bengalis here?" "Oh no, that's Gurkha," he told me. "They cook with mustard oil. They came from Nepal with the British army and some of them stayed on. We get on well with them."

Another piece of the puzzle explained.

Market vendors in Myitkyina sell butterfly beans, eggplants, small new potatoes, and more in a sunny spot in late afternoon.

pork strips with star anise

SERVES 3 OR 4 One evening in Mandalay I went out to supper at a little Shan restaurant with a German woman named Ann and a young monk friend of hers, even though he couldn't eat at that hour (see "Offerings at Dawn," page 263). Afterward we went to see the Moustache Brothers, a comedy troupe headed by three brothers. Their show was subversive, funny, and touching all at once. Now that is changing, for as Burma moves toward democracy, they don't have as much edgy material to play with.

This deeply flavored pork dish was another memorable star of that evening. There's definitely more than a hint of China in the flavoring (star anise, soy sauce, a touch of sweet), a reminder that the Shan come from the border regions of Thailand, Burma, and Yunnan. I like to serve it with something acidic, perhaps Succulent Grapefruit (or Pomelo) Salad (page 45), or a simple vinaigrette-dressed salad, to balance the smoky dark flavors of the pork.

About ¾ pound pork tenderloin or
boneless pork shoulder
½ teaspoon salt, or to taste
3 tablespoons peanut oil or rendered
pork fat
2 tablespoons crushed or minced garlic
2 teaspoons minced ginger

1 tablespoon Fermented Soybean Paste
(page 39) or store-bought, or substitute
1 teaspoon brown miso paste
1 cup water
2 star anise, whole or in pieces
2 teaspoons Palm Sugar Water (page 96)
2 teaspoons soy sauce
¼ cup chopped coriander (optional)

Cut the pork into strips about 1 inch long, ½ inch wide, and nearly ¼ inch thick. Place in a bowl with the salt and toss to coat; set aside.

Place a wok or heavy pot over medium heat. Add the oil or fat and toss in the garlic and ginger. Cook until they are well softened, then add the pork and cook, stirring it to expose all sides to the hot surface of the pan, until it has all changed color.

Stir the mashed soybeans or miso into the water, then add to the pan, along with the star anise, stir, and bring to a boil. Lower the heat and simmer for several minutes. Add the palm sugar liquid and soy sauce and simmer over low heat, half-covered, for another 10 minutes. Taste and add a little salt if you wish (the dish is traditionally a little salty).

Sprinkle on the coriander just before serving if you wish.

sweet-tart pork belly stew [MOO JAW]

SERVES 4 OR 5 This satisfying cross between a soup and a stew is aromatic with lemongrass. Traditionally the broth gets a tart edge from whatever leaf or fruit or flavoring is available. In Shan State, that might be hibiscus flower buds or unripe tomatoes or lime juice. You can also use tamarind liquid.

Serve over rice or over noodles or pasta, with a vegetable side.

About 6 cups water
2 teaspoons turmeric
1 tablespoon salt, or to taste
3 stalks lemongrass, trimmed, smashed, and cut into 1-inch lengths
1 pound pork belly, cut into ½-inch-wide strips about 1½ inches long

1 generous cup shallots, halved or quartered
1 cup garlic cloves, halved if they are large
1 cup hibiscus buds, or substitute ½ cup fresh lime juice or 1 cup finely chopped green tomatoes
¼ cup finely chopped coriander

Bring the water to a boil in a large pot. Add the turmeric, salt, lemongrass, and pork, cover, and bring back to a boil, then lower the heat to maintain a steady boil and cook until the pork is just cooked, 8 to 10 minutes.

Add the shallots and garlic, raise the heat slightly, and boil vigorously, half-covered, for 15 minutes.

Add the hibiscus buds (or other souring agent) and boil vigorously for another 10 minutes. Sprinkle on the coriander just before serving.

PORK BELLY SKIN: *Pork belly skin (sometimes called rind) is a great but often neglected ingredient. Use it to make your own lard and crispy pork cracklings. Slice it, then cut it crosswise into approximately 2-inch pieces. Place them in a wok or wide heavy skillet over medium heat. Move them around as they heat, and soon the fat will melt off them. Continue to cook over medium to medium-low heat until you have a lot of fat with cracklings floating in it. Let cool for 10 minutes, then pour the fat off into a glass jar; seal and refrigerate. Use this lard, clean and subtle, in making pastry or for frying. The crispy cracklings are a delicious snack and also a great crouton-like addition to a salad: see Chinese Kale (or Broccoli Rabe) with Pork Cracklings (page 54) for a Shan example—or a variation on Caesar salad for a Western one.*

three-layer pork with mustard greens and tofu

SERVES 4 In Burmese, as in Chinese and Thai, what we call pork belly in English is called "three-layer pork," a great description of the cut, and to me far more attractive sounding. Three-layer pork looks a little like pale slab bacon: meat layered with fat. It's a great way to give depth to a vegetable, as it does here.

Pickled mustard greens are widely available in Chinese grocery stores. In this Shan dish, their acidity balances the slight sweetness of the pork, and the tofu is a nice bridge between them. As is typical of Shan cooking, the ingredients come together in one pot, seasoned with salt, not fish sauce, and flavored with onion rather than shallot, as well as with fresh coriander.

This is traditionally served with rice, but it is also delicious with polenta.

2 pounds pork belly, to yield about 1¾ pounds trimmed of skin
¼ cup peanut oil or vegetable oil
1 medium to large onion, quartered and thinly sliced crosswise (about 1 cup)
Scant 2 cups Chinese preserved mustard greens (see Glossary), well rinsed and thinly sliced crosswise

A scant ¾ pound tofu, thinly sliced into bite-sized pieces
1½ teaspoons salt, or to taste
About ½ cup water
½ cup coriander leaves

Lay the pork belly on a cutting board, cut it across the grain as thin as possible, then cut the slices into 2-inch or so lengths. Set aside.

Place a large wok or wide heavy pot over medium heat. Add the oil, then toss in the onion and cook, stirring occasionally, until translucent and softened, about 5 minutes. Raise the heat to medium-high, add the pork, and cook, turning and pressing it against the hot surface of the pan, until it has all changed color and started to render its fat, 4 to 6 minutes. Toss in the sliced greens and stir well, then cook for several minutes, stirring occasionally, until heated through. Add the tofu and salt and carefully stir to mix thoroughly without breaking up the tofu.

Add the water, cover, and cook for 3 to 5 minutes, until the greens are a little more softened and the flavors are blended. Stir in the coriander, remove from the heat, and serve hot or at room temperature.

lemongrass-ginger sliders

MAKES 16 TO 18 SLIDERS; SERVES 4

Photograph on pages 194–95

The original Shan recipe is for meat balls made with ground beef or pork flavored with minced lemongrass, ginger, and garlic. I've found it easier in a North American kitchen to flatten the balls and cook them as sliders. They cook slowly in a little oil, which gives them a slight crust and succulent interior. You want some fat for tenderness, which is why the recommended cuts are flank steak or pork shoulder.

Traditionally the meat is chopped by hand, using two cleavers and alternating chop-chop-chop, as it's done by all the Tai peoples (the word for the technique in the Tai languages is *laap*). Hand-chopped meat has a different texture from ground meat, and I urge you to try it. And chopping the meat yourself means that you know the quality of the meat. You can instead chill the meat and use a food processor to grind it.

The Shan traditionally use minced shavings of green *makawk* wood (see Glossary) in the meatballs. They help hold the meat together. I use a little leftover rice instead.

1 pound boneless beef chuck or boneless pork
   shoulder, or 1 pound ground chuck
   or ground pork
¼ teaspoon turmeric
2 tablespoons minced lemongrass
2 tablespoons minced garlic
½ cup minced shallots

2 tablespoons minced ginger
1 teaspoon salt
¼ cup chilled cooked jasmine or other rice
½ teaspoon Red Chile Powder (page 28)
   or cayenne
¼ cup finely chopped Roma tomatoes
About ¼ cup peanut oil

If using meat that has not been ground: To hand-chop the meat, thinly slice it, then place the slices on a large cutting board. Holding a cleaver in each hand, chop the meat with alternating hands, chopping across the piled meat one way, then another, and repeating until finely chopped. Sprinkle on the turmeric and set aside in a large bowl. *Alternatively,* to use a food processor, cut the meat into 5 or 6 pieces and place in the freezer for 20 minutes. Transfer the meat to the processor, add the turmeric, and pulse to finely chop. Transfer to a large bowl and set aside.

If using ground meat: Place in a bowl, sprinkle with the turmeric, and set aside.

To make and cook the sliders: Combine the lemongrass, garlic, shallots, ginger, and salt in a large mortar or the food processor and pound or pulse to a coarse paste. Add the rice, chile powder, and tomatoes and pound or pulse again.

Add the flavor paste to the meat and knead it thoroughly into the meat. Shape the mixture into balls about 1 inch in diameter, then flatten each one gently into a thick patty. Set aside on a lightly oiled plate.

Place a large skillet over high heat. Add the oil, then lower the heat to medium-high and add the sliders, being careful not to splash yourself with oil; arrange the first ones around the edges of the skillet and work your way in to the center. Cook for 3 minutes or so, then use a wide metal spatula to turn the sliders over. As the meat starts to release water, raise the heat a little to evaporate it. Remove the sliders from the pan when they are firm to the touch or have reached the degree of doneness you like.

ABOVE: *In a Tai Koen temple in the center of Kengtung, large Buddha statues gleam in the half-light of a few candles.* **OVERLEAF:** *Lemongrass-Ginger Sliders, with pea tendrils draped on them, accompanied by various dipping sauces and condiments and by Everyday Cabbage-Shallot Refresher (page 220).*

spice-rubbed jerky

MAKES 1¾ POUNDS;
SERVES 6 TO 8

This jerky is hauntingly delicious as a snack with drinks or as part of a meal. The main ingredient for the recipe is time. The meat—beef or pork—is rubbed with a spice blend, then dried. Traditionally that would mean air-drying for 2 or 3 days, but I take a shortcut and dry it in a low oven for several hours. Just before serving, the meat is sliced and lightly shallow-fried.

SPICE PASTE
2 tablespoons coriander seeds
2 teaspoons turmeric
3 tablespoons minced ginger
3 tablespoons minced garlic
2 teaspoons cayenne
1 tablespoon salt

2 pounds boneless beef steak, such as flank or skirt steak, or boneless pork shoulder, or 1 pound of each
Peanut oil for shallow-frying

Use a spice or coffee grinder to grind the coriander seeds to a powder. Place in a mortar or a food processor with the remaining ingredients for the spice paste and pound or process to a paste.

Cut the meat across the grain into strips just under 1 inch wide and about 4 inches long. Place the meat in a bowl; if using both pork and beef, keep them in separate bowls. Add the spice paste, dividing it evenly if using both meats, and use your hands to rub it thoroughly into the meat.

To air-dry the meat: Hang the meat in a spot out of direct sunlight for 1½ to 2 days; it may take 2½ days if the air is very humid. It's easiest to do this by threading one end of each piece onto a long metal skewer, leaving ½ inch between the pieces so the air can circulate easily; you will need about six skewers. Then suspend the skewers so the strips of meat hang down freely and can air-dry. When ready, the meat will be lighter in weight but not completely dry.

To dry the meat in the oven: Lay the meat strips on a rack set over a roasting pan so the air can circulate. Place in the oven set to its lowest temperature (usually 150°F). Turn the meat after 1½ to 2 hours, and remove when it is lighter in weight but not completely dried out, about another hour.

Once dried, the meat can be refrigerated for as long as 3 days.

To cook the meat: Cut the meat strips crosswise into bite-sized pieces. Place a large wok or skillet over medium-high heat. Add about ½ inch of peanut oil, and when it is hot, slide in a handful of the meat, without crowding; you want each piece in contact with the hot oil. Cook, turning frequently, until tender, 3 or 4 minutes. Cook the remaining meat the same way.

Serve hot or at room temperature.

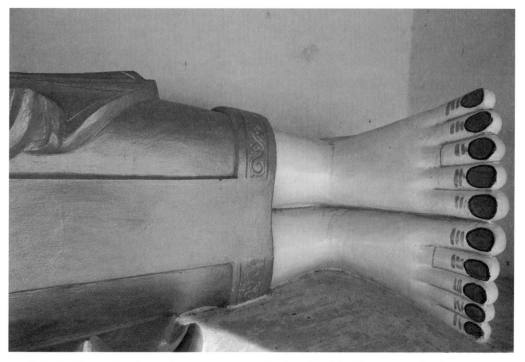

A reclining Buddha at a temple complex in Amarapura, not far from Mandalay. These statues often have spectacular feet.

CONDIMENTS AND SAUCES

IT'S THE EXTRA DISHES ON THE TABLE that make eating in Burma such a special pleasure, mouthful by mouthful.

Some of the sauces, like Tart-Sweet Chile-Garlic Sauce (in the Burma Basics chapter—see page 36), Kachin Salsa (page 200), and Sour-Plum Chutney with Chile Oil (page 202), have marked chile heat. Milder sauces include Fresh Red Chile Chutney (page 203), from Myitkyina, and Standout Tomato Chutney (page 206). Get familiar with them and then get creative, as Burmese cooks are: include a little ginger paste here or extra minced fresh herbs there, as the fancy takes you.

I've included several pungent sauces and one relish-like condiment that are almost always on the table at a rice meal in central and southern Burma. They are a bit of an acquired taste for foreigners (once you learn to love them, however, they're hard to pass up) because their pungency comes from fermented fish and shrimp paste. The sauces are a traditional dip and flavoring for the plates of raw and steamed vegetables (see page 217) that come to the table as part of a rice meal.

The palate fresheners are a cross between simple salads and fresh chutneys, blends of fresh ingredients without a dressing. Like the condiment sauces, they add another layer of flavor and variety to a simple rice meal, with very little effort.

kachin salsa [ZAP TOE]

MAKES A GENEROUS 1 CUP

Southeast Asian cooks know as well as Mexican cooks do how much flavor you can get from grilling vegetables before using them in salsas. Here whole tomatoes and green cayenne chiles are put on the grill (or into a heavy skillet on the stovetop) to get a little blackened and softened, then are processed to a salsa that has a touch of sweetness from the roasted shallots.

If you have Romas or other fleshy tomatoes, use them; if your tomatoes are juicier, the sauce will be a little runnier. I find myself spooning up the runnier version like a cold soup sometimes.

5 green cayenne chiles
3 medium tomatoes, preferably Roma (plum) or another fleshy variety
4 shallots, not peeled

1 tablespoon Dried Shrimp Powder (page 30)
¾ teaspoon salt, or to taste

Preheat a charcoal or gas grill until hot, or heat a cast-iron or other heavy skillet over medium-high heat.

Grill the chiles, tomatoes, and shallots on the hot grill or in the hot skillet, turning to expose all sides to the heat, until touched with black and very soft.

Peel off and discard any black areas or tough skin from the chiles and tomatoes. Cut off and discard the chile stems. Trim off the root ends of the shallots and remove the skins. Coarsely chop the chiles and shallots.

Place the chiles, tomatoes, and shallots in a food processor, add the shrimp powder and salt, and pulse several times until the mixture is reduced to a chunky sauce. Taste for salt and adjust if necessary. Serve warm or at room temperature. Leftovers will keep, refrigerated, for 3 days.

Condiments to complement a meal: Kachin Salsa (upper right) and Standout Tomato Chutney (page 206).

sour-plum chutney with chile oil

MAKES ABOUT 1½ CUPS

There's a sour plum in Southeast Asia sometimes called hog plum in English and that I know by its Thai name, *makawk*. I saw makawk for sale at the market in Hpa'an, capital of Karen State (see page 173), and later came across this yummy chutney in a small Hpa'an eatery. It's very simple: tart fruit stewed with a little palm sugar and heated with chile oil and garlic.

Because Southeast Asian sour plums have not yet come to North America, at least in any reliable way, I usually substitute tomatillos. Tomatillos are nothing like hog plums, but they have a similar tart edge. Green tomatoes are another option. I also make this with damson plums, an old-variety tart plum from the eastern Mediterranean that has a short season in early fall.

This is a great condiment for rice and for meat dishes of all kinds.

1 pound Asian sour plums, peeled and coarsely chopped, or substitute ¾ pound tomatillos, husked and rinsed, green tomatoes, or damson plums, coarsely chopped
¼ cup water
Scant 3 tablespoons chopped palm sugar or brown sugar

3 tablespoons peanut oil
3 or 4 bird (Thai) chiles or 3 red cayenne chiles, seeded and minced
1 tablespoon minced garlic
1 teaspoon fish sauce
½ teaspoon salt, or to taste
½ to 1 teaspoon Red Chile Oil (page 25)

Place the fruit in a pot with the water, cover, and bring to a boil over medium heat. Add the sugar and stir to dissolve it, then lower the heat and simmer, half-covered, until the fruit is very soft but not falling apart. If the pot starts to run dry, add a little more water as needed. If you are using plums, the pits will float to the surface as the fruit cooks; lift them out and discard.

Meanwhile, place a wok or a heavy skillet over medium heat. Add the oil, then toss in the chiles and cook for about 3 minutes, or until they are well softened. Add the garlic and cook for another 3 or 4 minutes, until golden. Remove from the heat.

When the fruit is cooked, add the chile mixture, fish sauce, and salt and simmer for another couple of minutes, until the oil rises to the surface. Add the chile oil and stir. Taste and adjust the seasoning with salt or fish sauce if you wish.

Let cool, then store in a well-sealed glass jar in the refrigerator; it will keep for 4 days or so.

fresh red chile chutney

MAKES A SCANT 1 CUP

Photographs on pages 37, 46–47, 160, and 227

This condiment, a milder fresh-chile cousin of Tart-Sweet Chile-Garlic Sauce (page 36), was served with the street-side rice crepes in Myitkyina (see page 240). The combo makes a wonderful late-afternoon snack. In Myitkyina the sauce is a bright red, but if you cannot find red cayennes or a red bell pepper, use green ones, and increase the sugar slightly. Notice that the garlic goes into the pot later, after the chiles, so it still has a little bite to it.

There's some sweetness from a little sugar and a touch of tartness from vinegar. You can vary the sauce in any way that suits you.

This makes a great pairing with roast pork or grilled beef.

2 tablespoons peanut oil or vegetable oil
Scant ⅛ teaspoon turmeric
4 red cayenne chiles, seeded and thinly sliced (about ½ cup)
1 small red bell pepper, cored, seeded, and thinly sliced (about ½ cup)
¼ to ½ teaspoon salt
¼ cup water
1 tablespoon minced garlic
1 tablespoon rice vinegar, or substitute apple cider vinegar
1 teaspoon sugar

Place a small heavy pot over medium heat and add the oil. When it is hot, toss in the turmeric and stir, then add the chiles, bell pepper, and salt and stir well. Cook for 2 minutes, stirring, then add the water. Once the water bubbles to a boil, cover and cook for 7 or 8 minutes, or until the chiles are softening well.

Add the garlic, vinegar, and sugar, stir well, and cook for about a minute, uncovered, stirring to prevent sticking. Remove from the heat and let cool before serving.

Store in a glass jar with a tight-fitting lid in the refrigerator for up to 4 days.

tamarind sauce

Like tamarind sauces in India, this is used as a dipping sauce for deep-fried snacks. It's also good drizzled on rice. The tartness of the tamarind is balanced by a little sugar, there's the pungency from the garlic, and the chile heat keeps the flavors alive in your mouth. Tamarind sauce is at its best freshly made.

¼ cup tamarind pulp (see Glossary), coarsely chopped
½ cup hot water
2 medium garlic cloves, minced (see Note)

3 green cayenne chiles, seeded and minced
½ teaspoon salt, or to taste
½ teaspoon sugar, or to taste

Place the tamarind pulp in a small bowl, add the water, and soak for about 10 minutes.

Mash the tamarind with a fork (or use your fingers) to separate the seeds and fibers from the pulp. Place a sieve over a bowl and press the tamarind through the sieve, using the back of a spoon to extract as much liquid as possible from the pulp; set the tamarind liquid aside.

If you have a mortar, pound the garlic and chiles to a paste with a pinch of salt. *Alternatively*, process the garlic and chiles to a coarse paste in a food processor.

Stir the paste into the tamarind liquid and add the sugar and salt. Taste and adjust the seasoning if necessary.

NOTE: *Garlic varies greatly in size, taste, and intensity. If your garlic is tender and sweet, use it as is. If it is dry and harsh-tasting, then fry it briefly in a little oil before adding it to the mortar; frying will soften its edge.*

tamarind chutney with shallots and dried chiles

In Pakkoku, a household of fabulous cooks (see "'Tribal Woman,'" page 113) showed me another take on tamarind sauce. Make the tamarind liquid as above. Soak 2 or 3 dried red chiles in warm water for 20 minutes, then drain, remove the stems and seeds, and mince; or pound to a paste in a mortar. Stir into the tamarind liquid along with a scant ½ cup thinly sliced shallots. Add 1 tablespoon fish sauce, taste, and add more if needed. Stir in ¼ teaspoon sugar—it's remarkable how it brings all the flavors together. Serve with meats, or rice or noodle dishes.

Tamarind pods are light brown, and contain a mass of pulp mixed with seeds and fibers; that mixture is sold in blocks as tamarind pulp. The pulp must be soaked in water to soften it (top) and then pressed through a strainer to produce tamarind liquid (bottom).

standout tomato chutney

MAKES A GENEROUS
3 CUPS

*Photograph on
page 201*

Of all the stars in the condiment universe, this tomato chutney really stands out. It's a cross between a flavoring sauce and a condiment, with mild heat.

I find myself making it frequently when tomatoes are in season (and even when they're not, substituting crushed canned organic tomatoes). The tomatoes that grow in the dry heat of Burma have a more intense flavor than ours, so it's important to cook the tomatoes down a little, as described below, to concentrate them.

Serve as a condiment to accompany any meal or, nontraditionally, as a sauce over rice noodles or pasta.

**1 tablespoon tamarind pulp (see Glossary),
    coarsely chopped**
¼ cup hot water
About 2 tablespoons chopped shallots
1½ teaspoons chopped garlic
Salt
**3 dried red chiles, soaked in water for
    10 minutes and drained**
Scant ¼ cup peanut oil
¼ teaspoon turmeric

**1 teaspoon shrimp paste (*ngapi*;
    see Glossary)**
**1½ pounds ripe tomatoes, finely chopped
    (about 3 cups), or 3 cups crushed canned
    tomatoes, preferably unseasoned**
¼ cup Dried Shrimp Powder (page 30)
**3 or 4 green cayenne chiles, seeded and cut
    lengthwise into 3 or 4 strips each**
About 1 tablespoon fish sauce, to taste
About 2 tablespoons chopped coriander

Place the tamarind pulp in a small bowl, add the hot water, and let soak for 10 minutes.

Mash the tamarind with a fork to separate the seeds and fibers from the pulp. Press the tamarind through a sieve set over a bowl, using the back of a spoon to extract as much liquid as possible from the pulp. Set the tamarind liquid aside; discard the pulp.

If you have a mortar, pound the shallots and garlic to a paste with a pinch of salt, then pound the chiles to a paste. *Alternatively*, mince the shallots and garlic to a paste with the salt, then mince the chiles. Set aside.

Place a wide heavy skillet or heavy pot or a wok over medium heat. Add the oil and turmeric and stir, then add the shallots and garlic and stir-fry for a minute or two. Add the reserved chiles and shrimp paste and stir briefly to blend. Add the tamarind liquid and tomatoes. Stir well, bring to a boil, then lower the heat slightly and cook at a strong simmer until the tomatoes are softened and a little thickened, about 10 minutes.

Stir in the shrimp powder and cayenne chiles and cook for several minutes, stirring occasionally to make sure that nothing is sticking to the bottom of the pan, until the chiles are softened. Add the fish sauce, then taste and adjust the seasonings if you wish.

Turn out into a bowl and let cool to room temperature. Stored in a well-sealed glass jar in the refrigerator, the chutney will keep for 4 days; bring to room temperature before serving.

Sprinkle on the coriander just before serving.

shan tomato chutney

In Shan State, this chutney's depth of flavor comes from toasted soybean disks instead of the dried shrimp powder and shrimp paste, and it is seasoned with salt rather than fish sauce. (The result is a vegetarian chutney.) Substitute ¼ cup crumbled toasted soybean disk (see Cooking with *Tua Nao*, page 41), or 1 to 2 teaspoons brown miso paste, for the dried shrimp powder and shrimp paste, and use 1 teaspoon salt instead of the fish sauce. Thicken with 2 to 3 tablespoons Toasted Chickpea Flour (page 32) if you wish.

Cherry tomatoes of various colors and sizes on sale at a small market in Kengtung, in eastern Shan State.

COOKS IN BURMA STILL WORK with hand-powered tools—mostly mortars and cleavers—rather than processors and juicers. While I don't yearn to return to hard labor in the kitchen, the contrast serves as a reminder that there are many ways to prepare food, and that low-tech tools can sometimes do a better job.

I'm thinking particularly of the mortar and pestle. Some mortars are better for one thing than for another, but a good solid stone mortar with a heavy, comfortable-in-the-hand pestle is a fine tool for many purposes. So is a large ceramic mortar with a wooden pestle. You can smash a clove of garlic or grind chopped shallots or ginger to a paste with a few swipes of the pestle. And you can blend ingredients together for a curry paste with just a little pounding. A mortar does the job so quickly, and is so easy to clean, that I'm never tempted to use the food processor—at least not for small quantities.

But when it comes to larger quantities, or to tasks like pureeing cooked beans into a soup, I am very grateful to have the processor; it does a great job in minutes.

There are many different mortar design options. In Burma, the two I've seen most often are the Rakhine mortar, a flat stone bowl with a stone pestle (it's great for grinding), and the tall brass mortar of central Burma with a wooden pestle.

If you have enough space, I urge you to find yourself a stone mortar. Get one that is large enough to hold a couple of cups, for it will be easier to use, with less risk of ingredients splattering. I promise that you'll soon find yourself reaching for it whenever there is garlic or ginger to crush to a paste, and wondering how you ever did without it.

CLOCKWISE FROM BOTTOM: *Stone mortars at a market in Kalaymyo, a largely Chin town on the border of Chin State. A man cooks supper in the evening at a small café in Hsipaw, in Shan State. A woman in Mrauk U deep-fries fritters in a wok.*

crispy shallot and dried shrimp relish [BALACHAUNG]

MAKES ABOUT 1 CUP The main ingredient of this central Burmese classic is dried shrimp powder fried in oil. The relish has salty depth and a pleasing chewy texture. Some versions of *balachaung* have more shrimp paste, which makes them more pungent, while others have more heat. Feel free to adjust the proportions.

1½ teaspoons tamarind pulp
(see Glossary), chopped
2 tablespoons hot water
About ¼ cup peanut oil
About ⅛ teaspoon turmeric
⅓ cup thinly sliced shallots (see Note)
6 to 8 medium cloves garlic, sliced,
about 2 tablespoons (see Note)

¾ cup Dried Shrimp Powder (page 30)
½ teaspoon Red Chile Powder (page 28), or
cayenne, or more to taste
1 teaspoon shrimp paste (*ngapi*; see Glossary)
dissolved in 1 tablespoon water
½ teaspoon sugar
¼ teaspoon salt

Place the tamarind pulp in a bowl, add the hot water, and let soak for 5 to 10 minutes. Mash with a fork, then press the tamarind through a sieve into a bowl, using the back of a spoon. Set the tamarind liquid aside; discard the pulp.

Place a heavy skillet or a wok over medium heat. Add 3 tablespoons of the oil, and when it is hot, add a pinch of turmeric and the sliced shallots. Cook, stirring occasionally, until the shallots are turning golden, 5 to 10 minutes. Lift them out of the hot oil, pausing to let excess oil drain off; set aside on a plate.

Add another pinch of turmeric and the garlic to the hot oil. Once the garlic turns golden (1 or 2 minutes), lift it out and set aside on the plate.

Add another tablespoon of oil to the skillet. Add ⅛ teaspoon turmeric, the shrimp powder, and chile powder and stir. The powder will foam as it starts to cook. Keep stirring until it reaches a paste-like consistency, about a minute, then add the tamarind liquid, dissolved shrimp paste, sugar, and salt and stir well. Cook until the shrimp powder has softened and the whole mass has blended together, about 4 minutes.

Stir in the fried shallots and garlic and transfer to a bowl. Let cool completely. Store in a glass jar. It will keep for a week in the refrigerator.

NOTE: *If you have fried shallots and fried garlic in your pantry, you can use them, rather than starting from scratch.*

"IF YOU'RE GOING TO Myitkyina, be sure to talk to Sister Mary," a foreigner in Rangoon told me. "She's been working with HIV/AIDS patients for years up there."

Sister Mary is a Columban nun from Ireland who is well into her sixties. The Columban order ran a large school in Myitkyina for decades, until the government closed all foreign-run institutions in the 1960s. Now the Columbans are back, in a quiet way. A small group of nuns from several countries (Korea and the Philippines, as well as Ireland) is working to help with AIDS and other public health issues in Myitkyina.

This nun is so amazing, I thought when I met her. I'd pedaled out to the hospice/shelter she helped set up on the outskirts of town. All the residents are HIV-positive—some there temporarily while their medications get figured out, others there to die. All cooking, cleaning, and maintenance is done by the residents. The vibe is open and friendly rather than glum. People live day to day in their situation and come to find community and purpose there.

Sister Mary fundraises in Ireland, and she also accepts donations. As I gave her mine, I looked into her wide clear face, ageless in its intelligence, determination, and good humor, and I wondered at her stamina. Perhaps it comes from religious faith, but I actually think it's an attitude, an innate toughness of spirit and a confidence in other people. Sister Mary believes that people can come through for themselves and one another if they're given positive encouragement, and a bit of a push from time to time.

A woman and a dog walk past low tables set up for late afternoon snacking in Myitkyina, in Kachin State.

pungent essence of burma

Pungent and mildly hot, *ngapi yei* is a must-have for Burmese and an acquired taste for foreigners. I have come to find it delicious. It's served in a bowl with a small spoon so diners can add it as they please. Used as a dip for steamed vegetables or drizzled on rice, it has a distinctive earthy taste.

Store in the refrigerator in a well-sealed glass jar. It becomes more yellow-green in color over time, as the turmeric is absorbed, and even more delicious to those who love it.

4 to 5 garlic cloves, not peeled
3 green cayenne chiles or 2 bird (Thai) chiles,
 or substitute 3 dried red chiles
2 tablespoons fermented fish paste (see Note)

1 cup water
¼ teaspoon turmeric
2 tablespoons Dried Shrimp Powder
 (page 30)

Preheat a charcoal or gas grill or place a heavy skillet over medium-high heat. Grill or heat the garlic and chiles, turning them to expose all sides to the heat. Let the garlic and fresh chiles scorch and blacken a little; however, if using dried chiles, just heat them to soften and be careful not to scorch them. Set aside to cool.

Meanwhile, place the fish paste and water in a small saucepan and bring to a boil. Stir in the turmeric, return to the boil, stirring occasionally, and cook down to about ½ cup liquid. Place a sieve over a bowl and strain the liquid through it; discard the solids.

Peel the garlic and pound it to a paste in a mortar, or mince it, then add to the liquid. Discard the chile stems and any very scorched patches, coarsely chop the chiles, and pound to a coarse paste in the mortar, or mince. Add to the liquid. Stir in the shrimp powder.

Store in a glass jar in the refrigerator for up to 3 days.

NOTE: *There are a number of preserved fish paste products sold in jars in Asian groceries. I use boneless pickled fish bottled in Vietnam; if necessary, you can substitute shrimp paste (ngapi; see Glossary), which will give a less earthy taste.*

THE PALE PINK ROBES of the nuns who walk in single file down the streets of Rangoon and Mandalay and the lanes of small villages are eye-catching, and their under-robes add an accent of intense golden orange. Unlike monks, these Buddhist nuns aren't out each morning collecting alms. Instead, they look for offerings of food or money as they need to—which can be weekly, or more frequently. They'll stop in front of a shop or small eatery and chant in their light voices to let people know they are there. If there's an offering made, they'll say a small blessing, then move on.

Some of the little ones, "nunlets" as I think of them, can't be more than six years old. They are led around by nuns who are still in their teens or twenties. Are the girls orphans who have been given shelter in the nunnery? What schooling do they get? What is their future? I have asked Burmese friends but have never been able to properly understand the shape of the nuns' lives. Older nuns are sometimes out and about on their own in the cities, wandering with a begging bowl and a parasol to protect them from the sun and rain. Do they like their independence? Are they lonely? I haven't had the courage to ask them, for I'm afraid of offending them.

There is another category of nun, a scholarly "dharma" nun. I've met a couple at Thamanyat Huang, a temple complex on a hill an hour east of Hpa'an. These nuns wear dark reddish-brown robes. To the outsider's eye, they look serious and intent, not exotic and butterflyish like their possibly less intellectual sisters. They study and meditate, as monks do. It feels as if they have chosen what they do. And it seems they get some respect for who they are. Nuns generally don't have the same status as monks, but these dharma nuns come close.

*Whether Buddhist nuns are walking along a track in rural Karen State (**OPPOSITE**) or a Rangoon street, their pink habits are a bright spot in the landscape.* **ABOVE:** *A golden Buddha at the temple at Myit Sone, north of Myitkyina.*

family ngapi sauce [NGAPI TAUN]

MAKES ABOUT
½ CUP

Another in the family of pungent village sauces from the Bamar tradition, this close relative of a southern Thai *nam prik* starts with shrimp paste (*ngapi*) that is toasted to soften its pungency and then stirred into a flavor paste. Unlike Pungent Essence of Burma (page 213), where preserved fish is a main ingredient, this one is made of garlic, green chile, and dried shrimp powder. Its Bamar name, *ngapi taun*, means "crushed or pounded *ngapi*." Serve with raw or steamed vegetables or to accompany a rice meal.

1 teaspoon shrimp paste
(*ngapi*; see Glossary)
3 green cayenne chiles, slit lengthwise
7 small or 3 large garlic cloves, not peeled
¼ cup Dried Shrimp Powder (page 30)

About 2 tablespoons fresh lime juice,
or to taste
About 1 tablespoon water
Salt

Preheat a charcoal or gas grill, if using.

Wrap the shrimp paste in foil and place on the grill or in a pan over medium-high heat to cook for about 3 minutes, turning it several times. It should be dried out and almost powdery when done. Set aside in a mortar if you have one, or in a small bowl.

Grill the chiles over a flame or in a heavy skillet over medium-high heat until softened and touched with black. Grill the garlic until touched with black, to sweeten its edge before you peel it.

Coarsely chop the chiles if you are using a mortar, or mince them if not, and add to the shrimp paste. Peel the garlic cloves and add to the mortar (if not using a mortar, mince the garlic and add to the bowl).

If using a mortar, pound the shrimp paste, chiles, and garlic together to make a smooth paste. *Alternatively,* mash with the back of a spoon. Stir in the shrimp powder thoroughly. Add the lime juice and water and taste. If you'd like a slightly more liquid sauce, add more water. Adjust for seasoning and sourness as you wish.

raw and cooked vegetable plate

The raw and parboiled vegetables that accompany every lunchtime rice meal in Burma are a kind of resting place, allowing for a pause in a meal of sometimes intense flavors. They can be eaten on their own or with a condiment or relish.

Set out a plate of raw and cooked vegetables whenever you serve a meal with complex or spicy flavors. You don't need to put out a dipping sauce or relish, but if you put out one or two, they do give your guests another layer of flavor and choice. (Don't limit yourself to the condiment choices in this chapter; you may have other salsas, homemade or store-bought, that would go well with the vegetable plate.)

PARBOILED VEGETABLE OPTIONS (PICK 3 OR 4)

Winged beans, yard-long beans cut into lengths, small round Thai eggplants, okra, cauliflower or broccoli florets, morning glory/water spinach, mustard greens or broccoli rabe, pea tendrils, cucumber vine tendrils, bean sprouts, soybean sprouts, daikon cut into sticks or slices, and/or small pieces of pumpkin or squash or luffa (see Glossary for further descriptions)

RAW VEGETABLE OPTIONS (PICK 3 OR 4)

Tender lettuce leaves, cucumber sticks, bean sprouts, carrot sticks, small wedges of cabbage, tender young wild lime leaves, small shallot chunks, onion root (see Glossary), zucchini sticks, and/or yard-long beans cut into 2-inch lengths (see Glossary for further descriptions)

PICKLED VEGETABLES (PICK 1; OPTIONAL)

Bamboo shoots, mustard greens, or other salty or sour pickled greens or vegetables (see Glossary)

CONDIMENT CHOICES (PICK 1 OR 2)

Standout Tomato Chutney (page 206)
Kachin Salsa (page 200)
Family Ngapi Sauce (opposite)
Pungent Essence of Burma (page 213)

Allow about 6 pieces of vegetable per person.

Bring a pot of water to a boil and add a little salt. Cook in batches, one vegetable at a time. Toss in the vegetable and cook until just softened, then remove with a spider or slotted spoon; set aside to cool.

Chop the cooked and raw vegetables into large bite-sized pieces as necessary and arrange on a plate (without seasoning them). Put out one or two dipping sauces.

shallot chutney with chiles

MAKES ABOUT 1¼ CUPS;
SERVES 4 When I was at lunch with Karen friends in a village near Moulmein, a Mon neighbor of theirs brought this contribution to the meal. She told me that it is eaten as a condiment or topping for rice. In poorer households in Mon State, it might be the only topping, in fact. There's a depth of umami flavor, a pungency from the dried shrimp powder and the touch of toasted shrimp paste.

Generous ½ teaspoon shrimp paste
(*ngapi*; see Glossary)
2 tablespoons minced seeded green
cayenne chile
1 cup shredded shallots (grate on a box grater
or pulse to shreds in a food processor)

1 tablespoon Dried Shrimp Powder
(page 30)
1 to 2 tablespoons fresh lime juice,
or to taste
1 tablespoon Shallot Oil (page 24)
Salt

Wrap the shrimp paste in foil, place in a skillet over medium-high heat, and cook on both sides for 3 minutes or so. It should be dried out, almost powdery. Set aside.

If you have a mortar, pound the green chile to a paste.

Combine the shallots, chile, and dried shrimp powder in a bowl and toss to mix. Stir together about 1 tablespoon of the lime juice, the shallot oil, and shrimp paste, pour over the shallots, and stir and turn to blend together. Let stand for 5 minutes before serving to give the flavors a chance to blend.

Just before serving, taste and add a little lime juice and/or salt if needed.

MAKES ABOUT 2½ CUPS;
SERVES 4 TO 6 ## shallot chutney with cucumber

This take on shallot chutney is a little more like a salad. Make the chutney and just before you taste for seasoning, add 1 to 1½ cups finely chopped English cucumber and 2 to 3 tablespoons chopped coriander (leave the skin on the cucumber if you wish for a little more color). Toss to mix well and proceed.

shallot-lime chutney

MAKES A SCANT ½ CUP;
SERVES 4

In this first cousin to the Mon recipe opposite, the shallots are soaked briefly in water to soften their edge, then tossed with fresh chiles. This hot fresh chutney is a welcome side condiment with any meal, but especially if you are serving a rich meat curry. Notice there is no shrimp paste or dried shrimp here, just fresh tastes and textures.

**½ cup thinly sliced shallots, soaked in water
   for 10 minutes and drained
1 green cayenne chile, or substitute 2 jalapeños,
   seeded and thinly sliced**

**2 tablespoons minced coriander
   (optional)
Juice of 1 to 2 limes
Scant ¼ teaspoon salt, or to taste**

Combine the shallot slices, chile, and coriander, if using, in a small condiment bowl. Squeeze on about 1½ tablespoons lime juice. Toss to mix well, then add the salt, mix again, and taste. Add lime juice and/or salt if you wish.

A man mends a fishing net in Moulmein, the port at the mouth of the Salween River.

everyday cabbage-shallot refresher

SERVES 4 Cabbage is readily available in the colder months, so this is an ideal winter dish. I like it with grilled fish or grilled meat, or with beef stew, because of its contrasting crispness and bright flavors. This can have a marked hit of heat (red cayenne chiles are very attractive against the green), or less heat if you reduce the amount of cayenne or use a milder chile.

Dressing the shallots 10 to 30 minutes ahead gives them time to soften and get a little milder. Then just toss with the crisp cabbage at the last minute (the photo shows Napa cabbage). Serve as a condiment.

Generous ½ cup thinly sliced shallots
1 red or green cayenne chile, seeded and minced, to taste, or substitute a milder chile such as a jalapeño or a Hungarian wax pepper

About 1 tablespoon fish sauce, or 1 teaspoon salt, or to taste
2 tablespoons fresh lime juice
About 2 cups grated or very thinly sliced Savoy, green, or Napa cabbage

Combine the shallots, chile, fish sauce or salt, and lime juice in a medium bowl and toss. Set aside for 10 minutes to half an hour.

Add the shredded cabbage and toss well. Taste for seasoning, and sprinkle on more fish sauce or salt if you wish.

MOSTLY RICE

IT'S NOT SURPRISING THAT RICE is mentioned in every chapter of this book: in this rice-eating land of Burma almost all dishes, from soups and salads to curries of all kinds, and condiments, are traditionally designed to be accompaniments to rice.

Beyond the meals centered around plain fresh rice, leftover rice is breakfast for many, lightly fried, with perhaps an egg or some cooked beans or meat on top. Rice is also cooked in coconut milk (see page 237), or with oil and flavorings (see Fried Rice with Shallots, page 226, and Peanut and Rice Porridge, page 234). Sticky rice is the everyday rice of the Tai Koen people in eastern Shan State; it's also the main ingredient in many of the dishes in the Sweets chapter.

Rice flour is used to make many noodles as well as sweet and savory confections of all kinds. Street-side snacks, from deep-fried crackers to savory crepes, are made from rice-flour batter (see the dosa-like Street-Side Rice Crepes, page 240, and Rice-Batter Crepes, page 242, an inventive cross between noodles and crepes).

From rice crepes, it's a short jump to oven-baked flatbreads. I've included the tender naan-style flatbread known as *nan-piar* in Burma (see page 244). There it's baked in street-side tandoor ovens, but the breads are easy to make in a North American home oven.

basic lunchtime rice

MAKES ABOUT 8 CUPS;
SERVES 6 TO 8
The classic rice of Burma is like Thai jasmine rice, delicately perfumed and aromatic as it cooks, and tender and slightly clinging when cooked. Use Thai jasmine as a substitute. This recipe for cooking the rice in a measured amount of water yields tender rice every time. It's always a good idea to make more than you need. Leftover rice makes wonderful fried rice (see page 226).

3 cups Burmese rice or Thai
jasmine rice

Water

Place the rice in a bowl or pot and wash throughly in several changes of water, swirling it around gently with your hand and then pouring the water off. Place in a heavy straight-sided pot (with a tight-fitting lid) or a rice cooker. Add water until the rice is covered by a depth equal to the first joint on your index finger: to measure, place the tip of your finger on the top surface of the rice.

Cover and bring to a boil, then reduce the heat to low and cook for 15 minutes. Remove from the heat. *Alternatively*, cover and turn on the rice cooker.

Let the cooked rice stand for 10 minutes. Take off the lid, moisten a rice paddle or a flat wooden spoon with cold water, slide it down the inside wall of the pot or cooker, and turn the rice gently. Repeat all around the pot, gently turning the rice from the outside in. Serve from the pot; keep it covered.

toasted rice powder

Used as a base for soup by the Kachin and also as a thickener in sauces, soups, and vegetable dishes, toasted rice powder is easy to make, and it keeps well. Place about 1 cup raw jasmine rice in a large heavy skillet over medium-high heat. Use a wooden spatula to move the rice around as the skillet heats, and continue cooking and stirring until all the rice is touched with light gold and aromatic, 5 minutes or so. Let cool for a moment, then grind to a powder in a food processor or, in batches, in a spice grinder or clean coffee grinder. Let cool completely, then store in a well-sealed glass jar.

After rice is harvested, the rice straw is gathered. Here three Karen guys are tying the load of straw down, before driving it back to their village, in Karen State.

fried rice with shallots

SERVES 3 OR 4 This simple way to use leftover rice is great for breakfast. Top it with a fried or poached egg or some cooked chickpeas (see below). Or serve instead of plain rice to accompany a meal.

2 to 3 tablespoons peanut oil
¼ teaspoon turmeric
Generous ½ cup sliced shallots
4 to 5 cups chilled cooked jasmine rice

1 teaspoon salt
1 cup green peas (optional)
2 tablespoons Fried Shallots (page 24)
Lime wedges (optional)

Place a wok or a heavy, deep skillet over medium-high heat and add the oil, then add the turmeric and shallots and stir-fry until the shallots are tender and translucent, about 5 minutes.

Raise the heat to high and use wet hands to break up any clumps as you add the rice to the pan. Add the salt and peas, if using, and stir-fry, pressing the rice against the sides of the pan to sear it. Continue cooking until the rice is hot (the peas should be cooked by then), add the fried shallots, stir-fry briefly, and transfer to a serving bowl. Serve with lime wedges on the side if you wish.

BREAKFAST RICE AND PEAS: *This rice is breakfast for many people in Burma, topped with some tender chickpeas or cowpeas (see Peas for Many Occasions, page 112), and maybe an egg or a little leftover meat curry. After getting up in the dawn hours to photograph markets, I've often found find myself looking forward to some version of the rice, peas, and fried egg combo around eight thirty. At home in Toronto, I top the rice with fresh coriander leaves or tender greens and a fried egg, and drizzle on one of the condiment sauces to give it a kick, most often Tart-Sweet Chile-Garlic Sauce (page 36).*

Fried Rice with Shallots, made with green peas. It's accompanied by a jar of Fresh Red Chile Chutney (page 203), a small bowl of cooked chickpeas (see Peas for Many Occasions, page 112), and, in front, a bowl of Fried Shallots (page 24).

IN 1980, on my first trip to Burma, there were few automobiles on the streets of Rangoon, and most of those were old British and American cars from the late 1940s and early '50s. There was a disturbing sense of stopped time, for the government had closed the country off and was trying to keep out modernity. Men all wore traditional Burmese *lungyi* (sarongs); the women were all in traditional long narrow skirts and fitted long-sleeved tops. I was struck, as visitors always are, by their grace as they walked down the street.

When I got up to the Inle Lake area, the feeling of stopped time—or perhaps timelessness is a better word—was even stronger. There were no cars, no motorcycles. People used oxen to pull their plows, and they traveled to village markets on foot or in open-back trucks that operated like buses. Out on the lake, men rowed their narrow wooden boats standing up, with one leg wrapped around the paddle, powering it.

I met some tourists from Rangoon who told me about a thousand-Buddha cave at a small place called Pindaya. They said there was a guy in the village who had taken them there in his big old 1948 car; perhaps he'd take me. Thanks to him, I went to the Pindaya caves the next day in stately comfort. The cave entrance was up a long flight of covered steps. The Buddhas—some heads, some full statues, in niches high on the

wall and in every cranny of the rock—gleamed white in the darkness. They were a magical, haunting sight.

Fast-forward thirty years: I was in another part of Burma, in Karen State, and headed out to see Buddha caves with a couple of other foreigners. This time I wasn't in a grand old car, but a metal cart attached to the back of a motorcycle. It was slow and pretty bumpy, but I was in good company, so the trip was entertaining.

The Buddha caves were amazing, especially the Kawgun site, a towering cliff face covered with Buddha statues. At the foot of the cliff, a procession of white and gold plaster Buddhas—some standing, some sitting in meditation—leads to a grotto. There's a temple too, tended by monks who live at a small monastery nearby. But everything is dwarfed by the cliffs—tall, slightly concave walls of pale yellow limestone covered with Buddhas of every shape and size, painted dark red and gold, fitted into niches or plastered onto the cliff face. The statues are so densely packed that from a distance the whole surface looks like a huge undulating embroidered shawl or a Persian rug.

Each of the statues in the Pindaya caves and on the cliff face at Kawgun is an offering, a form of prayer. This accumulation of prayer is a powerful testament to the enduring strength of Buddhism in Burma.

Scenes from the Buddha cliffs at Kawgun; the reclining Buddha (OVERLEAF) is spectacular.

sticky rice

SERVES 6

*Photograph on
page 164*

In most of Burma sticky rice is eaten only occasionally, as a sweet flavored with sugar and often coconut as well. But for the Tai Koen of eastern Shan State, it's a staple, eaten plain and unsweetened every day.

Sticky rice—or glutinous rice as it's also called—is traditionally steamed in a basket over boiling water, with no seasoning or oil. The rice is soaked before steaming, so that it cooks quickly and evenly.

The most satisfying version of sticky rice that I've seen in Tai Koen households is a blend of white and black sticky rice. When the two rices are soaked together, the black rice tints the water and the white rice. The cooked rice is an attractive pale purple. You can, of course, just make plain white sticky rice.

To cook sticky rice, steam in either a conical basket that fits into the neck of a pot (the two are sold as a unit in many Asian stores), or a wide steamer (with a lid) that fits tightly over a pot. A cheesecloth liner prevents the rice from sticking to the basket or falling through the slats or holes of a steamer.

I find that people eat a surprising quantity of sticky rice, so it's good to make more than you think you'll need. Put any leftovers to delicious use by transforming them into crackers, as described in the variation.

3 cups white Thai sticky rice, rinsed in cold water and soaked for 6 to 12 hours in plenty of water

⅓ to ½ cup black sticky rice, rinsed and soaked with the white rice (optional)

Drain the rice. Fill the lower "water pot" of your steaming arrangement (see the headnote) with about 3 inches of water. Put the steamer top on the pot, line it with cheesecloth, and add the rice. The water in the lower pot should not touch the rice. If using a steamer, fit the lid on; if using a conical basket, place a lid loosely over the rice.

Place the pot over high heat and bring to a boil. Lower the heat slightly, to maintain a strong boil, and cook until the rice is tender, about 35 minutes. The rice will be shiny and chewy but cooked through.

Turn the rice out onto a clean work surface; use a wet wooden spoon or spatula to spread it out and then to fold the edges of it back over to make a pile. Pull the rice together with your hands and transfer to a basket with a lid, or a deep bowl, and cover with a damp cloth to prevent it from drying out. Invite your guests to use their hands to serve themselves chunks of rice, or put out a wooden spoon for serving.

rice cracker snacks

These are a treat for breakfast and even better as a snack or appetizer, served on their own or alongside a salsa or dip of any kind.

If you have sticky rice left over, pull off clumps of rice about 2 tablespoons in size and shape each into a roughly formed flat disk about 2 inches across. Press firmly to shape the disk, but don't mash it. They'll look like slightly lumpy large cookies. Set on a baking sheet, covered loosely with a cloth, to dry for 2 or 3 days.

To make the crackers, heat about 1½ inches of peanut oil in a stable wok or wide shallow pot over medium-high heat. To test, toss in a little of the sticky rice; if the oil bubbles around it, it is ready. Add the rice disks one at a time, without crowding; you don't want them to stick together. The rice will puff a little in the hot oil and turn white. Use a slotted spoon to keep the crackers from sticking to each other and to turn them over after a minute or so. Fry until puffed on all sides, then lift out and put on a paper-towel-lined plate. Repeat with the remaining crackers.

inle lake rice with garlic oil

SERVES 4 The Intha people of Inle Lake claim this recipe is theirs, but so do the Shan near the lake. Whoever thought of it, this cooked rice kneaded with cooked potato (potatoes are grown up in the hills above the lake) and/or with cooked, flaked boneless fish, is a real keeper. Serve the rice-potato blend instead of plain rice, or serve the fish version as a one-dish meal with a side of cooked vegetables. Put out Red Chile Oil (page 25) or another chile-hot condiment.

2 cups freshly cooked jasmine rice
2 cups crumbled boiled potato
1 cup poached or grilled, deboned, and flaked fish (optional)

About 2 tablespoons Garlic Oil plus 2 tablespoons Fried Garlic (page 25)
¼ to ½ cup chopped coriander (optional)
1 teaspoon salt, or to taste

Place the rice and potato in a bowl and use your hands to blend and knead them together. Add the fish, if using, and repeat the kneading. Add a little salt and the oil and knead together. Taste and add more salt as needed. Mix well, then serve topped with the fried garlic and a sprinkling of coriander if you wish.

peanut and rice porridge [KHAO POON TUA LIN]

On my first morning in Kengtung, the cultural center of the Tai Koen people in the eastern part of Shan State, I stared at a pale pink-mauve mass, like tinted soft polenta, that steamed in the cool morning air, and couldn't imagine what it was. The vendor at the small morning market saw my puzzlement, so she scooped out a ladleful, poured it into a bowl, and handed it to me with a spoon and a "taste it, go ahead" gesture. Smooth on the tongue, rich-tasting... it took a moment, because the combination was so unexpected: a puree of peanuts and rice! As I ate the rest of my sample I watched people flavor their porridge.

Some people order rice noodles topped with the porridge as a sauce, along with condiments such as shallot oil, soy sauce, and fresh herbs. Others use it like polenta, as the base of their morning bowl, topped with meat sauce (like the sauce for Shan Village Khaut Swe, page 266), blanched pea tendrils, and various condiments. Then every customer carefully stirs the whole combination to blend everything.

The Tai Koen name of this dish means "rice noodles with peanuts"; in Burmese the name is *ni bei thamin san*, "peanuts with rice." It's become a favorite in our house, especially on chilly days, as a substitute for plain rice with supper. I like to stir in shallot oil just before serving, as well as a dash of soy sauce, and some fresh coriander leaves and bright green pea tendrils.

1 cup raw peanuts, in their papery skins, rinsed

About 5 cups water

1 cup jasmine or other long-grain tender white rice

1½ teaspoons salt, or to taste

1 tablespoon peanut oil

2 tablespoons Shallot Oil (page 24), or to taste

Soy sauce (optional)

OPTIONAL TOPPINGS AND FLAVORINGS

1 cup coriander leaves

2 cups pea tendrils, blanched in boiling water for 1 to 2 minutes and coarsely chopped

Red Chile Oil (page 25)

Chopped Roasted Peanuts (page 35)

Lightly toasted sesame seeds (see page 32)

Kachin Salsa (page 200) or Tart-Sweet Chile-Garlic Sauce (page 36)

Place the peanuts in a wide heavy pot with a tight-fitting lid, add 3 cups of the water, and bring to a vigorous boil over medium-high heat. Cover, lower the heat to maintain a steady low boil, and cook until the peanuts are tender, about 1 hour.

Meanwhile wash the rice in several changes of water, swishing it around gently in the water.

[Continued]

Peanut and Rice Porridge, topped with peanuts, chile oil, sesame seeds, and blanched pea tendrils. At top are small bowls of flavorings (clockwise from top left): sesame seeds, Red Chile Oil (page 25), and Kachin Salsa (page 200) topped with thinly sliced green cayenne chile.

When the peanuts are tender, add the rice and salt, along with enough water to cover by 1½ inches or so. Stir and raise the heat to bring back to a boil, then cover, lower the heat to maintain a simmer, and cook for 20 minutes, or until the rice is tender.

Turn out into a food processor (you may have to work in batches) and process to a smooth puree. Transfer the mixture back to the pot, add hot water as necessary to give it a soft texture, and stir in the peanut oil. (You can make this ahead and then reheat it just before serving; the mixture thickens as it stands, so you will want to add another ½ cup or more water and stir it in as you are heating it.)

Transfer to a large bowl and stir in the shallot oil, then taste for seasoning and add salt or soy sauce if you wish. You don't want it highly seasoned, because this—like plain rice—is meant to be a neutral background to other flavors. (For a more highly seasoned version, see below.) Serve with the toppings and flavorings of your choice.

noodles with peanut-rice sauce

You can use the porridge as a sauce or dressing for rice noodles. Allow 1 pound dried noodles or 1½ pounds fresh noodles for 4 people. Once the sauce is ready, bring a large pot of water to the boil and drop in the noodles. Fresh noodles will be ready in a minute or two; dried noodles will take longer to soften fully. Drain, then distribute among your guests' bowls. Add a little shallot oil and toss, to prevent the noodles from sticking. If the sauce is very thick, add hot water to loosen it. Stir in 1 to 2 tablespoons soy sauce or another 1 to 1½ teaspoons salt, to taste. Top each serving of noodles with a generous portion of sauce and some coriander leaves and raw or blanched pea tendrils. Invite your guests to add flavorings as they wish and to stir the whole mass together. Serve with sliced tomatoes or chopped cucumber and a chile-hot condiment sauce.

perfumed coconut rice

SERVES 8 This luxurious version of "plain rice," which is delightfully aromatic as it cooks, is a good choice for special occasions. It pairs well with a chicken curry or with Kachin Pounded Beef with Herbs (page 178). There are many versions of coconut rice. Some of them are a little sweet, but this one is just lightly perfumed with shallots, a single clove, and a little cinnamon, and it's salted, rather than being left unseasoned as plain rice is.

3 cups jasmine rice
1 tablespoon peanut oil or vegetable oil
3 or 4 small shallots, cut lengthwise in half or into quarters (about ¼ cup)
1 clove

One 2-inch piece cinnamon stick, broken in half
¼ teaspoon turmeric
2 teaspoons salt
1½ cups canned or fresh coconut milk
About 2½ cups water

Wash the rice by immersing it in a bowl of cold water, swishing it around, and draining; repeat two or three times. Set aside.

Place a pot with a tight-fitting lid over medium heat. Add the oil (don't skip it, or the coconut milk will make the rice stick to the bottom of the pot), then add the shallots and cook, stirring occasionally, for 3 or 4 minutes. Add the rice, clove, cinnamon stick, turmeric, and salt and stir gently. Add the coconut milk and 2 cups of the water, then measure the depth of the liquid: place the tip of your index finger on the top surface of the rice—the liquid should come up to your first joint. Add water if needed. Bring to a boil, then cover, lower the heat to medium-low, and cook for 5 minutes. Lower the heat to the lowest setting and cook the rice for another 15 minutes. Remove from the heat and let rest for 5 minutes.

Shake the pot gently, then remove the lid and use a wet rice paddle or flat wooden spoon to turn the rice: slide the paddle or spoon down the inside wall of the pot or cooker and turn the rice gently. Repeat all around the edges of the pot. Cover until ready to serve, hot or at room temperature.

LEFTOVERS: *The coconut milk makes each rice grain tender and separate, so that leftover rice doesn't clump at all; it's also very flavorful. It doesn't need refrying. Warm it over steam or in the oven, or serve it at room temperature, topped simply with cooked beans or an egg and perhaps some fried shallots or greens.*

IN MAY 2008, Cyclone Nargis devastated parts of the Irrawaddy Delta with wind and rain and flooding, killing over 100,000 people. Twenty months later in Rangoon, I met an English woman who'd gone to Burma right after the cyclone. Despite the government's resistance to offers of outside help, she had taken a truckload of relief supplies down to the delta. She was interested in getting back there, to a town called Bogole, to see how rebuilding efforts were going, and I was happy to keep her company.

We applied for travel permits in a sleepy office that looked like a scene in a movie set in the colonial 1930s. The next day at the dock downtown, we had our permits carefully checked, and walked onto a crowded ferry to cross the Yangon River. The other shore was a different world: poorer, slower, and quieter than the busy city across the way.

We found a share-taxi headed to Bogole, an old suspension-challenged station wagon. Soon we understood why the suspension was shot. The road—sometimes paved and pitted, sometimes just dirt—wound past tall palm trees, small huts on stilts, and rice fields still sickly from their inundation in salt water during the cyclone.

The other passenger in the taxi was a young Burmese working for an NGO in Bogole. We bombarded him with questions. He told us that a disproportionate number of women had been killed in the cyclone, and that many families were fragmented. It was hard to imagine how whole communities could find their feet again, with so much social, emotional, and material loss. He told us that most of the ducks and pigs had died in the storm, and that nearly all the water buffalo—the essential beast of burden for farmers in the delta—had been swept away. Later, at his office in Bogole, we saw a job posting advertising a "buffalo procurement" position.

On the plus side, donations by people in the rest of Burma and by foreigners meant that Bogole was doing pretty well. In town, we saw new schools, the classes full of lively children, and mothers with plump, healthy-looking babies. Building supplies were stored in sheds along the riverside.

But when we went out in a boat to poke around in the waterways out of town, the basic level at which people were living was dismaying. Only half an hour from the relative prosperity and full markets of Bogole, families were still "housed" in makeshift lean-tos and shelters, essentially roofs with no walls. They were doing what they could to improve their situation: men were working on mangrove restoration projects (the mangroves stabilize the shoreline and protect the land) and there were vegetables growing by every shelter. Children played on the riverbanks.

Images from the Irrawaddy Delta. CLOCKWISE FROM BOTTOM: *Early morning in Bogole. An older woman whose face shows the wear and strain of life. A classroom of children in a newly built school near Bogole, less than two years after Cyclone Nargis. A tiger shrine, with Buddha statue behind, at a temple in Pathein.*

street-side rice crepes, myitkyina style

MAKES ABOUT 12 CREPES; SERVES 4 These beautiful crepes (called *yei mont* in central Burma and *mok ghieh-ba* in Kachin State) are made at markets all over Burma. They are close first cousins of *dosa*, the crepe-like flatbread of southern India, but like other dishes in Burma that probably originated in the Indian subcontinent, they have taken on a distinctive identity.

The batter is made of rice flour and unlike *dosa* batter, it is not fermented, instead whisked up just before it's needed. The crepes are cooked on one side only, in a very lightly oiled skillet. They are sprinkled with a little oil as they cook and then topped with an eclectic, attractive mixture of textures and flavors: finely chopped tomato (the vendors use scissors to cut off thin wedges), minced scallions, coriander, a scattering of cooked chickpeas or cowpeas, minced green chile, and often strips of fresh coconut. The crepe is folded over the toppings and served as a half-moon, sometimes accompanied by a dipping sauce, such as red chile chutney.

Cooking these takes practice, as any crepes do, so you may have to discard the first one or two. You will need a well-seasoned cast-iron or other heavy skillet 7 or 8 inches in diameter (it's more difficult to heat a larger pan evenly). It's useful to have a pastry or other brush for dabbing a little oil on the breads as they cook.

BATTER
¾ cup rice flour
½ teaspoon salt
¼ teaspoon baking soda
1½ cups lukewarm water
Scant 1 teaspoon minced ginger
   (optional)
About ½ cup peanut oil

TOPPINGS (ALL OR SOME, AS YOU PLEASE)
¾ cup cooked chickpeas or cowpeas
   (see Peas for Many Occasions, page 112)
   or green peas
¾ cup thin tomato wedges, preferably
   Roma (plum) or another fleshy tomato
1 cup coarsely chopped coriander
½ cup minced scallions
¼ cup minced seeded green cayenne chiles
   (optional)
½ cup fresh coconut strips
   (optional; see Glossary)
Fresh Red Chile Chutney (page 203)
Tart-Sweet Chile-Garlic Sauce (page 36)

Combine the rice flour, salt, and baking soda in a bowl and whisk in ½ cup lukewarm water until you have a perfectly smooth thick batter. Add the remaining 1 cup water and stir or whisk to incorporate it. (You may think there is a typo in the recipe because the batter is so thin. Don't worry!) Stir in the ginger, if using.

Place a well-seasoned 7- or 8-inch skillet over medium heat. When it is hot, add about 1 tablespoon oil and use a heatproof spatula to spread it over the pan, then wipe away the excess with a paper towel. Quickly stir the batter, then scoop up about 2 tablespoons of it and pour it onto the center of the skillet. Tilt the pan so the batter flows over it. It will move quickly across the pan's surface, making a lacy pattern; if there are any large gaps, dab on a little extra batter to fill them. Let the crepe cook for about 30 seconds, then brush the center very lightly, barely touching it, with a little oil, or dribble on a few drops of oil. Use your spatula to see if the crepe is starting to crisp at the edges; once it is, drip a few drops of oil under the edges in a couple of spots.

Make this first crepe plain, so that you can get comfortable handling it: fold it in half, flip it over for 15 seconds, and transfer it to a plate.

Repeat with the remaining batter and oil, stirring the batter each time before you start, but with subsequent crepes, sprinkle toppings on one half of the crepe once it has started crisping at the edges: a scant tablespoon each of peas and chopped tomato, a teaspoon each of coriander and scallions, and a pinch of minced green chile as well as a little coconut, if you want. Fold the crepe over the toppings, flip it over for 15 seconds, and use a spatula to transfer it to a serving plate or individual plate; serve hot or warm with a chutney or sauce.

Street-side crepes in Mandalay.

rice-batter crepes [KHAO SOY KHEM NOI]

**MAKES ABOUT
7 CREPES; SERVES 4**

The inventiveness of people who work day to day with basic ingredients is almost limitless. These steamed savory crepes are made in Kengtung, north of the Golden Triangle; I've never seen them anywhere else. The alternate title above is in Tai Koen, the majority language in Kengtung; and the Shan name is *khao soy biu bang moh*. They're kind of a cross between noodles and crepes.

Each morning in the local market, kids and adults sit on low benches as the crepe maker keeps two pans going, steaming the crepes by floating the pans in big pots of water. Once the first layer of batter is cooked, she asks whoever is next what he or she wants as flavoring and topping. The choices include soy sauce, fish sauce, pea tendrils, lettuce greens, and chopped roasted peanuts. She drizzles on the flavorings, and often a little sugar, adds another layer of batter, and then sprinkles on greens and herbs. The pan goes back into the pot to steam for another couple of minutes, then she carefully rolls up the crepe and hands it to the waiting hungry customer on a small plate.

These are a great option for people who are gluten-intolerant.

BATTER
1 cup rice flour
¼ cup tapioca flour
¼ cup cornstarch
2 cups lukewarm water
¼ teaspoon salt

OPTIONAL FLAVORINGS AND TOPPINGS
Soy sauce
Rice vinegar or black rice vinegar
Fish sauce
Garlic Oil (page 25) or Shallot Oil (page 24)

Red Chile Oil (page 25)
Sugar
Chopped Roasted Peanuts (page 35)
1 cup coriander leaves, coarsely chopped
**1 to 2 cups torn or coarsely chopped lettuce
    leaves, fine pea tendrils, or other tender
    greens**
**Fresh Red Chile Chutney (page 203),
    Tart-Sweet Chile-Garlic Sauce (page 36),
    or Kachin Salsa (page 200) (optional)**

Whisk together the batter until very smooth. Pass it through a sieve if you are having trouble getting rid of lumps.

Put the flavorings and toppings of your choice by your stovetop.

Lightly oil an 8- or 9-inch shallow cake pan. Make sure it floats. Pour 2 inches of water into a wide shallow pot and bring to a boil. Pour the batter into the oiled pan (if it is 9 inches in diameter, you'll need about 3 tablespoons; use 2½ tablespoons for an 8-inch pan). Tilt the pan to spread the batter all over, then use tongs to place the

At a small morning market in the old Tai Koen capital Kengtung, in eastern Shan State, steamed savory crepes are made to order.

pan in the boiling water. Cover the pot and steam until the crepe is cooked through, 2 to 3 minutes. It should be translucent and lifting away from the pan a little.

Lift the pan out with tongs, splash on a teaspoon or more of soy sauce, vinegar, fish sauce, and/or garlic or shallot oil; a dab of chile oil; a sprinkle of sugar; and a couple of tablespoons of peanuts. Pour on a scant 3 tablespoons batter and swirl to spread it (it will become stained as it mixes with the darker condiments, which is fine), then top with the coriander and other greens too if you wish. Put back into the pot with tongs, cover, and steam until the greens have wilted and the top layer of batter is cooked through and translucent, about 3 minutes.

Lift the pan out with tongs and set on a work surface. The crepe is like a large noodle sheet: use a round-tipped spatula to help lift an edge of the crepe, then roll it up, loosely lift it out of the pan, and place on a plate. Repeat with the remaining batter and flavorings/toppings.

Serve plain or with a dipping sauce.

tender flatbreads [NAN-PIAR]

Known as *nan-piar*, these fine tender flatbreads are closely related to Indian naan and are made in markets in many parts of Burma. Usually they're baked in a tandoor oven (for which a baking stone in a regular oven is a good substitute). The breads are slightly sweet and leavened with both yeast and a little baking soda.

Make the dough about 2 hours before you want to bake the breads. Or make it the night before, and shape and bake the breads in the morning. The breads bake in a couple of minutes. Serve for breakfast or as a snack anytime, spread with almond butter or topped with slices of firm cheese (and see Sweet Flatbread Breakfast, below). This is a large recipe that yields about 2½ pounds of dough. You can bake half the dough one day and then save the rest for the next day.

1¾ cups lukewarm water
½ teaspoon yeast
5 to 5½ cups all-purpose flour, preferably
    unbleached

2 tablespoons sugar
1 egg
2 teaspoons salt
½ teaspoon baking soda

Put the water in a large bowl, sprinkle on the yeast, and stir. Add 2 cups of the flour and stir to make a smooth batter. If you have the time, let rest for 20 minutes.

To make the dough by hand: Sprinkle on the sugar, add the egg, and stir in thoroughly. Add 2 cups of the flour, the salt, and the baking soda and stir to incorporate. Add another ½ cup of the flour and stir. Once you can pull the dough together into a ball, turn out onto a dry, generously floured surface. Knead, incorporating more flour only as necessary, until smooth, soft, and elastic.

To make the dough using a food processor: Combine the batter, sugar, and egg in the processor and process briefly to blend. Add 2 cups of the flour, the salt, and the baking soda; process to blend. Then add another cup of the flour and process until a ball of dough forms. Process for another 10 to 15 seconds. Turn out onto a lightly floured surface and knead for a minute, incorporating more flour only as necessary. The dough should be smooth, soft, and elastic.

Set the dough aside in a tightly covered bowl, and let rest for 1½ to 2 hours; you can also let it rest overnight in a cool place if you wish.

Twenty minutes before you wish to bake, place a rack in the center of your oven, lay a baking stone, pizza stone, or a surface of unglazed quarry tiles on it (see Glossary), and preheat the oven to 500°F.

Meanwhile, dust your work surface with flour, turn out the dough, and cut it in half. Set half aside covered in plastic wrap (if you won't be using it until the next day, refrigerate until 1 hour before you wish to bake). Cut the remaining dough in half, and then in half again. Cut each quarter into 3 equal pieces—you will have 12 pieces altogether. Roll each piece firmly between your lightly floured palms to make a smooth ball, then flatten each to a 2-inch disk on the floured surface. Set aside, loosely covered with plastic wrap, for about 15 minutes.

Working with one disk at a time on the lightly floured surface, press first one side and then the other into the flour, then roll out to a round 7 to 8 inches in diameter, working with short firm strokes of the rolling pin and rolling from the center outward; rotate the bread a quarter turn or so after each stroke of the pin. (This technique helps prevent the dough from sticking to your work surface as you roll it out.) Set aside and repeat with another disk. Stretch each bread a little more with your hands, so it's as thin as possible.

Transfer one bread onto a baker's peel lightly dusted with flour or the floured back of a baking sheet and use the peel or sheet to transfer the bread onto the hot baking stone or quarry tiles. Repeat with the other bread. Bake for 2 to 3 minutes, or until they are touched with color on the bottom and have little bubbles on top but are still soft and pale, then remove and wrap in a cotton cloth to stay warm and soft. Repeat with the remaining dough.

Serve as a snack or to accompany any meal: the breads are thin and seductive, so allow 3 per person.

rangoon tea-shop banana flatbreads

At my favorite tea shop in Rangoon, the breads are pale yellow and sweet. The baker's secret ingredient is ripe banana. To try this, substitute 1½ cups water mixed with ½ cup pureed very ripe banana for the water in the recipe, then proceed as above.

sweet flatbread breakfast

Spread *nan-piar* with lightly mashed tender cooked chickpeas or cowpeas (see Peas for Many Occasions, page 112), sprinkle on a little sugar if you wish, and roll up. Cut into 2-inch pieces and eat with pleasure, to accompany tea or coffee. This combo of bread and cooked peas, with or without sugar, is known as *nan-piar bei-leh*.

NOODLES

WHILE THE NOONTIME MEAL for most Burmese is centered around rice, many people eat noodles at other times of day. The best-known Burmese noodle dish is *mohinga*, a breakfast favorite that comes in many versions (see page 255).

Other delectable noodle dishes include Mandalay Noodles with Chicken Curry (page 270) and the coconut-sauced noodle dish called *ohn-no khaut swe* (see page 251). My personal favorites are the Shan noodles with a tomato-y pork sauce (see page 266) and the egg noodles with coconut milk and pork, called *swe daung khaut swe* (pronounced "sway dong kao sway") on page 248.

There's a huge fascinating world of noodles in Burma. They can be made of rice flour, wheat flour, or even chickpea flour. They can be fine rice vermicelli, or the fat round noodles called *mondi* from Mandalay, or flat ribbons, fresh or dried. Most of these noodles are found in this chapter, but see Soups for bean threads and Mostly Vegetables for Shan tofu noodles.

egg noodles
with pork in coconut sauce [SWE DAUNG KHAUT SWE]

When I was in Dawei, in southern Burma, I had a long conversation with a follower of the Sitagu Sayadaw (see page 93) from Rangoon. But we weren't talking Buddhism, we were discussing food—specifically, noodles and where to find them in Rangoon. He gave me directions to several noodle shops there, including what is now my favorite, an unassuming place called Osaka. It's near the Yegyaw market, at the eastern edge of the downtown, and it specializes in this spectacular noodle dish, pronounced "sway dong kao sway" in Burmese. Egg noodles are topped by pork in a coconut milk sauce, with a light broth served alongside to sip between mouthfuls of noodles. The other accompaniments all play a lively role in giving the dressed noodles texture and layers of flavor. It's hard not to go there every day for breakfast when I'm in Rangoon, and when I'm not, this recipe is a good backup.

You can omit the broth or substitute any light broth for it.

BROTH
Scant ½ pound pork shoulder, chopped
½ pound pork bones
6 cups water
3 shallots, coarsely chopped
1 stalk lemongrass, trimmed and smashed
2 tablespoons fish sauce

SAUCE
1 pound boneless pork shoulder, cut into
   bite-sized slices
¼ teaspoon turmeric
About 1 teaspoon fish sauce
¼ cup minced shallots
1 tablespoon minced garlic
2 dried red chiles, soaked in water for
   10 minutes, drained, and minced
¼ cup peanut oil
1 teaspoon shrimp paste (*ngapi*; see Glossary),
   dissolved in ¼ cup water
2 tablespoons Toasted Chickpea Flour
   (page 32)

¼ cup water
¾ cup canned or fresh coconut milk
   (see Glossary)
½ teaspoon finely ground black pepper,
   or to taste
Salt (optional)

About 1 pound thin egg noodles
1 tablespoon Shallot Oil (page 24)

ACCOMPANIMENTS
About 1½ cups Fried Noodles (recipe follows)
½ cup coriander leaves and tender stems
2 limes, cut into wedges
1 cup finely shredded Napa cabbage or other
   chopped fresh greens such as Romaine
   lettuce or Belgian endive
½ cup thinly sliced shallots, soaked for
   10 minutes in cold water, drained, and
   squeezed dry
¼ cup Red Chile Oil (page 25) or store-bought

Make the broth: Place the pork and bones in a pot with the water, shallots, and lemongrass. Bring to a boil and skim off any foam, then add the fish sauce, lower the heat, and simmer for 1 hour. Strain the broth (you will have about 5 cups). Set aside.

Place the sliced pork in a shallow bowl, add the turmeric and fish sauce, and turn to coat the meat; set aside. If you have a mortar, pound the shallots to a paste, then pound the garlic and chiles to a paste; set aside.

Heat the oil in a wok or heavy pot over medium heat. Add the shallots and cook for about 3 minutes, or until well softened and translucent. Add the garlic, chiles, and the dissolved shrimp paste and cook for a minute, then add the sliced pork. Cook, stirring and turning, for several minutes. Add the toasted chickpea flour to the water, stirring until smooth, and add to the pork. Stir briefly, then add the coconut milk and black pepper and simmer for another 5 to 10 minutes. Taste and adjust the seasoning if you wish, by adding a little fish sauce or salt.

Meanwhile, reheat the broth and let simmer. Bring a large pot of water to a boil. Add the egg noodles and cook until just tender, 5 to 7 minutes (less if using fresh noodles). Drain and transfer to a large bowl. Drizzle on the shallot oil and toss gently to coat.

Set out large bowls for your guests. Distribute the noodles among the bowls, then ladle the sauce over. Sprinkle on the fried noodles and coriander and squeeze on a little lime juice. Serve the broth in small bowls. Put out a tray with the other accompaniments.

fried noodles

MAKES ABOUT 1½ CUPS To make fried noodles for a topping, break or cut about 1 cup of dried egg noodles into approximately 3-inch lengths. Heat 1 inch of peanut oil over medium-high heat in a stable wok or a wide shallow pot. When the oil is hot, toss in the noodles. If they start to brown immediately, lower the heat slightly. Fry, moving them around to prevent scorching, until they crisp and curl and just start to change color. Use tongs or a spider to lift them out of the hot oil, pausing to let excess oil drain off, then transfer to a plate. Pour off the oil; it can be used for another purpose.

Fried noodles will keep for a week if stored, once completely cooled, in a well-sealed glass jar.

KENGTUNG is an old princely kingdom and a center of Tai Koen culture that dates back more than six hundred years. The town is a long way from central Burma, and very isolated. It's a two-day drive from there west to Taunggyi, the capital of Shan State, but that road is closed. So is the road to the Chinese border, a couple of hours north, which has a wild reputation for drugs, gun-running, and gambling. The only access to Kengtung is by airplane from Taunggyi or by road from Thailand.

I traveled from Thailand to Kengtung with a friend, arriving just before dark. We didn't want to waste a moment of our short time there, so we set out from our guesthouse on foot that first evening. With little electricity in the town and no moon, the stars gleamed in the black night. We found our way uphill through the remains of a gate in the old city wall and then down a steep slope to the lake in the middle of town. We were looking for a café, bar, or any sign of life, but the streets were deserted, the bars empty.

Two days later, in the middle of a hot sunny afternoon, we walked down the same steep hill to the lake. We had a better understanding of the town by then, for we'd poked around the main market, chatted with people at cafés and temples, and walked miles. As we neared the water, we heard an unexpected sound: "Hotel California," the old Eagles song, was playing at full blast inside one of the houses that faced the lake.

A skinny young Chinese man appeared in a doorway. When he saw us, he waved us over and then he invited us into his place. He had a huge collection of music videos and pirated CDs, mostly covers by Asian artists of rock-and-roll tracks from every decade. He was a guide who was out of work because, with the road to China closed, there were no Chinese tourists. His solace is rock music. And so he sits all day in that house by the lake, smoking cigarettes, listening to music, and dreaming of the USA.

Detail of a beautiful chedi on the outskirts of Kengtung. Before independence in 1948, the town was the capital of the largest of the Shan states. Kengtung lies a half-day's drive north of the Golden Triangle, the place where the borders of Thailand, Laos, and Burma meet.

coconut sauce noodles [OHN-NO KHAUT SWE]

SERVES 6 This rich meal-in-a-bowl is the one many foreigners say is their favorite dish from Burma. The Burmese name, pronounced "oh-no kao sway," is a simple compound of the terms for coconut (*ohn-no*) and noodles (*khaut swe*).

Ohn-no khaut swe in its most elaborate form also includes fish balls, given as optional in the recipe. I love the chicken sauce-broth so much that I often serve it on its own over rice or pasta, with simple cooked greens or a green salad on the side. Lime wedges and a chile sauce such as Tart-Sweet Chile-Garlic Sauce (page 36) or Sour-Plum Chutney with Chile Oil (page 202) are good condiments for the table.

I prefer dark meat, so I begin with about 2 pounds chicken legs (two whole legs), but you can use breasts if you prefer. I cut most of the meat off the bones, and use them to make the stock, but you can use boneless chicken and already-made broth (both options are set out below).

2½ pounds bone-in chicken legs or breasts; or
   1½ pounds boneless chicken

BROTH (IF USING BONE-IN CHICKEN)
5 cups water
3 or 4 slices ginger
2 shallots, halved

1 teaspoon fish sauce
1½ teaspoons salt
4 cups Basic Chicken Broth (page 76) or canned
   broth, if using boneless chicken
¼ cup Toasted Chickpea Flour (page 32)
¾ cup water
3 tablespoons peanut oil
¼ teaspoon turmeric
1½ cups minced shallots, plus (optional)
   1 cup small whole shallots

1 tablespoon minced garlic
1 cup canned coconut milk
1½ pounds fresh egg noodles or
   1 pound dried egg noodles

ACCOMPANIMENTS AND TOPPINGS
About 1 cup Fish Balls (page 133; optional)
About 1 cup Fried Noodles (page 249; optional)
2 hard-cooked hen or duck eggs, sliced
   (optional)
2 limes, cut into wedges
Red Chile Powder (page 28)
1 cup thinly sliced shallots, soaked in water for
   10 minutes, drained, and squeezed dry

If you are using bone-in chicken, cut the chicken off the bones. Set the meat aside.

To make the optional broth: Place the bones in a medium pot and add the water, ginger, and shallots. Bring to a boil, half-cover, lower the heat, and simmer for an hour. Remove the bones, ginger, and shallots, or strain the broth into a large

saucepan. You should have about 4 cups broth; add water if necessary. (The broth can be made ahead and stored, once completely cooled, in a well-sealed container in the refrigerator; it can also be frozen.)

Meanwhile, about 30 minutes before the broth is ready, chop the reserved chicken meat or the boneless chicken into 1-inch pieces. Place in a bowl, add the fish sauce and ½ teaspoon of the salt, and mix well. Cover and set aside for 20 minutes.

Bring the chicken broth to a simmer.

Put the chickpea flour in a small bowl, add ½ cup of the water, and whisk to blend it into a paste, then stir in the remaining ¼ cup water. Scoop out some warm broth and whisk or stir it briskly into the chickpea mixture so there are no lumps. Add it all back into the broth and whisk to incorporate it smoothly. Set aside.

Place a large wok or wide heavy pot over medium-high heat. Add the oil and then the turmeric. Stir, then add the minced shallots and cook, stirring frequently, for 4 minutes or until translucent. Add the garlic and cook for about 30 seconds, then add the chicken and stir-fry until all the meat has changed color. Add the chicken broth and the remaining 1 teaspoon salt, then add the coconut milk and whole shallots, if using, and bring to a boil. Lower the heat and simmer until the oil rises to the surface, about 10 minutes.

Meanwhile, put on a large pot of water to boil. Put out six large soup bowls.

Drop the egg noodles and fish balls, if using, into the boiling water. Lift out or drain when the noodles are cooked through, about 4 minutes for fresh noodles, 7 for dried. Place about 1 cup noodles in each soup bowl. Ladle over the sauce generously. Top with 2 or 3 fish balls, if using, some fried noodles, and several slices of egg, if you wish. Put out the remaining fish balls, fried noodles, and egg slices on a platter, along with the lime wedges, chile powder, and shallot slices, so guests can top their soup as they wish.

Coconut Sauce Noodles topped with sliced shallots, fried noodles, slices of hard-boiled egg, a sprinkling of chile powder, and a squeeze of lime. More accompaniments await in the background.

WHAT MAKES A DISH mohinga rather than something else?

Mohinga is made of a broth poured over fine rice noodles (rice vermicelli). You could think of it as the Burmese equivalent of Vietnamese pho, the rice noodle soup that has become well-known in North America. Pho is usually made with beef broth, mohinga with a delicate fish broth. There are pieces of banana stem in the broth (mostly for texture rather than flavor, although they are also believed to have health benefits), and there's always a selection of toppings and accompaniments. Mohinga is a classic breakfast food in Burma, sold at street stalls and in little cafés, even in some tea shops.

In Rangoon, and in central Burma generally, the broth is clear, with a little fish in it and some banana stem; it comes with a wide choice of deep-fried toppings. In Dawei, in the south, mohinga has lots of fresh fish in it, may have tomato for a little acidity, and is flavored with galangal as well as ginger and shallots. In Rakhine State, along the west coast, mohinga generally has hot chile and no galangal and is served with an array of chile pastes.

I ate out with some people from Rangoon while I was in Dawei. I asked them about the local mohinga. They thought it was too thick, too heavy. Dawei people said Rangoon mohinga was too thin and watery, and Rakhine people told me there was not enough flavor in it! It's just a fact: the mohinga from your home region is the one you prefer. No wonder, for mohinga is comfort food, a taste of home.

When I arrived in Dawei and asked about mohinga, several people told me that I'd find a great version at this small café. Good advice, it turned out—it was so delicious, I went back there every day.

west coast mohinga

SERVES 6 Rakhine State is known for its spicy cuisine. More chiles and chile powder are used in dishes and even more chile pastes are out on the table as condiments. This version of mohinga is a good example.

Here fish is poached to make a broth, then the flesh is lifted off the bones, flaked, lightly fried in turmeric-flavored oil, and served on top of the noodles. The mohinga can be served with all the suggested extras, or you can simplify and omit some.

One 1¾- to 2-pound whole fish such as carp, trout, or snapper, or several smaller fish, cleaned and scaled

BROTH
5 cups water
½ teaspoon shrimp paste (*ngapi*; see Glossary)
About 2 tablespoons coarsely chopped galangal (see Glossary)
2 tablespoons coarsely chopped garlic

TAMARIND LIQUID
1 heaping tablespoon tamarind pulp (see Glossary), cut into chunks
½ cup hot water

RED CHILE PASTE
Generous ¼ cup dried red chiles
¼ cup hot water
⅛ teaspoon salt
1 tablespoon peanut oil

2 tablespoons peanut oil
¼ teaspoon turmeric
5 inches banana stem, peeled, sliced, soaked in cold water for an hour, and drained (see Glossary; optional)
2 teaspoons fish sauce
2½ to 3 pounds fresh rice vermicelli or thin rice noodles (flat or round) or 1½ pounds dried rice vermicelli or narrow dried rice noodles

OTHER ACCOMPANIMENTS AND FLAVORINGS
About 2 tablespoons Shallot Oil (page 24) or Garlic Oil (page 25)
About 3 tablespoons Toasted Chickpea Flour (page 32; optional)
About 3 tablespoons fish sauce
½ cup chopped coriander
About ¾ teaspoon white or freshly ground black pepper
Green Chile Paste (page 153; optional)

Rinse the fish thoroughly; set aside.

Pour the water into a wide pot or deep wide skillet and set over medium-high heat. Add the shrimp paste and stir to dissolve it, then add the galangal and garlic. If the fish is too long to fit comfortably in the pot, cut it crosswise in half (leave the head on; it will add flavor). Slide the fish into the water. Once the water comes to the boil, lower the heat to maintain a gentle simmer and poach for about 4 minutes. Turn the fish over and poach for another 3 to 4 minutes, or until just cooked through.

[Continued]

West Coast Mohinga, topped with flavorings and accompanied by small bowls of broth and red chile paste.

Use a spider or tongs to lift the fish out of the liquid and onto a platter. (Set the broth aside.) Let cool briefly, then lift the flesh off the bones, remove and discard the skin, and set the flesh aside to cool.

Return the bones to the broth. Raise the heat to medium-high and simmer vigorously for 10 minutes or so. Strain the broth; discard the solids. Add water to the broth if necessary to bring it up to 4 cups, and set aside.

Place the tamarind pulp in a small bowl, add the hot water, and stir and mash with a fork. Set aside to soak for 10 minutes.

Meanwhile, make the chile paste: Break off and discard the chile stems; discard the seeds if you want less heat. Place the chiles in a small pan with the hot water, bring to a boil, and boil for a minute or two, until softened. Transfer to a mortar or a food processor, add the salt, and mash or process to a paste.

Heat the oil in a small skillet over medium-high heat. Add the chile paste and cook until it sizzles, a minute or two. Transfer to a small condiment bowl; set aside.

Mash the soaking tamarind again with a fork or your fingers to get it to dissolve. Place a sieve over a medium bowl and pour in the tamarind mixture; press the mixture against the mesh of the sieve with the back of a spoon to extract as much liquid as possible. Discard the solids and set the liquid aside.

Pull the fish apart into flakes, discarding any stray bones. Squeeze out any excess liquid from the fish and add it to the broth.

Place a heavy medium skillet or a wok over medium heat, add the 2 tablespoons oil, and stir in the turmeric. Add the fish and cook, using a spatula to stir it and separate it further into flakes, until it has dried out a little and has all been exposed to the hot oil. Turn out into a bowl and set aside.

About 10 minutes before serving, place the broth back over medium heat, add the soaked banana stem, if using, and the fish sauce, and bring to a simmer.

Meanwhile, put out six large soup bowls. Pour about 8 cups of water into a large pot and bring to a boil. Add the noodles. If using fresh noodles (they'll be heated and tender after 30 seconds or so), use a spider or tongs to lift them out of the hot water and distribute them among the bowls. If using dried noodles, bring the water back to the boil and cook until tender, 3 or 4 minutes. Drain and distribute among the bowls.

Add 1 teaspoon or so of the shallot or garlic oil to the noodles in each bowl and turn to coat them. Sprinkle about 1 teaspoon toasted chickpea flour, ½ teaspoon fish sauce, 1 teaspoon tamarind liquid, a generous pinch of coriander, and ⅛ teaspoon black pepper over the noodles in each bowl and toss to mix and blend. Sprinkle the flaked fish onto the noodles and toss again.

Pour the hot broth into individual small bowls and serve alongside the bowls of noodles. Put out the chile paste(s) and small bowls of the remaining tamarind liquid, chickpea flour, fish sauce, and coriander, so guests can adjust flavorings as they wish.

As I pedaled around exploring the lanes and markets of Mrauk U, I was a surprising and odd sight to some people—including this young mother, standing outside the house of her extended family.

rangoon mohinga

SERVES 6 Mohinga as it's made and served on the street in Rangoon can be a multilayered, extraordinary dish. The trick is to find a cook who cares a lot—look for a busy stall—and then keep going back to her each day.

Here's one welcoming take on mohinga, not chile-hot, broth. I've included banana stem in case you have access to it, but you can make the soup without it. Do make at least one of the fried toppings.

One 2- to 2½-pound catfish or other freshwater fish such as tilapia or trout, or several smaller fish, cleaned and scaled

BROTH
4 cups water
1 teaspoon shrimp paste (*ngapi*; see Glossary)
1 teaspoon turmeric
3 garlic cloves, smashed
3 slices ginger
2 stalks lemongrass, trimmed and smashed

½ cup minced shallots
1 tablespoon minced lemongrass
Salt
1 to 2 teaspoons minced ginger
1 tablespoon minced garlic
¼ cup oil
¼ teaspoon turmeric
½ teaspoon Red Chile Powder (page 28) or cayenne
1 tablespoon fish sauce, or to taste
¼ cup Toasted Chickpea Flour (page 32) or Toasted Rice Powder (page 224)

1 cup water
5 inches banana stem, peeled, soaked in cold water for an hour, sliced, and drained (see Glossary; optional)
10 small whole shallots, or 5 larger ones, cut in half
Finely ground black pepper
1½ pounds fresh rice vermicelli or rice noodles or 1 pound dried rice noodles (see Glossary)
1 to 2 tablespoons Shallot Oil (page 24)

OPTIONAL TOPPINGS AND CONDIMENTS (CHOOSE ANY OR ALL)
Deep-Fried Chayote Fingers (page 125)
Fish Cakes (page 133), fried and cut into thin slices
Red Chile Powder (page 28)
1 cup minced scallion greens
3 hard-boiled hen or duck eggs, cut into wedges or slices
2 limes, cut into wedges
½ cup Fried Shallots (page 24)
1 cup chopped coriander

Rinse the fish thoroughly; set aside.

Pour the water into a wide pot and add the shrimp paste, turmeric, garlic, ginger, and lemongrass. Add the fish and bring to a boil. Lower the heat and simmer, covered, for about 20 minutes. Remove the fish and set aside to cool for a moment.

Strain the broth into a pot, discarding the solids, and set aside.

Pull the cooked fish off the bones, flake, and set aside. Add the bones and skin to the broth and boil for another 10 minutes, then strain and discard the bones and skin. Set the broth aside.

If you have a mortar, pound the minced shallots to a paste; set aside. Pound the lemongrass to a coarse paste with a pinch of salt; set aside. Pound the ginger and then the garlic and mix together with the lemongrass. *Alternatively,* combine the lemongrass, ginger, and garlic in a food processor, add a little salt, and process to a coarse paste.

Heat the oil in a wok or heavy skillet over medium heat, add the turmeric, chile powder, and pounded or minced shallots, and cook for several minutes, until the shallots are softened. Add the lemongrass-ginger paste and cook until aromatic, 3 minutes or so, stirring to prevent sticking. Add the reserved fish and the fish sauce and cook for several minutes more to blend flavors. Turn out and set aside.

Bring the broth to a boil. Stir the toasted chickpea flour or rice powder into the water, then stir into the broth. The broth will bubble and foam a little as it thickens. Add the fish mixture and the banana stem, if using, and cook at a low boil for about 10 minutes. Add the whole (or halved) shallots and black pepper and simmer for another 5 minutes or so, until the shallots are cooked. Taste and add fish sauce or salt if needed.

Meanwhile, bring a medium pot of water to a boil. Add the noodles and boil gently until softened, about 1 minute for fresh noodles, 5 minutes for dried. Drain and transfer to a large bowl. Drizzle on the shallot oil and toss gently to prevent the noodles from sticking together.

To serve, put out a platter with the toppings and condiments of your choice. Set out a large bowl for each guest. Place a generous cup of noodles in each bowl, top with some fried shallots, and ladle the soup over, making sure that each serving has some fish and whole shallots in it. Top with the coriander, and invite your guests to add other toppings as they wish.

MONKS OF EVERY AGE are treated with respect in Burma. Women make sure not to touch them, and everyone opens a path to let them pass through a crowd or lets them go ahead when there's a line. Every boy from a Buddhist family spends some time ordained as a monk, usually entering a monastery for just a few days in a celebratory ceremony at around the age of eight. The family gives a party, and guests donate supplies to the monastery in honor of the occasion. Later on, a young man will spend a month or more as a monk, his head shaved, living in a monastery.

To an outsider, the most obvious rule followed by monks is that they must go out and accept alms every morning. At dawn all over the country, monks of all ages walk barefoot in single file through the streets, each carrying an alms bowl. Householders who have prepared rice and other food stand waiting by the side of the road. As the monks pass, the laypeople put a small amount of their offering in each monk's bowl, accepting the monk's blessing.

Once the alms round is completed, the monks return to the monastery. Most of these morning offerings become the monks' breakfast. Their big lunch, taken just before noon, is often paid for by donations. They then take no food or drink until the next morning.

Mandalay and the towns surrounding it have the greatest number of monasteries, many of them renowned centers of Buddhist scholarship. Some monasteries have also begun to take an active role in these towns and villages, establishing clinics and schools for children and families in need.

In September 2007 the monks of Burma engaged openly in political action. During this period—known as the Saffron Revolution ("saffron" because Buddhist monks in many places, though not in Burma, wear saffron yellow robes)—they marched in peaceful protest against the government. The demonstrations started in the town of Pakkoku, on the Irrawaddy River north of Bagan, and spread to Rangoon, Mandalay, and elsewhere. When the army opened fire, many monks as well as laypeople were killed or injured. Many others were imprisoned; they were released in 2012 as the country opened to democracy.

These days, monks are treated with extra respect by the people. They've earned it.

TOP LEFT: *The morning alms round takes a long line of monks through the main market in Hpa'an, in Karen State.* LEFT: *In Moulmein a woman places rice in the bowl of a small monk, while those ahead of him rush to catch up to the procession of older monks up the street.* ABOVE: *At a monastery in Mandalay, a monk's begging bowl and several small steel cups (for holding liquids) sit out drying on a wooden step.* OVERLEAF: *Monks line up outside a temple in Myinkaba, south of Old Bagan.*

shan village khaut swe

SERVES 4 OR 5 Once the capital of a Shan princedom, Hsipaw is five hours northeast of Mandalay on the road to Lashio and the Yunnanese border. The town is small: after a few minutes' walking, you can be out in the countryside, with the sounds of birds and the wind in the trees.

Just outside town one day I came upon a small family-run noodle stand and stopped for a bowl of *khaut swe* (pronounced "kao sway"), rice noodles topped with simmered meat and pea tendrils. It's a first cousin of the noodle dishes found at morning markets along the Mekong River in Yunnan and Laos. In Kengtung, farther east, a version of these noodles, called *khao soi*, is sold streetside for breakfast every morning.

The five-spice powder, a reminder that China is a short distance away, gives the tomato-laden chopped-pork sauce a little warmth. There's no chile in the sauce itself; instead, diners can add chile powder or chile oil if they want. There are many other possible condiments—choose the ones you like. I sometimes make the sauce as a topping for rice, adjusting the recipe by adding extra water to make it more liquid.

3 tablespoons peanut oil

¼ teaspoon turmeric

1 cup thinly sliced shallots

1 tablespoon minced garlic

¾ to 1 pound pork tenderloin or boneless pork roast, such as shoulder, cut into cubes less than ½ inch across

2 cups crushed or finely chopped tomatoes

1 tablespoon Fermented Soybean Paste (page 39) or store-bought, or substitute 1 teaspoon brown miso paste

1 tablespoon fish sauce

1 teaspoon Five-Spice Powder (recipe follows), or substitute ½ star anise, ground, ¼ teaspoon ground cinnamon, and ⅛ teaspoon ground cloves

½ teaspoon salt, or to taste

OPTIONAL TOPPINGS AND CONDIMENTS (CHOOSE ANY OR ALL)

About 2 cups pea tendrils, raw or briefly blanched in boiling water

2 tablespoons Chopped Roasted Peanuts (page 35)

Red Chile Oil (page 25) or Red Chile Powder (page 28)

3 tablespoons chopped pickled Chinese mustard greens (see Glossary)

½ cup Palm Sugar Water (page 96)

2 tablespoons Garlic Oil (page 25) or Shallot Oil (page 24)

1½ pounds fresh rice noodles or 1 pound dried rice noodles (see Glossary)

Heat the oil in a large heavy pot or a wok over medium-high heat. Add the turmeric and then the sliced shallots and cook until the shallots are translucent, 3 or 4 minutes. Add the garlic and cook for another minute.

Add the pork and stir and turn to expose all surfaces to the hot oil. After several minutes, once all the meat has changed color, add the tomatoes and bring to a boil. Reduce the heat to medium-low and simmer for about 10 minutes. Add the mashed soybeans or miso paste, fish sauce, five-spice powder (or alternative spices), and salt, and stir to blend into the sauce. Taste for seasonings, and add extra salt if necessary.

Meanwhile, bring a large pot of water to a boil.

Put out the optional toppings and condiments, and set out the individual bowls for your guests near your stove. Drop the rice noodles into the boiling water and boil gently until softened, about 1 minute for fresh noodles, 4 minutes for dried noodles. Drain and then distribute the noodles among the bowls. Top each pile of noodles with a generous helping of meat sauce.

Invite your guests to add the toppings and condiments as they like.

five-spice powder

MAKES A GENEROUS
¼ CUP

Five-spice powder is traditionally made of a blend of cassia (cinnamon), star anise, cloves, fennel, and Sichuan pepper. You can buy five-spice powder, but blends and freshness vary, so do try making your own.

About 2 tablespoons star anise pieces
2 tablespoons fennel seeds

One 1-inch cassia (cinnamon) stick
2 teaspoons Sichuan peppercorns
Scant ½ teaspoon ground cloves

Combine the star anise, fennel, and cassia in a spice or coffee grinder and grind to a powder. Pick over the Sichuan peppercorns and discard any black seeds. Add the peppercorns to the grinder and grind to a powder.

Transfer to a clean, dry jar, add the ground cloves, and mix, then seal well. Store in a cool, dry place.

OVERLEAF: *Shan Village Khaut Swe, with side dishes of extra toppings: blanched pea tendrils, peanuts, and pickled mustard greens.*

mandalay noodles with chicken curry

SERVES 6 This Mandalay classic, called Mandalay *mondi* locally, is a dish of fat round rice noodles. Mondi noodles are topped with a little chicken curry and served with a small bowl of broth alongside, as well as an array of toppings and condiments. The cooked noodles are tossed with oil and a little toasted chickpea flour, which gives them a textured surface.

Traditionally a whole chicken is used: the meat goes into the curry sauce and the carcass and bones are used to make the broth. You can, if you like, take a shortcut and use store-bought stock and boneless chicken.

One 3- to 4-pound chicken or 1½ pounds boneless legs and breasts, rinsed

BROTH (IF USING A WHOLE CHICKEN)
8 cups water
2 slices ginger
1 large or 2 small shallots, quartered
1 large or 2 small garlic cloves, smashed

CURRY SAUCE
¼ cup peanut oil
¼ teaspoon turmeric
½ cup minced shallots
2 tablespoons minced garlic
1 cup water
2 tablespoons fish sauce
½ teaspoon salt, or to taste

4 cups Basic Chicken Broth (page 76) or store-bought (if using boneless chicken)
1½ to 2 pounds fresh round rice noodles, or 1 pound dried rice noodles (see Glossary)

GARNISHES AND CONDIMENTS
About 2 tablespoons Shallot Oil (page 24)
½ cup Toasted Chickpea Flour (page 32)
3 to 4 tablespoons Fried Shallots (page 24)
3 to 4 tablespoons Chopped Roasted Peanuts (page 35), ground finer
2 hen or duck eggs, hard-boiled, cut into slices (optional)
2 limes, cut into wedges
Red Chile Powder (page 28)
½ cup chopped coriander
1 cup Fried Noodles (page 249)
12 Fish Balls (page 133; optional)
2 tablespoons minced scallion greens

If using a whole chicken, cut off the legs, then cut the meat off the breast and legs. Cut the meat into approximately 1-inch pieces and refrigerate. Or cut the boneless chicken into 1-inch pieces and refrigerate.

To make the optional broth: Place the chicken carcass, wings, and bones in a large pot. Add the water, ginger, shallots, and garlic and bring to a boil. Lower the heat and cook at a simmer for about 1 hour. Remove from the heat.

When the broth has cooled, lift out the chicken pieces and discard. Strain the broth through a sieve into a pot and discard the solids. Set the broth aside. (The broth can be made ahead and stored, once completely cooled, in a well-sealed container in the refrigerator for up to 3 days; it can also be frozen for up to 1 month.)

Heat the oil in a large wok or a wide pan over high heat and stir in the turmeric. Lower the heat to medium-high, toss in the minced shallots, and cook for 3 to 4 minutes, until translucent. Add the garlic and cook for another minute or so. Add the chicken and cook, stirring frequently, until it has all changed color, about 7 minutes.

Add the water, fish sauce, and salt. Bring to a boil, then lower the heat and simmer for 15 minutes, or until the chicken is very tender. Taste for salt and adjust if necessary. Set aside.

Meanwhile, 10 minutes before you want to serve, bring the chicken broth to a boil over medium-high heat, then keep at a simmer over low heat. Set out six wide soup bowls or plates.

Bring a medium or large pot of water to a boil. Toss in the noodles and cook until tender, 1 minute or so for fresh noodles, 3 to 5 minutes for dried rice noodles. Drain and immediately transfer onto the soup bowls or plates. Sprinkle about 1 teaspoon shallot oil and 1 tablespoon chickpea flour onto each serving and toss gently. Top each serving with some chicken and sauce, then sprinkle with 1 or 2 teaspoons fried shallots, a teaspoon or so of peanuts, a slice of hard-cooked egg, if using, a squeeze of lime, a pinch of chile powder, and about 2 teaspoons chopped coriander. Top with a couple of tablespoons of fried noodles, if using.

Invite guests to use forks and spoons to mix their noodles and toppings together Burmese-style. While they do that, add the fish balls, if using, to the simmering chicken broth and cook for 3 minutes. Ladle the broth (and fish balls) into small side bowls, top each with minced scallion greens, and serve. Put out the remaining toppings on a platter or in small bowls so that guests can add extra if they wish.

seafood noodle stir-fry [KAGYI KAI]

SERVES 4 Every little roadside eatery in the southern coastal town of Dawei serves a version of this dish (pronounced "ka-gee kai"). The usual combination is squid, shrimp, and mussels or oysters. If you can find only two of the three kinds of seafood called for, increase the quantity of each, or add another that you like. In Burma the shrimp are cooked head-on and in the shell. Guests then suck all the flavor possible from them as they eat. If you prefer, you can remove the heads, or the heads and the shells, before you cook them.

The shrimp paste gives a depth of flavor, but you can omit it if you wish and just add a little extra oyster sauce or soy sauce. In my experience, the noodles in Dawel are always mild. That's why the dish is served with hot condiments even though there are no chiles in the recipe. But sometimes as a variation I toss a couple of minced chiles in with the shallots and shrimp paste.

I like to serve one of the palate fresheners as a side, most often Shallot Chutney with Chiles (page 218). You can also put out a plate of sliced cucumbers or chopped tomatoes.

¾ pound head-on shrimp or
   ⅔ pound headless shrimp
¼ pound shelled mussels or oysters (from
   8 to 10 mussels or oysters; see Glossary)
¼ pound cleaned squid
1 tablespoon Fermented Soybeans Paste
   (page 39) or store-bought, or substitute
   1 teaspoon brown miso paste
½ cup water
1 pound fresh rice noodles or ¾ pound
   dried rice noodles (see Glossary)
¼ cup peanut oil
½ cup thinly sliced shallots
¼ teaspoon turmeric
1 tablespoon thinly sliced garlic

1 teaspoon shrimp paste
   (*ngapi*; see Glossary; optional)
3 scallions, cut into 1-inch lengths
3 to 4 cups bean sprouts, rinsed
1 teaspoon salt
2 tablespoons oyster sauce or soy sauce
1 tablespoon minced Chinese celery leaves
   or coriander

ACCOMPANIMENTS
3 or 4 limes, cut into wedges
Red Chile Oil (page 25) or store-bought
   (optional)
Sweet-Tart Chile-Garlic Sauce (page 36) or
   other tart-hot condiment sauce

Rinse the shrimp. Remove and discard the shells and heads, if you wish; set aside. Rinse the mussels or oysters; chop into bite-sized pieces if they are large, and set aside. Rinse the squid, chop the tentacles, and cut the bodies crosswise into ¼-inch-wide rings or strips; set aside.

Stir the mashed soybeans or miso into the water and set aside.

If using dried rice noodles, soak in a large bowl of cold water for 10 minutes, then drain and set aside.

Heat 2 tablespoons of the oil in a wok or large heavy skillet over medium-high heat. Set 2 tablespoons of the shallots aside and add the remaining shallots and a pinch of turmeric to the hot oil. Stir-fry for several minutes, until the shallots begin to soften. Add the garlic and stir-fry until lightly brown and beginning to crisp, 2 minutes. Use a slotted spoon to scoop out the shallots and garlic, pausing to let the excess oil drain off, and set aside.

Add the remaining turmeric, the reserved sliced shallots, and the shrimp paste, if using. Stir to dissolve the shrimp paste in the oil, then stir-fry until the shallots are translucent, about 2 minutes. Add the squid and scallions, increase the heat to high, and stir-fry for 1 minute. Add the mussels or oysters and shrimp and stir-fry for 1 minute, then add the soybean or miso mixture. Cook for another minute or two, until the shrimp have just changed color, then turn out into a bowl and set aside.

Unless your wok is huge, you'll need to cook the noodles in two batches: Divide the sprouts, noodles, and reserved cooked seafood in half; for each batch, use 1 tablespoon oil, ½ teaspoon salt, and 1 tablespoon oyster sauce or soy sauce. Put out a large platter. Place your wok over high heat and add the oil. Add the bean sprouts and salt and stir-fry for 2 minutes, or until the sprouts are just starting to wilt. Add the noodles and cook for 1 minute or so, pressing them against the hot sides of the wok, then turning them and pressing again. If using soaked noodles, cook them for an extra 2 or 3 minutes, until softened. Add the reserved seafood together with the oyster sauce or soy sauce and stir-fry gently, for a minute or so, until well combined. Add the chopped herbs and turn out onto the platter. Repeat with the second batch of the ingredients.

Serve on the platter or on individual plates. Top with the reserved fried shallots and garlic and squeeze on lime juice generously. Put out the remaining lime wedges and other condiments, along with a palate-refreshing side, if you wish.

seafood noodles with egg

Sometimes these stir-fried noodles are made with only one or two kinds of seafood, and with thin strips of omelet. Make a simple 2- or 3-egg omelet (see Easy Coriander-Tomato Omelet, page 121, for guidance). Let cool for 5 minutes. Slice into ½-inch strips. Add to the noodles when you add back the seafood.

SWEET TREATS

IN BURMA SWEETS ARE A PLEASURE for the moments in the day when you're not eating a meal and just want a little pick-me-up. Most of them are made from rice or rice flour and sweetened with palm sugar in inventive combinations with coconut or banana, or sesame seeds and peanuts.

One place to find sweet treats is at morning markets; another is in tea shops, especially in the afternoon. Many sweets, such as Doughnut Rings Dipped in Palm Sugar Syrup (page 284) and Street-Side Seductions (page 294), as well as the wonderful Shan Burmese version of fried bananas, Fried Sesame-Seed Bananas (page 300), are made and sold by street vendors, especially in the cities. They're also a big favorite at temple festivals. Other sweets are made in home kitchens. That's where I learned to make Magic Rice Balls (page 290) and the sweet morning treat Sticky-Rice Sweet Buns with Coconut (page 286).

semolina cake [SHWE GYI MONT]

SERVES 8 This recipe will look strange to you if you are a cake maker: that's because it's a Burmese version of Indian semolina halvah, not a classic cake. You toast the semolina flour first, add the liquids and cook it over low heat, and then bake it. (It's all easier than it sounds.) The result is a tender, delicious cross between cake and sweetmeat.

This modern "fancy" version of halvah includes eggs, which make the cake a little firmer. If you want to try an eggless version, see Classic Burmese Semolina Cake (page 278).

1 cup semolina flour (see Glossary)
1 cup packed brown sugar or granulated sugar
½ teaspoon salt
1 cup canned or fresh coconut milk
1 cup warm water
4 large eggs, lightly beaten

¼ cup peanut oil
¼ cup golden raisins (optional)
4 tablespoons butter, melted
3 tablespoons blanched almonds, sliced
   (optional)

Place a cast-iron or other heavy skillet over medium heat and add the semolina. Cook, stirring frequently to prevent scorching, until the flour starts to change color markedly, becoming a golden brown. Remove from the heat and continue stirring for a minute or so as the pan cools down, then transfer to a bowl. Add the sugar and salt and stir in, then stir in the coconut milk and water. Stir in the eggs, cover, and set aside for 20 to 30 minutes.

Place a rack in the top third of the oven and preheat the oven to 350°F. Set out an 8-inch cake pan or cast-iron skillet

Heat a heavy skillet or a large wok over medium heat. Add the oil, then pour in the semolina mixture and cook, stirring frequently with a wooden spoon to prevent sticking. The liquid mixture will start to thicken and get stickier. When it is quite sticky and thickened, about 20 minutes, remove from the heat and stir in the raisins, if using.

Transfer the mixture to the pan and smooth the top. Drizzle on the melted butter, sprinkle on the sliced almonds, if using, and put in the top third of the oven. Bake for 20 minutes, or until the cake feels firm when pressed lightly on the top. For an attractively browned top surface, you can place the cake under the broiler for a minute or two.

Remove and let stand for at least 1 hour to firm up before you slice it. Turn it onto a plate if you wish, or serve from the pan.

classic burmese semolina cake

SERVES 5 OR 6 Because this cake is tender and a little fragile (no eggs to help it firm up), I make it in a small pan, so that slices are easier to handle. I bake the cake in a cast-iron skillet, but you can also use a cake pan or even a pie plate. The taste is very light and clean. Include a few golden raisins if you like and/or top this with slivered almonds. This is a very handy cake if you are serving pure (non-egg-eating) vegetarians or vegans (use oil rather than butter for vegans).

I serve this from the pan.

½ cup semolina flour (see Glossary)
½ cup packed light brown sugar
¼ teaspoon salt
1 cup canned or fresh coconut milk

1 cup lukewarm water
4 tablespoons butter or ¼ cup peanut oil
2 tablespoons golden raisins (optional)
1 tablespoon thinly sliced almonds (optional)

Place the flour in a heavy skillet and toast over medium-high heat until aromatic and touched with golden brown. Transfer to a bowl and add the sugar and salt, then add the coconut milk and water and stir to make a smooth batter. Set aside for 20 to 30 minutes.

Place a rack in the center of the oven and preheat the oven to 350°F. Set out a 6-inch cast-iron skillet or cake or pie pan.

Place a heavy skillet or wok over medium heat and add the butter or oil. When the butter has melted or the oil is hot, add the batter and cook, stirring frequently with a wooden spoon to prevent sticking, for about 20 minutes, until thickened and sticky. If you wish, add the raisins about 5 minutes before it's done.

Pour the batter into the pan. Sprinkle on the sliced almonds, if using. Bake for about 20 minutes, or until a skewer inserted into the center comes out clean. It will still be very soft when done; let cool completely, a couple of hours, before serving.

deep forest monklets' sticky rice cake

SERVES 8 One day I went on an excursion up the Dokhtawaddy River from Hsipaw with several other travelers. An hour brought us to a small landing stage overhung with vines. We walked past fields of pineapple and along a path to a Buddhist monastery called Lwe Yung, the Deep Forest Monastery. The main temple was a beautiful place, built of wood and up on stilts, so it caught the breezes. The young monklets, from five to twelve years old, were hanging out in the temple under the benign, distracted supervision of the abbot (all the other senior monks were away). He was clearly loved as well as respected by the young ones.

After we had looked around, we were offered tea and a sweet treat, small pieces of "cake" made from sticky rice flavored with sesame seeds, sugar, and peanuts. It's easy to make, the boys said as they ate with us, and they told me what to do.

1½ cups white Thai sticky rice (see Glossary)
⅓ cup unsalted raw peanuts
½ to ⅔ cup chopped palm sugar or packed brown or granulated sugar (see Note)

⅓ cup sesame seeds
¾ teaspoon salt
2¼ cups water

Rinse the rice in cold water, drain, and place in a small pot with a tight-fitting lid or in a rice cooker. Add the peanuts, sugar, sesame seeds, salt, and water and stir to mix well.

If using a pot, bring to a boil over high heat, then cover tightly, reduce the heat to low, and cook for 30 minutes, until the rice is tender. *If using a rice cooker,* cover and turn it on (it will automatically turn to "warm" when the rice is done).

Let the cooked rice stand, covered, for 10 minutes.

Lightly oil an 8-inch square baking pan or 8-inch pie plate. Transfer the rice mixture to the pan, mixing and blending it gently as you do so to distribute the flavorings (as the rice cooks, the sesame seeds end up on top, and you want them scattered throughout). Smooth the top gently without pressing down too hard, and let stand for 30 minutes to firm up.

Cut into squares or wedges. This keeps well for 3 days, covered—do not refrigerate (it toughens the sticky rice).

NOTE: *Palm sugar or brown sugar, which makes a beige-colored cake, gives a more interesting smoky taste than white sugar. Two-thirds of a cup of sugar reproduces the sweetness of the monklets' cake, but is sweeter than I like; I use ½ cup palm or brown sugar.*

sticky rice cake with ginger and coconut

When I spent a morning cooking with Mimi in Rangoon (see Mimi's Bean Soup with Tender Leaves, page 98), one of the many things I learned was the name for the "monklet" cake: it's called *htamanei* in Burmese. Mimi's version is a more sophisticated cake than the monklets', made with fresh ginger and coconut shavings. There's a warm hit from the ginger and a lushness from the coconut.

Add 3 tablespoons ginger cut into matchsticks when you put the rice and flavorings on to boil, and use ⅔ cup sugar. When you transfer the cooked rice to the baking pan or pie plate, mix in ½ cup or more deep-fried coconut shavings (see below). Or just press them into the surface as a sweet and delicious topping.

fried coconut strips

MAKES ABOUT 1 CUP

Serve as a topping for sweets of all kinds or use as an ingredient in other sweet treats.

1 coconut, or about 1½ to 2 cups frozen grated coconut

About ¼ cup peanut oil or coconut oil

If using a coconut, crack it open (see Glossary) and use a coconut scraper, a potato peeler, a very coarse grater, or a bottle cap to scrape long, flat strips of flesh from the coconut. If using frozen coconut, put it out on a plate to thaw, then squeeze out the excess water and pat dry.

Heat about ¼ inch of oil in a wok or a small heavy skillet over medium heat. Add the coconut strips or thawed coconut and stir-fry, stirring constantly to prevent burning, until touched with golden brown. Lift it out with a slotted spoon or tongs, allowing excess oil to drain, then transfer to a paper-towel-lined plate. Leftovers, once cooled, can be stored in the refrigerator.

Sticky Rice Cake with Ginger and Coconut

SAI IS A TALL, good-looking man with a wide face and a full white beard. He and his wife own a little tea shop in Hsipaw, near the edge of town. I stopped by there one day for tea and we fell into conversation. Sai told me about his father, who had died the previous year at the age of ninety-four. He'd come to Burma from India with the British during World War II, then stayed on. He started a yogurt business when Sai was a boy, using milk from local cows, but few people up here in Shan State, near the Chinese border, were prepared to eat yogurt. Sai ate a lot of it when he was growing up—he says he has his father to thank for his height and good health.

Sai offered to take me out of town on his motorcycle to see some food sights. Our first stop was at a peanut-oil press powered by a water mill. It was in a large, airy post-and-beam building that looked like a kind of cluttered wooden cathedral, built over a stream. The whole place smelled invitingly of peanuts. The mill was quiet that day; the owner was busy replacing one of the huge wooden paddles, so the press wasn't operating. The only action was the frolicking of some fine-boned cats on the wood floors.

Then we rode out to a hamlet where the main business is salt. The villagers pump saltwater from wells in the ground, boil it, and pour it into shallow pans to evaporate, leaving behind the salt. In this region, people have always relied on salt wells. Once, in places like this, the people who controlled the salt grew rich on the trade, but with modern transportation local sources of salt are not so important anymore and salt sells for very little.

Finally, we bumped up a small dirt road to a small village that produces another staple: sugar. On the sloping hillside above the settlement grew tall stands of sugarcane. Stacks of cut cane lay all around. In an open-sided shed, men were feeding teak logs into a large fire pit. At one end of it, a chimney billowed pale smoke. In a long metal pan that lay over the fire, liquid sugar gave off thick steam as it boiled down. Once it becomes solid, the sugar is cut into large blocks and sold in the Hsipaw market.

Next morning at the market before dawn (see "Market by Candlelight," page 67), the taste of sticky rice sweetened with smoky local sugar transported me right back to the sugar village.

Tastes of Hsipaw. **CLOCKWISE FROM TOP LEFT:** *Salt from a village salt well. Blocks of cane sugar. Thick cane sugar syrup, with a smoky taste and aroma from the fire it's been cooked over, gets poured into molds; once it has set, it's cut into blocks and taken to the market for sale. A woman fries doughnuts in a wok.*

doughnut rings dipped in palm sugar syrup

MAKES 12 DOUGHNUTS;
SERVES 6 These doughnuts with a difference are made from sticky rice flour. Common in Shan markets in northern Burma, from Kalaw to Hsipaw, they're also made and sold in northern Thailand, in towns where there are large populations of Shan people.

Street-side cooks deep-fry them in plenty of oil, in large woks, and their doughnuts are about 3 inches across. My home-style method produces smaller versions of the doughnuts, fried in less oil, in small, manageable batches.

Because there is no wheat flour in the doughnuts, they are delicate when cooked. As they cook in the hot oil, they puff up and become hollow. They're best eaten hot and fresh, but I also like how, once they cool, they soften and sag a little.

You can make the doughnuts with white rice flour only (use 1 cup in that case), but I love the purple-gray tint that black sticky rice flour gives, so I grind a little raw black rice to a powder in my coffee grinder or food processor and add it to the dough.

Traditionally these are drizzled with a little palm sugar syrup after cooking. I prefer a more indulgent approach. I serve them with small bowls of palm sugar sauce, so that guests can dip their doughnuts into it as they eat. Heaven!

**Scant 1 cup white sticky rice flour
(see Glossary), plus a little extra
flour for shaping**
**1 tablespoon black sticky rice flour
(see the headnote; optional)**
¼ teaspoon baking soda
¼ teaspoon salt
½ cup water

PALM SUGAR SYRUP
½ cup palm sugar shavings
½ cup water

Peanut oil for deep-frying

Combine the rice flours, baking soda, salt, and water in a medium bowl and stir to make a dough. Smear it with a wooden spoon or your hand to blend it until very smooth (if it is too stiff or dry, add another tablespoon or so of water, and blend it in). Let stand for 5 minutes.

Put a little rice flour on a plate and put out a second plate. Scoop up 2 teaspoons of the dough. If it is sticky, touch it lightly to the rice flour, then roll it into a ball between your palms and set it on the other plate. Repeat with the remaining dough. You should have 12 balls of dough. Set aside for 30 minutes to firm up.

Meanwhile, prepare the sugar syrup: Combine the palm sugar and the ½ cup water in a small heavy saucepan and bring to a boil over medium heat, stirring to dissolve the sugar. Remove from the heat and transfer to one or more small bowls.

Doughnuts frying at the market in Hsipaw.

When ready to proceed, put out two lightly oiled plates or a lightly oiled baking sheet. Pick up a ball of dough and gently roll it back and forth between your palms to make a small rope about 4 to 5 inches long. Press the ends together to make a ring and set on one of the plates or the baking sheet. Repeat with the remaining balls.

Pour 2 inches of oil into a large stable wok, a wide pot, or a deep-fryer and heat over medium-high heat to 350°F. If you don't have a thermometer, stand a wooden chopstick or wooden spoon handle in the oil; if the oil bubbles up gently along the wood, it is at temperature. (This deep-frying is done at a lower temperature than most, so that the insides of the doughnuts get cooked before the outsides burn.) Put out a spider or slotted spoon and another large platter or plate.

Slide 3 or 4 dough rings into the hot oil, without overlapping, then lower the heat slightly and let them cook, the oil bubbling up around them, for about a minute. (If the rings start to brown in the first minute, lower the heat a little more.) Gently turn them over and continue cooking until they are browned and firmer, 3 to 4 minutes. Use the spider or slotted spoon to lift them out, pausing to let excess oil drain off, and onto the plate.

Serve immediately (the doughnuts soften as they cool), with the small bowls of palm sugar syrup for dunking.

sticky-rice sweet buns with coconut

MAKES 8 BUNS;
SERVES 4 TO 6

These treats are a breakfast or anytime pleasure served with fresh fruit and tea or coffee. Cooked sticky rice (left over from the night before, or cooked fresh for the purpose) is wrapped around shaved coconut and palm sugar, and the filled "buns" that result are quickly fried to golden. I love the smoky hit of palm sugar when you bite through the crisp outer layers of fried rice kernels into the meltingly sweet center.

Make them just before you want to serve them. Allow one or two per person. The originals were deep-fried, but they work well shallow-fried in a cast-iron skillet or wok.

2 tablespoons fresh or defrosted frozen grated coconut (see Glossary), minced, or substitute a scant 2 tablespoons dried unsweetened grated coconut plus 1 tablespoon warm water

3 tablespoons chopped dark palm sugar, minced
About 2 cups cooked sticky rice, at room temperature
Peanut oil for shallow-frying

Place the coconut and palm sugar in two bowls by your work surface; if using dried coconut, place it in a bowl, add the warm water, stir well, and let soak for 5 minutes.

Make sure your work surface is absolutely dry (a wet surface will make the rice slippery rather than sticky, so that it won't stick to itself when you are shaping the buns). Turn the rice out onto it. Flatten the mass of rice with the palm of your hand, then use a rolling pin to roll it out to an approximate 9-inch square. Use a dough scraper or a knife to cut it into 4 strips, then cut these crosswise in half, so you have 8 rectangles, about 4½ inches long.

Work with one strip at a time: With your thumb, make a dent about 1 inch from one end of the strip, place 1 teaspoon palm sugar and a scant teaspoon coconut in it, fold the strip over, and press on the edges to seal. You'll have a flattened rectangular package about ½ inch thick and 2 inches long. Place on a plate, and repeat with the remaining strips and filling.

Put a plate and a spider or a slotted spoon by your stovetop. Place a wok or wide heavy skillet over high heat, add peanut oil to a depth of ½ inch, and heat to about 360°F. (If you don't have a thermometer, test the temperature by standing a wooden chopstick or wooden spoon handle in the oil; if the oil bubbles up vigorously along the wood, it is at temperature.) Slide in one bun, and then a second. The oil will bubble up as the buns start to cook. The rice on the outside will puff up a little and start to turn golden, about 2 minutes. Use the spider or slotted spoon to turn the buns over and fry the second side until well touched with gold, another 2 to 3 minutes. Flip back onto the first side to deepen the color a little, then lift out of the oil, pausing to let excess oil drain off, and put on the plate. Cook the remaining rice buns the same way. Once you are used to the process, you will probably find that you can cook more than 2 at once. (Once the oil has cooled, store it in a clean, dry glass jar and reuse it for stir-fried dishes.)

Serve warm or at room temperature; these are best soon after they are cooked.

In my notebook I called these two charmers "goofy girls." Wearing their mother's lipstick, they played at looking serious for a moment and then burst into big smiles at the market in Mrauk U, in Rakhine State.

WHEN THE BRITISH captured Burma's southern coast in the First Anglo-Burmese war in 1826 (see Burma over Time, page 306), Moulmein, at the mouth of the Salween River, became their chief commercial city. The main business was the export of teak and other tropical hardwoods. Logs were hauled by elephants to the banks of the Salween and its tributaries in dry season, then floated downriver when the waters rose during monsoon season.

These days Moulmein is a quiet place in a beautiful location. Golden-roofed temples stand silhouetted on a ridge above the town. A huge new bridge spans the Salween, bringing traffic and the railway from Rangoon and the rest of the country. (Before the bridge was built, everything had to cross the river by ferry to reach Moulmein, which lies on the southern bank.) I stayed in a small guesthouse on the Strand Road, overlooking the river's expanse and not far from the market. It's mesmerizing to be in that huge open-skied wide-water landscape, like floating in space, especially in the pale dawn.

Down the road was a small Mon tea shop/restaurant, where I went early each morning to taste new dishes. I'd often see the local *nan-piar* (flatbread)

seller there, stopping by with a basket of flatbreads, samosas, cooked beans, and sweet pastries on her head.

One day I caught a bus out to a small village where there's a well-known temple called Kyaikmaraw. A woman I met on the bus showed me around and afterward invited me to meet her aunt and uncle, whose house was opposite the temple. The aunt was spry and lively and spoke some English. The uncle was alert, but his legs were paralyzed. As we sat on the floor in their airy front room sipping our milk tea, a neighbor massaged the uncle's legs, rubbing them up and down, with cut lime halves, to stimulate the circulation.

In the warm air, lulled by the conversation, I felt myself gradually falling into a drowse. They noticed me struggling to stay awake and told me to just give in to it. The aunt had already nodded off. People nap in the heat of the day—it's a normal pleasure in Burma. I lay right down on the mat where I was sitting, relieved to be able to let myself drift off. Their voices were a soft sound track for my dreams as I slipped away.

An hour later I was awake again, refreshed. It was time to thank my hosts and catch the bus back to Moulmein.

OPPOSITE, UPPER RIGHT: *A woman sits by tall ornamental wooden doors at a temple complex on a hill overlooking Moulmein.* TOP LEFT: *A mother and child near a mosque in Moulmein.* MIDDLE LEFT: *Stacks of huge crispy rice-paste crackers are sold at village markets in the Inle Lake area.* LEFT: *A bus is not always a bus in Burma. Here, waiting to leave Moulmein for some smaller nearby villages, the "bus" is the back of a very old truck with bench seating, open sides, and a wooden roof. The woman in the front chatted to me after I took this photo, and later showed me around the Kyaikmaraw temple.*

magic rice balls [MOUN LON YEI BO]

MAKES 32
FILLED BALLS
OR ABOUT 125
SMALL BALLS The Burmese name of these treats—traditional food at the Burmese water festival, in mid-April—translates as "sweets rising in the water." The balls, made of a rice dough wrapped around small chunks of palm sugar, are dropped into a pot of boiling water. They swell as they cook and bob to the surface; when done, they are translucent, so they look a little like large peeled lychees. The magic comes when you bite into them, for each one hides a smoky, sweet molten core of palm sugar.

Smaller balls made of the same dough but without a filling are served topped with a light sugar syrup and a sprinkling of coconut shavings.

I usually make only the larger balls, but the traditional way is to divide the dough in half and make both filled balls and smaller ones.

1 cup sticky rice flour (see Glossary)
½ cup rice flour, plus more for dusting
About ¾ cup lukewarm water

FOR FILLED BALLS
About ⅓ cup dark palm sugar (or maple sugar) chopped into small chips the size of a half-peanut

FOR SMALLER BALLS IN SYRUP
1 cup or more Sugar Syrup (recipe follows), or substitute maple syrup
Grated fresh coconut or defrosted grated coconut (see Glossary), toasted

Combine the two flours in a medium bowl, then add about ½ cup of the water and stir to mix well. Dribble in a little more water and stir some more. You want a smooth dough that is not too soft or sticky. If you find the dough is a little too soft to work with, turn it out onto a work surface dusted with plain rice flour and roll it around to incorporate a little more flour, then return it to the bowl. Set aside for a moment.

Put out a small bowl of water for moistening your hands as you work. Set out a serving plate for the larger balls or a shallow bowl for the smaller syrup-coated balls. Pour 4 inches of water into a wide pot and bring it to a boil.

To shape the larger balls: Once you have made a few, you will be able to estimate how much dough you need by eye, but to start with, it's helpful to divide the dough, measuring out what you need. Cut the dough in half and set one half aside in the bowl, loosely covered with plastic wrap to prevent drying out.

[Continued]

Magic Rice Balls, two ways: the smaller ones in sugar syrup with a topping of coconut, with a bowl of the larger ones behind.

Place the remaining dough on a work surface lightly dusted with rice flour and use a dough scraper or knife to cut it in half and then in half again. Cut each of these pieces into quarters, to give you 16 pieces in all.

Lightly moisten your palms with water. Place a piece of dough on the palm of one hand and, with your other thumb, make a large dent in the center, flattening it a little. Place 2 or 3 chips of sugar in the hollow, and pull the sides up around to cover it. Roll the ball lightly between your palms to smooth it out and set aside on a plate, When all 16 balls are shaped, drop them into the boiling water. The balls will sink and then slowly rise back to the surface. Let them bob there for about 5 minutes, then use a spider or a slotted spoon to lift them out onto the waiting plate. Repeat with the remaining dough.

To shape the smaller balls: Cut the dough in half and set one half aside in the bowl, loosely covered with plastic wrap. Place the remaining dough on a work surface lightly dusted with rice flour and cut in half and then in half again. Shape balls from one piece at a time, to start; each of these small pieces will yield 16 small rice balls (cut each into 4 pieces, then divide again into quarters). Quickly roll the pieces into balls between your palms and drop them into the boiling water; they will swell and bob up to the surface very soon. Let them cook for 2 or 3 minutes longer, then lift them out with a spider or slotted spoon and transfer to the shallow bowl. Drizzle on some syrup, turning them so all surfaces get coated; this prevents them from sticking together as they cool. Repeat with the remaining dough. Top the pile of rice balls with the coconut.

sugar syrup

<table>
<tr><td>MAKES ABOUT
1 CUP</td><td>1 cup water
1 cup granulated sugar or
   1¼ cups palm sugar</td><td>¼ teaspoon rose water (optional)</td></tr>
</table>

Pour the water into a small pot set over medium heat, add the sugar, and bring to a boil, stirring to dissolve the sugar. Add the rose water if you wish, and simmer for 1 minute before removing from the heat.

tapioca-coconut delight

SERVES 6 TO 8 In this delicious cross between a custard and a pudding, cooked tapioca is topped with a layer of creamy coconut-milk custard. The contrast between the soft chewiness of the tapioca and the smoothness of the custard is a pleasure. With 3 tablespoons sugar, the pudding is sweet but not intensely so; you may prefer to use 4 tablespoons sugar. I like to mix white and green tapioca pearls so the tapioca layer is bright green. Use the regular ones, not the big pearls that are used for bubble tea.

Serve this chilled in small bowls as dessert or as a sweet treat. Top each serving with slices of mango or peach if you wish.

TAPIOCA
3 cups water
¾ cup regular tapioca pearls
   (white, colored, or a mixture)
About ½ cup hot water, or as needed
Pinch of salt
¾ cup sugar

CUSTARD
4 large egg yolks
3 to 4 tablespoons finely chopped palm sugar
   or brown sugar
2 tablespoons rice flour
1 cup thick canned or fresh coconut milk
   (see Glossary)
¼ teaspoon vanilla extract

Pour the 3 cups water into a wide pot and bring to a boil. Sprinkle in the tapioca and bring back to a boil, then lower the heat to maintain a strong simmer and cook, half-covered, stirring occasionally, until thickened, about 15 minutes. Add water if the pan starts to run dry; I usually have to add between ¼ and ½ cup hot water at this point. Add the salt and continue to simmer until the tapioca is tender, another 5 minutes or so.

Add the sugar and stir well, then cook for a few minutes more. Pour into a 7-inch square cake pan or an 8-inch pie plate that is at least 2½ inches deep. Refrigerate for at least 30 minutes, until firm.

Whisk the egg yolks well, add the sugar, and whisk again. Sift the flour into the coconut milk and stir to make a smooth paste, add the vanilla extract, then add to the eggs and whisk or stir until you have a smooth batter.

Transfer to the top of a double boiler and cook, stirring frequently, until smooth and thick, 5 to 10 minutes (if the custard starts to clump, lift the pot away from the heat, toss in an ice cube, and stir, then resume cooking and stirring over lower heat). Pour the custard on top of the tapioca and smooth. Let cool for 5 minutes, then refrigerate. Serve chilled on its own or with fresh fruit.

street-side seductions [AH-BOH]

MAKES ABOUT
8 CREPES

I came across a vendor making these sweets one sleepy Sunday afternoon in Rangoon. She had two bowls, one of batter, the other of filling, and two small charcoal burners going. On each was a curved metal pan, like a miniature wok but much heavier.

She added a little of the thin batter to one of the pans, lifted it to swirl the batter around, and put it back on the fire. It crisped up almost immediately on the hot metal surface. Then she ladled some of the filling onto the center of the crepe and covered the pan with a lid. A minute later, she turned the confection out onto her work surface. It was beautiful and delicate and looked like a Sri Lankan hopper, a bowl-shaped curve of fine crisp crepe, but with a thickened bulge of filling at the base.

I thought she'd just hand it to me, but no, rather shockingly, she folded two sides over the middle, breaking the delicate structure, and handed it to me all flattened. At the first bite I was in heaven, since the lush coconut-milk filling was a perfect creamy complement to the fine outer shell.

With specialized *ah-boh* pans not available outside Burma, the best implement to use is a cast-iron skillet (a wok is not heavy enough). The heavy skillet gives the right texture, even though the curved-bowl shape is missing.

I've experimented with using all rice flour as well as a mix of all-purpose and rice flour. Both work fine, but the mixture of flours gives more crispness. If you're serving these for dessert, serve them straight from the pan, with a scoop of sorbet on the side, for a great contrast of texture and temperature.

By the way, the man who first told me the Burmese name for these blushed a little when I asked him what they were called. I didn't understand his embarrassment until later, when I learned that *ah-boh* also means "vagina" in Burmese.

BATTER
1 cup rice flour plus a scant ½ cup
   all-purpose flour, or 1½ cups rice flour
1½ cups lukewarm water
⅛ teaspoon salt
1 tablespoon sugar
¼ teaspoon baking soda

FILLING
6 tablepoons thick coconut milk, canned or
   fresh (see Glossary)
3 tablespoons sugar
2 tablespoons rice flour
¼ teaspoon baking soda

Peanut or vegetable oil for surfaces

Whisk the batter ingredients together in a medium bowl until perfectly smooth. Set aside to rest for 30 minutes. Mix the filling ingredients together in a bowl until perfectly smooth; set aside.

Heat a 7- or 8-inch cast-iron or other heavy skillet over medium heat. Add a little oil and then after 20 seconds wipe the pan out with a paper towel. Place the pan over medium-high heat. Stir the batter. It should be very liquid; add a little more lukewarm water to thin it if necessary, and stir again. Pour a scant ¼ cup batter into the pan and lift and tilt the pan so the batter flows out to the edges. Cover and cook for 20 seconds or so. Spoon 1 generous tablespoon filling onto the center of the crepe, cover, lower the heat slightly, and cook for 1 minute. Check to see if the filling has set; if not, cover and cook a little longer.

Take the pan off the heat, fold the crepe in half, and transfer to a plate. Repeat with the remaining batter and filling.

Lifting an ah-boh *out of the traditional curved pan, streetside in Rangoon.*

AT SHWEDAGON AND other temples, people continually make offerings at small animal shrines. They pour cupfuls of water onto the Buddha statue, light candles, kneel in prayer. I hadn't realized what these shrines were until a friend asked me my birth day. She was astonished that I didn't know. Everyone in Burma knows what day of the week he or she was born on.

In Burma every day of the week is represented by an animal. It's astrological (different animals are associated with different characteristics), but it's also a matter of knowing what animal is looking out for you, and at which shrine you should be praying. It turns out that my birth day is Saturday, so my birth animal is a dragon. Those born on a Wednesday also need to know what time of day they were born, for Wednesday morning is an elephant with tusks, and Wednesday afternoon an elephant without tusks. There's a shrine for each of the eight animals of the Burmese zodiac at Buddhist temples. The other animals are the tiger (Monday), lion (Tuesday), rat (Thursday), guinea pig (Friday), and finally the Garuda, a mythical winged creature of Buddhist legend that is Sunday's animal.

Long ago, before the arrival of Buddhism, the people of this region worshipped and made offerings to the *nats,* the spirits of the jungle and the rivers, and also to the animals. They still do, at *nat* shrines all over Burma, and at the animal shrines at every Buddhist temple. Finding astrological animals at a Buddhist shrine is convincing evidence of the remarkable way Buddhism has absorbed and been energized by the local culture.

The interweaving of animist beliefs and Buddhism is everywhere in Burma. OPPOSITE, TOP: *Four nuns join other pilgrims at Shwedagon; throughout the year monks, nuns, and laypeople from all over the country visit this holy site.* LEFT: *At Mount Popa, east of Bagan, there are many animal shrines and statues, and people leave offerings at them, as someone has done at this huge tiger statue.* FAR LEFT: *A reclining Buddha at Shwedagon.* OVERLEAF: *This detail at Shwedagon shows a glittering glass-tiled* naga *(a snake-dragon) guarding a shrine; on the left a Buddhist guardian bears strands of jasmine flowers.*

fried sesame-seed bananas

MAKES 24;
SERVES 6 TO 8

There are versions of sweet banana treats all over Southeast Asia. Sometimes the bananas are fried in a batter until crisp, sometimes they're cooked in oil or lightly grilled, sometimes they're simmered in sweetened coconut milk.

These fried bananas are meltingly lush, and they're given an extra layer of flavor by a squeeze of lime juice. (Some friends like a little dusting of chile powder on top as well, for that hot-sweet-tart hit.) You can also serve them with tart-sweet mango or lime sorbet. They're good for dessert, but almost better as a snack. Make plenty, for it's hard to turn down second helpings.

Choose ripe bananas that are still firm. Cutting regular bananas crosswise in half mimics the size of the small sweet bananas that are used in Southeast Asia. If you do come across a hand of small sweet bananas, by all means use them.

The sesame seeds in the batter give a pleasing crunch that turns to chewiness as the bananas cool, as well as a mild sesame flavor.

BATTER
1 cup rice flour
¼ cup tapioca flour
2 tablespoons sugar
¾ teaspoon salt
¾ cup water
1 cup sesame seeds

6 bananas or 12 small tropical bananas
Peanut oil for deep-frying
3 limes, cut into wedges, or sorbet or ice cream
    for serving (optional)

Combine the flours, sugar, and salt in a bowl. Slowly add the water, stirring to make a smooth, thick batter. Stir in the sesame seeds. Set aside for 30 minutes.

Peel the bananas. If using large bananas, cut crosswise in half. Cut the pieces or the small bananas lengthwise in half (in either case, you will now have 24 pieces). Set aside.

Put out a slotted spoon or a spider by your stovetop along with one or two plates. Set a deep-fryer, stable wok, or wide heavy pot over medium heat. Add 2 inches of oil, raise the heat to high, and heat until the oil reaches 360°F. Use a thermometer to check the temperature, or drop a dollop of batter into the oil: If it sinks slowly to the bottom and then rises to the surface, the oil is at temperature. If it bobs right up without sinking or darkens immediately, the oil is too hot—lower the heat slightly; if it doesn't rise to the surface, the oil is not yet hot enough.

[Continued]

Fried Sesame-Seed Bananas with a squeeze of lime. On the left is a spider, a useful mesh-basket tool for lifting food out of hot oil.

Stir the batter, then drag 1 piece of banana through the batter and slide it carefully into the hot oil. Repeat with 2 or 3 more pieces, one by one. Fry, moving the pieces around carefully and keeping them from sticking to one another, until lightly golden and crispy. Lift out of the oil with the spider or slotted spoon, pausing to let excess oil drain off, and transfer to a plate. Repeat with the remaining bananas and batter.

Serve hot, with the lime wedges, sorbet, or ice cream, if you like.

cook's treat: fritters

There's usually a little batter left over when the bananas are all fried. Stir in some unsweetened dried coconut (about 3 tablespoons for ¼ cup batter). Use a teaspoon to scoop up dollops of batter and slip them into the hot oil. The delicious fritters will puff a little and be lightly golden and ready in a couple of minutes.

This little tea shop is just down the street from where I usually stay in Rangoon. It's got a few tables, some under a tree and others by the wall, opens well before dawn, and serves not just tea and coffee but also an array of noodle dishes.

drinks in burma

TEA SHOPS

All through the day, it's in tea shops that the main culinary traditions in Burma converge in a fascinating way. The foods in the larger tea shops in towns and cities range from Indian-style snacks, such as samosas, parothas, and *nan-piar* (flatbreads), to steamed dim sum, to Burmese classics like mohinga and semolina cake. The only problem for me is deciding what to order. My favorite for a long time was *nan-piar* fresh from the tandoor oven, topped with cooked chickpeas. That remains a hard-to-beat option for me, but once I forced myself to try other dishes, I got hooked on those possibilities too: delicate samosas, Burmese noodle salad, and more....

Tea shops are lively places to hang out, watch the passing scene, sip a tea or coffee, and take a pause from the efforts of the day. Sometimes there are women in a tea shop, a pair of them chatting, or as part of a young couple, but more often tea shops are filled with men, in twos and threes, sometimes in a larger group, talking and smoking.

In the morning tea shops are bustling with people in a rush, there to have a drink and a bite to eat before heading off to work. But after the morning rush they empty out. There's another crowd at lunch, another pause, and then comes what I think of as the heart of tea shop culture. Starting in the middle of the afternoon, tea shops fill up again, but the pace is more leisurely. There's a great feel to the tea shops in the afternoon, an ease and a visible relaxation of the pressures people feel at other times of day.

TEA-SHOP DRINKS

Tea originated in this part of Asia, and still grows wild—not in the lowlands and steamy deltas, but up in the mountains where Yunnan meets Burma's Shan and Kachin states and over toward Assam in India. Tall trees of wild tea (*Camellia sinensis, var. assamica*) grow there. Tea is now cultivated near Mandalay and farther into the hills in Shan State, and Burma is producing some very fine teas, from white and green teas to oolongs and earthier black teas.

Clear pale tea is drunk as a thirst quencher instead of water, as it is in much of China. Hot tea is also cooling in the heat.

Milk tea is a whole other thing—an intense burst of flavor and hit of energy—with its milk, sugar, and strong black tea base. This way of drinking tea apparently came to Burma from England, since in this part of the world tea is traditionally drunk clear and unsweetened. The same strong tea that is used for milk tea is available in tea shops, served without milk and called "black tea." It comes with several wedges of lime, and with sugar on the side or already added. Dark, intense, and refreshing, it's my favorite tea-shop drink.

Coffee has come into the country only relatively recently. Coffee beans are grown on plantations in most of Burma's neighbors—in Cambodia, Thailand, and Vietnam—but you'd never know that here. Most coffee comes as instant coffee, in sachets "made in China," often labeled "3-in-1" because it's premixed with a form of whitener and some sugar. The result, when made with boiling water, is not what I'd call coffee, just a brownish drink. Still, many people have a taste for it. Black coffee, usually made with instant coffee but sometimes brewed, is becoming more available in the urban tea shops. It is served with sugar and a slice or two of lime. The combination is a Burmese invention, I'm sure, and unexpectedly delicious.

European-style coffee made in espresso machines has recently arrived at expensive cafés and restaurants in Rangoon, just as it has already in Thailand.

A GLIMPSE OF BEER AND LIQUOR

Out in Rakhine State they make a fermented beer from sticky rice called *loh-zah*. The rice is cooked in water and then the water is left to ferment for a day into a slightly cloudy alcoholic liquid that is drunk from a bowl. It's rather like the barley- or rice-based beers of Nepal and Tibet.

In Shan State, as in Laos, Thailand, and Yunnan, *lao khao*, meaning "rice liquor," is made by the Shan and the Tai Koen. The Pa-O and Intha people around Inle Lake also make it. It's a clear distilled liquid that can be mild and easy to drink or harsh, depending on the skill of the maker. *Lao khao* is served at weddings and funerals and on other special occasions. And when people are laboring hard all day, for example at rice harvest, the occasional nip of *lao khao* helps them keep going.

In the central and southern areas of the country, where sugar palms (also known as toddy palms) grow, local people tap the palms for their sweet sap. The sap is used to make sugar but is more valued as a lightly fermented drink called *htan yei* ("toddy" in English). In some villages it is distilled to make a liquor called *arrack*.

Apart from local beers and liquors, usually made in villages and hard to find in the cities, there is an increasing variety of commercially brewed beers and distilled liquors, served in little beer halls and some restaurants. Quality varies, but they are generally very drinkable and welcome on a hot day, if chilled. Sometimes one or more is available on tap. The best-known liquor is Mandalay rum. It's easy to sip when it's diluted with soda water and plenty of freshly squeezed lime juice.

Finally, Burma is starting to produce wine at several vineyards in the Inle Lake area. The industry is young but European winemakers are working to bottle light, drinkable reds and whites.

All over Burma the innate generosity of the culture is on display: clay pots of clean water are set out in shelters by the side of the road, inviting the passing stranger to quench his or her thirst. This eye-catching water stop is in Bhamo, in Kachin State.

BURMA OVER TIME

BURMA'S LONG HISTORY STARTS WITH the early peoples who settled along the coast and in the Irrawaddy Valley, the advent of Buddhism more than two thousand years ago, the arrival of Bamar and Shan peoples from the north, and the rise of Bamar and Shan city-states and kingdoms. The colonial period, beginning with the First Anglo-Burmese War in 1824, ended with independence in 1948. Recent history begins with independence and touches on the complicated events since then, from the military coup in 1962 to the recent opening of the country to democracy.

The Annotated Bibliography (page 351) lists a number of books about Burma, written over the years and from many perspectives. In the meantime, here is a quick summary of Burmese history. You may find it helpful to consult the map on page 7 from time to time, since terrain and geography have played an important role in events.

In a village outside Hpa'an a woman's hat hangs on a post outside her house.

EARLY HISTORY

Archeologists tell us that there were agricultural settlements in the Irrawaddy Valley more than twenty-five hundred years ago, and these eventually developed into small city-states. The Pyu people, farmers and traders who controlled the area, spoke a Tibeto-Burman language. As early as two thousand years ago, they were trading gold, silver, and other valuables from the valley and surrounding hills with China and India.

Farther south, even before the time of Alexander the Great (some twenty-three hundred years ago), there was trade between southern India and the coastal area of Burma around Moulmein. The first kingdom for which there are records is Subanabhumi, a Mon kingdom that stretched north from Moulmein and was dominant in the region in the ninth through twelfth centuries (perhaps earlier—experts differ).

It was the strong trading connection between southern India and Burma that brought Theravada Buddhism to Burma, and from there into present-day Thailand, Laos, and Cambodia. With Buddhism came written scriptures. (Theravada scriptures are written in the Pali language, rather than the Sanskrit of Mahayana Buddhism, and the practices and beliefs are somewhat different.) Kings and other rich patrons established monastic centers of learning, and once Buddhism fell into decline in India, Burmese scholarship became the most respected in the Pali tradition. (The tradition of monastic learning continues in Burma today.)

Starting fifteen hundred to two thousand years ago, the Tai peoples of southern China (ancestors of the present-day Shan, Tai Koen, Lao, and Thai) started moving south into Laos, Thailand, Vietnam, and northeastern Burma. During the same period, people from the Nanzhao kingdom in the Dali/Lake Erhai area of Yunnan began to migrate south and west. It's generally agreed that they are the forebears of the current majority Bamar population of Burma and the source of the Burmese language. They displaced or absorbed the Pyu in the rich Irrawaddy Valley in central Burma, in the area around present-day Mandalay and Bagan (or Pagan, as it may be written).

There are few written records of the early centuries of Bamar control in this region. Detailed history starts with King Anawrahta (also spelled Aniruddha), who is in many ways the founder of Burma. Starting in 1044, he conquered huge territories from his base in Bagan, and by the time of his death his armies controlled much of present-day Burma. In Bagan itself, Anawrahta built temples and palaces; the ruins still remind visitors of that early glory.

Over the ensuing centuries a series of kings took power, fought to expand their kingdoms, and rarely died in their beds, just as Europe's history from 1200 to 1600 involved wars and power struggles. The kings in the Irrawaddy Valley also had to face invasions from the north, including the Mongols in 1271 and the Qing (Manchu) army in the 1760s. In each case the invaders eventually were repelled. The Bamar kings built a succession of capital cities in the region around Mandalay and Bagan (the remains of which now attract tourists).

Portuguese and other European traders began doing business with Burma starting around 1500, bringing goods from Europe and other Asian regions and trading them for gold, silver, jade, and precious stones.

The most memorable of the Burmese kings in this era, still celebrated today by the Burmese army, is King Bayinnaung, who in the mid-1500s conquered almost all of present-day Burma, as well as Thailand and Laos. His capital was at Ava, which is on an island in the Irrawaddy River just south of present-day Mandalay. (Early writers about Burma often refer to the country as Ava.)

Two centuries later, another powerful king, Alaungpaya, began campaigns in the 1750s that resulted in the reunification of a then-fragmented kingdom. He conquered the Mon kingdom, whose capital was Pegu (now called Bago) and which controlled the Irrawaddy Delta. He also attacked eastward and south, conquering the Tenasserim coast (then under Thai control) and the whole of what is present-day Thailand, and sacking the Thai royal capital Ayuthaya in 1767.

But in the early nineteenth century, the military confidence of the Burmese ran up against the expansionist plans of the British in India. The result was the First Anglo-Burmese War, in 1824, which ended with the defeat of the Burmese in 1826 and the ceding to Britain of most of the coast, from Arakan in the west to Tenasserim, the tail-of-the-kite strip in the far south.

COLONIAL PERIOD

By the Treaty of Yandabo, Britain, the victor in the 1824–1826 war, was entitled to huge indemnity payments from Burma, which impoverished the country. The British set up a trading port at Akyub (present-day Sittwe) at the mouth of the Kaladan River on the Arakan (now Rakhine) coast. They developed what became their principal trading city for most of the nineteenth century, Moulmein, at the mouth of the Salween River, southeast of Rangoon. They also began to exploit the rich hardwood forests of Burma, cutting teak trees up the Salween River and its tributaries and floating them downstream to Moulmein.

Because of historical trading ties, the population of Burma already included people from present-day India and Bangladesh, but once the British arrived there was an influx of South Asians from British India. These newcomers settled in Mandalay, Rangoon, and Moulmein, as well as other towns, starting businesses and small manufacturing concerns.

In the late 1850s, after the accession of King Mindon, the Burmese capital was moved from Ava to a newly built complex at Mandalay, a few miles up the Irrawaddy. A generation later, in 1885, during the third Anglo-Burmese War, the British marched up the Irrawaddy Valley from Rangoon and captured Mandalay and the king, Thibaw, whom they sent into exile in India. The British then loosely controlled the whole of present-day Burma. The extraction of teak up-country, as well as trade in gold and forest products and rice, continued to grow. During their tenure in Burma, the British built railways to link Rangoon with Myitkyina in Kachin State and Lashio in Shan State, as well as to Tavoy/Dawei in Tenasserim. They also brought in steamships to provide transport on the Irrawaddy, another way of linking the north and center of the country to Rangoon.

Meanwhile, the Shan princes remained autonomous in their small states, and so, generally speaking, did the Kachin, Karen, and Chin in their hills. Missionaries from Britain and the United States began to convert many Kachin, Karen, and Chin to Christianity.

The Japanese invaded Burma in 1942, and in a few short weeks, they had marched all the way north to Myitkyina, as the British army retreated. Some Burmese at first welcomed the Japanese, as a way of ridding themselves of colonial rule, and fought alongside them. But eventually the pro-Japanese elements in Burma came to realize that they had traded one occupying power for another. Independence was the only answer.

The tide turned in July 1944, when the British-Indian army and special forces from Burma defeated the Japanese at Imphal and Kohima. The Japanese retreated south through central Burma and along the Arakan (Rakhine) coast, surrendering in August 1945. The fighting and sabotage that took place during the war left the country with no infrastructure: railways, bridges, and roads were damaged, and agriculture had been seriously disrupted. Many people suffered from malnutrition, many had lost their homes and livelihoods, and many had died.

INDEPENDENCE

After the defeat of the Japanese, the British returned to power in Burma. Concerned about the potential for civil war and the fracturing of the country, Aung San, a young politician, and other Bamar leaders met with representatives of many of the non-Bamar peoples at a conference in Panglong in February 1947. There they hammered out the Panglong Agreement, which affirmed their commitment to a "union of Burma."

The Panglong Agreement was not to everyone's taste. Many in the newly formed Burmese army and others, too, feared that giving power and standing to non-Bamar peoples was risky. They

Early morning near Bothataung temple in the eastern part of Rangoon. The cycle rickshaws are distinctive, with two passenger seats set back to back, beside the man pedaling.

did not want the country to splinter, instead favoring a strong centralized model of government in which there was not much room for dissent or difference. The decision to assassinate Aung San that July seems to have originated with this faction.

After intense negotiations, independence from Great Britain came six months later, on January 4, 1948. (The British were in a hurry to divest themselves of their colonies: India and Pakistan had been granted independence the year before.) The various non-Bamar peoples—especially the Karen and Shan—had pressed for some autonomy, a kind of federal structure, without success. The Shan princes had agreed to join the union of Burma, with the proviso that if it didn't suit them, they would be free to leave in ten years' time.

The new country, still in ruins following the war, faced many difficulties. Aung San, the man who everyone had assumed had the vision and ability to lead the country in its first years. was no longer alive. Fighting, demonstrations, and lawlessness broke out all over at independence. There was also an invasion by Chinese forces, who were fighting out the end of the Maoist revolution, and the Karen, Mon, and Rakhine began their battles for their own states. Still, now that the nation was self-governing, with a parliament, a prime minister, and a president, many Burmese were hopeful that they were on the way to a prosperous future.

During the 1950s the army started businesses in order to raise money to modernize, and it slowly gained economic power. But it was stretched thin as it fought various factions in the border areas. In 1959, in an effort to restore order, the army seized power temporarily; it soon passed authority back to a civilian government.

And then in March 1962, the army, under General Ne Win, again overthrew the government and seized power. (Observers have suggested that the army saw itself as the only stabilizing influence in Burma.) The Shan princes were all put in prison, and none of them was seen again. A "socialist" model was established, with industries nationalized, South Asians and foreigners expelled or discouraged from staying, and most links to the outside world, including diplomatic connections, weakened or severed. The economy went into a tailspin. And the army under Ne Win ruled with a heavy hand, with no dissent tolerated.

Thus began twenty-five years of political and economic isolation. Few visitors were allowed in, very few Burmese except those connected to the government could get passports to leave, and the economy stagnated, with no exports and few, if any, legal imports. There was little or no government investment in infrastructure, and only the black market flourished.

In addition, the civil wars raged on in the outlying areas: the Kachin and Mon joined the Karen and Shan in battling for independence or at least autonomy from the central government. Their armies sheltered in the hills and largely supported themselves by trading in opium and heroin; the Karen also traded teak and other hardwoods from the forests.

RECENT EVENTS

In 1988, with the economy in ruins and the education system failing, the students of Burma began a series of pro-democracy demonstrations in Rangoon, Mandalay, and elsewhere. The movement caught fire and by early August it had become an outpouring of longing and hope, with thousands out in the streets on August 8. (The protests are referred to by pro-democracy activists as 8-8-88 or the Four Eights, and that anniversary is marked each year.) The protests were smashed by the army in the next five days as they fired on demonstrators, killing hundreds.

But then the army withdrew—no

In February 2012 Aung San Suu Kyi flew to Myitkyina, on her first visit since being released from house arrest. I was lucky to be there at the same time. It was amazing to see flags, banners, and posters of the NLD (her party, now in opposition) and to feel the excitement and confidence of the crowd as she spoke at this huge rally.

one really understands why—and by mid-August people began to meet and talk about change. Demonstrations, political meetings, and union meetings bloomed. It was a time of hope and optimism, as people exercised freedoms they hadn't had for a quarter century. Aung San Suu Kyi, daughter of the assassinated hero Aung San, mentioned earlier, happened to be in Burma visiting her invalid mother that month (Suu Kyi had been living in England with her English husband and their two sons). The pro-democracy movement sought her help, and when she was one of the speakers at a rally in late August, the crowds were enormous and energized.

The flowering of hope continued for only a few weeks. On September 18, the army went back into action, killing hundreds, a foretaste of what would happen in Beijing's Tiananmen Square the following year. At the same time, the army put a new constitution in place, setting up the State Law and Order Restoration Council (SLORC) under a new leader, Than Shwe, to rule the country. Many students were arrested, and many others fled to the border areas, especially the Thai border. There they tried to join forces with the Karen and Shan armies that had been battling the central government for more than twenty years. It was a difficult time for these other nationalities. Their distrust of Bamar people was deep, and yet here were (mostly) Bamar students who wished to help fight the central government.

Rather than return to England, Aung San Suu Kyi stayed in Burma, and with other people who had been political leaders at one time or another—some of them even former members of the military dictatorship—established a political party, the National League for Democracy (NLD). For a while the government allowed her to speak and meet with people, and to make trips out of Rangoon, but in 1989 she was placed under house arrest.

Surprisingly, in 1990 the Burmese government called national elections, presumably because it assumed there would be no strong opposition. But Aung San Suu Kyi became the figure around whom opposition to the government took shape. The result was that the NLD won a huge majority.

The government refused to step down. Many Burmese were put in jail, and Aung San Suu Kyi remained under house arrest until 1995. (In 1991, when she was awarded the Nobel Peace Prize for her "nonviolent struggle for democracy and human rights," her husband and sons accepted the award on her behalf.) Many more activists fled over the border to Thailand as the government embarked on a reinvention of the status quo: Burma was renamed Myanmar, Rangoon became Yangon, and it was announced that a new capital would be built between Mandalay and Rangoon, to be called Naypyidaw. (This was consistent with the history of Burma, in which kings would, on taking power, decide to build a new capital and abandon the previous one.)

At the same time the government, which had been running short of foreign currency, began trading with China. The Chinese invested in the ruby and sapphire mines, the jade mines, and other natural resources. As a result, SLORC had money to buy tanks and equipment so that the army could fight the rebels in the border areas. No longer was there a black market in goods long unavailable in Burma; instead, the country became a huge open market for Chinese manufactured goods, which poured across the border from Yunnan.

By the mid-1990s, the regime had succeeded in pushing back the rebel armies to the border areas, and in negotiating cease-fires with the leaders of some of them. Following these cease-fires, the government opened new areas of the country to tourism. Some Burmese held out hope that the army would also loosen restrictions on speech and political activity. It never happened. The country was newly open for business, and there was a sense of growing prosperity for friends of the government and for some in the cities, but not for any kind of democracy. Political prisoners in Rangoon's Insein Prison and other prisons around the country numbered in the thousands.

Western countries imposed sanctions, starting in the 1990s (these are now being eased in response to positive political changes in Burma). However, because of the China trade, these sanctions were not very effective. And the discovery of huge oil and gas deposits in the sea off the Burmese coast meant that the government became even less vulnerable to sanctions.

The Burmese army continued a campaign of burning and destruction of villages and of rape and forced labor in the dissident areas, creating a floating population of internally displaced people. Many of them found their way over the borders into India, Bangladesh, or Thailand; others just existed hand to mouth in the hills of Kayin, Kayenni, Mon, Shan, Chin, and Kachin states. (A number of the books in the Annotated Bibliography give a detailed picture of the situation.)

In September 2007, monks began a peaceful demonstration against the government, initially prompted by a rise in fuel prices. It soon mushroomed into massive demonstrations, as thousands of ordinary citizens joined the monks, and the movement became known as the Saffron Revolution. Nineteen years after 8-8-88, technology had changed; this time there were videos of the demonstrations, and people all over the world watched what was happening on their televisions and computer screens. However, once again the army moved in, shooting and beating demonstrators, including monks and nuns. Many monks were jailed; others fled the country.

In 2010, the military regime did away with its uniforms and declared itself a civilian entity. Than Shwe retired. When a national election was held, under a constitution that gave the military the balance of power, Aung San Suu Kyi, who had been rearrested in 2003, was once again under house arrest and both she and her party were declared ineligible to run. Nevertheless, with a few of the trappings of democracy in place, some opposition candidates succeeded in getting elected. Observers all agreed that in substance things had not changed: in the outlying parts of the country, the Burmese army still engaged in battles with one or another rebel army, and made vicious attacks on villages, as it had been doing for decades. (Over the years a huge percentage of Burma's resources has gone to maintain the military, at enormous cost to the whole country.)

After the 2010 elections, Aung San Suu Kyi was released from house arrest. She was able to speak to the outside world through electronic media, and began to speak to Burmese in small gatherings. But the big shift happened following her meeting with President Thein Sein in August 2011: the government suspended construction of a huge controversial dam on the upper Irrawaddy; about two hundred of the two thousand political prisoners were released; the government lifted blocks on many websites, giving people much more access to the outside world of opinion and commentary and news; and the restrictions on Aung San Suu Kyi's political activity were lifted.

With all this loosening and political evolution, the streets and tea shops of Rangoon felt quite different when I next visited Burma, in November 2011. People told me the changes of the preceding three months were exhilarating. Pictures of Aung San Suu Kyi and her father were posted on walls and printed in magazines and in the newspapers, and people chatted more openly and loosely in tea shops. Everyone looked more relaxed and less anxious. Early in 2012, many more political prisoners were released, including those who had been leaders of the demonstrations in 1988 and 2007.

The changes had a huge impact all over the world. Foreign governments that had shunned Burma began to respond positively to the changes. U.S. Secretary of State Hillary Rodham Clinton, as well as her counterparts from Britain, France, and other countries, traveled to Burma to meet with both President Thein Sein and Aung San Suu Kyi, and countries suspended or dropped sanctions and upgraded their level of diplomatic relations with Burma.

It's important to remember in all this—both the long years of oppression and the current era of more open politics—that people in Burma have found ways of living with dignity and good humor, despite the pressures on them. They have a strong sense of who they are, and like people all over the world, they are concerned about taking care of their children and keeping a roof over their heads and food on the table; they also like to joke and play when they can. Their news has for years

A man looks at the huge array of papers and magazines for sale in Rangoon in February 2012. With press restrictions relaxed, the media can cover stories that previously would have been censored, such as hip-hop bands, news of Aung San Suu Kyi, etc.

come from government-controlled media, but now the news has turned positive, and they have access to a wider range of internet sites, as well as newspapers and magazines that are much less censored.

And so Burma's history continues to evolve. As I write, in May 2012, there's a lot of optimism, both in Burma and outside the country. Burmese are relieved that there is more freedom of speech and the promise of more democracy and civil rights. They know that there is powerful opposition to the pro-democracy reforms in the army and elsewhere among the older leadership, but even so people are no longer afraid to talk politics and express opinions. And in the by-elections held in April, Aung San Suu Kyi and other opposition candidates won all but one of the forty-five contested seats.

But as Aung San Suu Kyi said at a big rally I attended in Myitkyina in February 2012, there is an urgent need for national reconciliation, and for a "Panglong Agreement for the twenty-first century." Until then there will be fear and uncertainty in many non-Bamar parts of the country. For example in 2011, after a seventeen-year-long cease-fire with the Kachin Independence Army, the Burmese Army moved in fresh troops and began attacking Kachin villages, creating tens of thousands of internally displaced people. Word is that the army is out of control. And so other groups—the Wa and Karen, for example—fear similar attacks.

Nonetheless, as this book goes to press, positive political change seems to be continuing. (For current news on Burma, the best sources are *The Irrawaddy* and *Mizzima*, both published online.) There will of course be many bumps in the road. But the country that looked as if it would forever be locked in a totalitarian purgatory now seems to be committed to a new era of openness. With its rich layers of culture, huge natural resources, and strategic location between China and India, Burma is set to become a powerhouse in Southeast Asia and a major player on the international stage.

TRAVELING IN BURMA

NOW THAT THE POLITICAL SITUATION HAS EASED dramatically and the country's politics are more open, Burma has become a very attractive destination. The best times to go, in terms of weather, are from early November until the end of February, the dry season. Temperatures cool down and the skies are generally clear. The first months of rainy season (June and July) are another good time, for the countryside is green and lush; skies may be gray and it rains sometimes, but then it clears and the light is beautiful.

I suggest that you read *The River of Lost Footsteps* by Thant Myint-U or Amitav Ghosh's sweeping historical novel *The Glass Palace* to give yourself some perspective before you go. (If you have time, look at some of the other books mentioned in the bibliography as well.)

Travel rules and details about visas and flights can change from one day to the next, but some things about travel in Burma are likely to remain stable for a while. Check online for updates to what follows, but here are the most immediate practical things to keep in mind.

- Foreigners need a visa to travel in Burma. Applications can be made at any Burmese embassy; people who are known pro-democracy activists, as well as journalists and lawyers, have been refused in the past, but this seems to be changing.

- If you stay at small-scale local hotels and guesthouses and avoid government transport and guides, you can ensure that most of what you spend will go to local people rather than to the government. Travel by bus is convenient, though not quick; travel by plane is expensive and, if you book it inside Burma, has to be paid for in cash.

- There are opportunities for volunteering as a language teacher or donating your skills in another area, especially at some of the monastery-run schools. Check online before you go to get guidance about volunteer opportunities.

- Burmese is not an easy language for speakers of Indo-European languages (see A Note on Language, below), but you can learn some basics, so get a phrase book or a basic language book (I like Gene Mesher's *Burmese for Beginners*) and leap in. Many Burmese speak some English, especially in tourist areas, and many older people in the cities speak beautiful English, but trying your tongue at Burmese is fun and rewarding.

- There is not yet any international cell phone service in Burma. Local mobile phones are evolving and gradually becoming more available and affordable. There are internet cafés in the cities, and many cafés have Wi-Fi; so do most hotels, in the lobby if not in individual rooms. As of early 2012, many of the government firewalls have come down, so access to the outside world is much easier. Nevertheless, a note of caution: there is still a lot of government surveillance of the internet so it's best not to engage in political discussion with people at internet cafés, or even online while you are in the country; it puts others at risk.

- Very few places take credit cards, and if they do, a hefty commission is charged for each transaction, so come with cash—U.S. dollars in clean, uncreased notes. (As of spring 2012, there are still no ATMs.) Other currencies will not be accepted: hotels, travel agencies, airlines, and others require that you pay in U.S. dollars. The best rate of exchange is for large bills, but you will need small bills to pay taxis and for tickets on trains, ferryboats, etc. You can change money at your hotel; the best black market exchange rates have traditionally been at the Bogyoke Market in Rangoon (also known by its old name, Scott Market).

A NOTE ON LANGUAGE

If you go to the National Museum of Myanmar in Rangoon, an echoing high-ceilinged building, you will find yourself first at a display about the development of the script used to write Burmese. For the non-Burmese-speaking foreigner, it's a bit of a leap into the deep end of the culture—at least that's how I felt about it when I went for the first time. Now I have come to appreciate it as an introduction to the complex history of the dominant Bamar culture in the region. The language is part of the Tibeto-Burman family of languages. It's tonal, there are no genders, and verbs are positioned at the end of the sentence. The writing is very beautiful to look at, all stylized loops and curves, like very round primary school alphabets. It derives from Mon and from Pali, the language of the Theravada Buddhist scriptures, but has gradually evolved over the centuries.

GLOSSARY

ARAKAN: See **Rakhine people; Rakhine State; Rohingya.**

ARECA NUT: The nut from *Areca catechu*, a palm indigenous to Southeast Asia, is an important crop in southern Burma. It is wrapped in a pepper leaf along with slaked lime and often other flavors (for example, tobacco, cassia, or sweet coconut) and chewed as a stimulant, especially by people in the countryside. In English the wad is often called "betel nut." The teeth and lips of habitual users are

ARECA NUTS

stained dark red, a result of the active ingredients in the areca nuts that are released by the lime.

BAMAR: The name given in English to the people who constitute the dominant population in Burma. The current government has rejected the words *Bamar, Burma,* and *Burmese,* insisting instead that the word *Myanmar* be used as the name of both the country and its people.

BAKING STONE; PIZZA STONE; QUARRY TILES; UNGLAZED QUARRY TILES: The porous unglazed clay of a baking stone or a pizza stone gives the bottom surface of oven-baked breads a great crust. Unglazed quarry tiles, laid on a rack in your oven with a 1- to 2-inch space between the edge of the tiles and the oven wall (to allow hot air to circulate), are another option. Place the stone or tiles in the oven before you preheat it for baking. Allow an extra 10 minutes after the oven has reached temperature for the stone or tiles to get completely heated through before you start baking.

BANANA; BANANA FLOWER; BANANA STEM: The banana plant, *Musa acuminata*, is native to Southeast Asia. Bananas grow in bunches, called "hands," at the end of a tall stem. Bananas come in many varieties, from small and sweet to large and much less sweet. In Burmese they are *ngepyaw thi.* Banana leaves are used for wrapping foods before steaming them. In Burma **banana stem** (actually the "stem" of the plant is a pseudostem, being composed of bundles of leaves) is an important ingredient in mohinga, the complex noodle soup that is the Burmese national dish (see "Mohinga Variations," page 255). The Burmese term for banana stem is *ngae pyaw oo.* **Banana flower** is eaten as a vegetable in Southeast Asia. It is large, beautiful, cone-shaped, and red-purple. In Burma it is cooked, then chopped and made into salad (see page 57); in Thailand and Laos the salad is more often made from chopped uncooked banana flower.

In Rakhine I was told a cure for stomachache: Boil a whole banana, including the skin, then eat it. A man staying at my guesthouse took the advice. Whether it was the banana, or just the passage of time, the pain he'd had the night before was gone by morning.

BASIL: *Occimum basilicum*, the intensely flavored version of basil that is commonly called Thai basil (*bai horapha* in Thai), with its purplish flowers and stems, is always handy to have around if you are cooking recipes from Burma. Use it torn as a garnish and flavoring on everything from Shan Tofu Salad (page 51) to Tamarind-Pumpkin Curry (page 103) and thick soups. You can substitute

Mediterranean basil, but since that doesn't hold its flavor as well when warmed, add it at the last moment.

BEAN THREADS: See **noodles**.

BEN OIL: See **moringa**.

BLANCHING; PARBOILING: The process of immersing food in boiling water to lightly cook it or soften it is usually called blanching. A closely related technique is parboiling, which involves immersing food in boiling water for a specific length of time. The two terms are often used interchangeably. A number of the recipes here call for blanching pea tendrils or other greens before adding them to noodle soups, or parboiling or blanching greens before using them as an ingredient in a salad.

BOTTLE GOURD: See **gourds and summer squashes**.

BROCCOLI RABE: Often called *rapini*, its Italian name, *Brassica rapa* is botanically a close relation of the turnip. It has yellow flowers, much finer darker green stems than broccoli, and a complex nutty flavor that is tinged with bitterness. It's

BANANA STEM

widely used in Southern Italian cooking. I love it, and often stir-fry it with garlic for a simple green side dish. It also makes a good salad, lightly boiled or steamed, coarsely chopped, and then dressed with either Burmese salad flavorings or a simple vinaigrette seasoned with a dash of soy sauce as well as salt.

BUDDHISM: Buddhists follow the teachings (called *dhamma*) of Gautama Buddha, who lived and taught in northern India about 2,550 years ago. There are a number of schools of Buddhism. The chief division is between Theravada, also called Hinayana, or "lesser path," which is the form of Buddhism followed in Burma, as well as in Sri Lanka, Thailand, Laos, and Cambodia, and Mahayana, or "greater path," various forms of which are followed in India, Tibet, Japan, China, and Vietnam.

Although the majority of Bamar people are Buddhists, some Bamar and a large proportion of the non-Bamar peoples were converted to Christianity in the nineteenth and twentieth centuries. (To some extent the central government has used Buddhism as a marker of nationalism, to try to create divisions between Buddhists and Christians who are in opposition.) Underlying Buddhist beliefs and practices in Burma is the "old" religion, a form of animism in which spirits, known as "nats," are worshipped and looked to for help. The animist beliefs of pre-Buddhist Burma infuse daily life for many Buddhists. (See "What Day Are You?," page 297.)

Monasteries are called *kyauntaik* or *kyaung*. Other structures, often loosely termed pagodas in English, include temples, called *pahto* or *paya* in Burma, and the solid round or domed structures called *chedis*. Most temple complexes consist of covered pavilions, with Buddha statues in them and space for people to sit or kneel on the floor, and a number of *chedis* of various sizes.

In Theravada, the scriptures are written in Pali, a language that followed Sanskrit, and so the religious centers of learning in Burma are called Pali universities in English. (And see "Offerings at Dawn," page 263; "Nuns," page 215; "Meeting Monk," page 93.)

CASSIA; CASSIA STICK; CINNAMON; CINNAMON STICK: *Cinnamomum cassia* is a tree that is closely related to the tree that gives true cinnamon, which is *Cinnamomum verum.* In both, the flavor is in the bark. It is rolled into cylinders to make cassia sticks (or cinnamon quills). Cassia (*thit jabou* in Burmese), rather than cinnamon, is widely used in Southeast Asia, and it is often used as a less expensive alternative to cinnamon in North America. Its flavor is hotter and harsher, less perfumed, than that of cinnamon.

CELERY LEAVES: *Apium graveolens.* These can be mistaken for coriander leaves, but they are larger and coarser, and if you rub them a little, their strong celery aroma is easy to smell. They are widely used in China. In Burma, where they are called *tayoka nanan,* they're used in some soups, especially in the winter months; they are believed to be good for high blood pressure.

CELTUCE; STEM LETTUCE: *Lactuca sativa,* var. *asparagina* is a variety of lettuce that has a thick stem (it resembles a broccoli stem) and a tuft of

CELTUCE

green leaves on top. Both stem and leaves are edible. The stem is usually peeled, cut into fine strips, and then simmered or stir-fried. Celtuce grows well in tough conditions and tolerates dry and cold better than most greens, so that people living in the hills of Shan State, Kachin State, and over the border in the hills of Yunnan and Thailand grow it as a winter vegetable.

CHAYOTE: *Sechium edule* is a member of the cucumber family but looks more like a large, hard, slightly lumpy green pear. It's originally from Central America. The Burmese call it *suka thi.* It has one seed, in a small core like an apple core, unlike most cucumbers and squash. The skin is peeled off, always (it has a stickiness in it that must be removed). The fruit grows on a climbing vine, the tender leaves and tendrils of which (*suka ywet*) are used blanched in salads and also cooked in soups (see Mimi's Bean Soup with Tender Leaves, page 98). In Burma some people call chayote "Gurkha gourd" (*gurkha thi*). Perhaps it came into the country with the Gurkhas (who are from Nepal and were in the British-Indian army). Chayote are now widely available in North America in well-stocked supermarkets and in Asian and Mexican groceries.

CHEDI: A conical dome of stone or brick, sometimes coated in gold, marking a memorial shrine and containing Buddhist relics; sometimes written *zedi.* The Sanskrit word for the same structure is *stupa.* The huge golden dome of Shwedagon is a (Mon-style) *chedi;* so are the smaller bell-shaped structures around many temples. The umbrella-like structure at the top of every *chedi* is called a *hti.* See also **Buddhism.**

CHICHARRONES: See **fried pork skin; pork cracklings; pork skin.**

CHICKPEAS; CHICKPEA FLOUR: *Cicer arietinum* is a round legume that grows, as all peas do, in a green pod. When fresh it can be cooked and eaten like green peas. Most often, however, it is taken from the pod and dried. In dried form it keeps well. In India dried chickpeas are known as Bengal gram or *channa;* they may be whole or split. In Mexico they are called *garbanzos,* and that is the name many people in the United States know them by. In Burma chickpeas are cooked like dal, boiled in water until tender, and eaten for breakfast with flatbread, or turned into soup. (See Index for recipes.) Chickpeas are also ground into flour, one called *besan* in northern India; the Burmese name is *pei hmont sein.* The Shan stir **chickpea flour** into hot water to make a thick soup, which can also be set aside to firm up into a yellow, jelly-like food, Shan tofu (see page 126). The flour is also used in Burma as a thickener and a flavoring, after being dry-roasted briefly to cook it (see Toasted Chickpea Flour, page 32).

CHILES; CHILE POWDER; ROASTED CHILE POWDER; CAYENNE CHILES; BIRD CHILES; DRIED RED CHILES: The general Burmese word for chile is *nagyok thi* (pronounced "na-jok tee").

   Fresh Chiles: There are small very hot chiles, called *kala aw thi* in Burmese and *prik ee noo* in Thai, both red and green, but milder cayenne chiles are more common, long and slender and medium-hot, either red or green. Whole **green cayenne chiles** are used in a few curries, especially in the Rakhine area, on the west coast, where the taste is generally for more chile heat than in the center of the country. Then there are milder sweet rounded red chiles that are used in some condiments, and substituted for hotter chiles by those who prefer mild taste. **Jalapeños** can be substituted for green cayennes, though they have a different flavor; they are usually a little less hot than cayennes. **Serranos** are another possible substitute for cayennes; they are smaller and hotter than cayennes, so proceed with caution.

   Dried Chiles: In Burma cooks can buy a wide variety of dried red chile products, from dried red cayenne chiles (*ngayoke thi chauk*) to dried Thai chiles (much hotter) and dried round red chiles (mild and sweet). Dried red cayennes are the ones I use and the most commonly used in Burma: They're shiny, dark red, and 3 to 5 inches long, usually labeled "Product of Thailand" or "Product of India." They can be hot to very hot, depending on where they were grown. Dried chiles can be used whole, or soaked and pounded to a paste, or ground to a powder that is then used as a flavoring. See also Red Chile Powder, page 28.

CHIN; CHIN STATE: Chin people speak a language related to Burmese and now live mostly in Chin State, in Burma, as well as in the Indian states of Manipur, Mizorum, and Nagaland. They have had an ongoing independence struggle with the central government, but the conflict is now confined to a small area of Chin State. Many Chin people have fled to Malaysia and into India. In the nineteenth and early twentieth centuries, many Chin were converted to Christianity by Western missionaries. For more, see "News of Chin State," page 118.

CHINESE CELERY: See **celery leaves.**

CHINESE KALE: Often known by its Chinese name, *gai lan,* this green, *Brassica alboglabra,* looks like a distant cousin of broccoli. It has white flowers, thick tender stems, and slightly tough leaves. Chop the stems, then stir-fry or steam-cook them.

CHIVES; GARLIC CHIVES; CHINESE CHIVES: The fine tender green hollow round stems of European chives are not found in Burma but make a good substitute for fresh greens in some dishes; their botanical name is *Allium schoenoprasum.* In Burma, especially in Kachin and Shan states, the greens on offer in the markets often include Chinese chives, *Allium chinense,* which have flat green blades and look like grass. Because their taste is more like garlic than the onion flavor of European chives, the other common name for Chinese chives is garlic chives. They can be chopped fine and used fresh, but are more commonly stir-fried.

CILANTRO: See **coriander leaves; roots; seeds.**

CINNAMON; CINNAMON STICK: See **cassia.**

CLOVES: The dried buds of a tropical tree native to the Molucca Islands of Indonesia, cloves (*Eugenia caryophyllata*) have an intense aroma and an almost burning taste. The name derives from *claves,* the Latin word for "nails," and in fact cloves look like small nails, with a stem and a rounded head. Clove oil has medicinal properties and is often used to dull the pain of toothache by people who lack other analgesics.

COCONUT; FRESH COCONUT; COCONUT STRIPS; GRATED COCONUT; FROZEN COCONUT; TOASTED GRATED COCONUT; COCONUT MILK: Coconuts grow on a tall palm tree (*Cocos nucifera*) that is salt tolerant, so it thrives in delta areas and along coastlines. The fruit has a hard husk and is lined with sweet white crisp flesh that has a high oil content. In Burma the word for "coconut" is *ohn thi.* Coconut is used mainly for sweet dishes in Burma, although coconut milk is also an essential ingredient in several noodle dishes, including Coconut Sauce Noodles (page 251) and Egg Noodles with Pork in Coconut Sauce (page 248).

Coconut flesh can be grated or finely sliced into strips and used fresh, toasted, or fried as a sweet topping. When buying a coconut, hold it in your hand. It should feel heavy and should have coconut water inside. To crack it, apply a heavy screwdriver point to the "eye" of the coconut, a flattened spot on the husk, then tap the other end firmly with a hammer. The coconut should crack open. Catch the coconut water in a bowl. It is a delicious, slightly sweet clear liquid.

If you have a coconut scraper, use it to scrape out the flesh. Otherwise, improvise a scraper. The easiest way is to take a metal bottle cap with a wavy sharp edge, flatten it slightly to make it easier to hold, and then use the edge to scrape out the **strips of fresh coconut.** Use the flesh to make coconut milk (see below) or eat it fresh, or use as a topping for cakes or other desserts. Because of its high oil content, fresh coconut flesh does not keep well, so it is often sold in North America as **frozen grated coconut** or **desiccated coconut shreds.** (The latter are often sweetened. The sweetened form is not a substitute for unsweetened grated coconut, fresh or frozen or desiccated.) To toast fresh coconut strands, place in a heavy skillet over medium heat and keep it moving on the pan so it changes color but does not scorch. Remove when just turning a pale brown. To toast frozen grated coconut, chop it into small pieces and put it in a wide heavy skillet set over medium heat. Stir it with a wooden spatula as it heats; the ice will melt and the water sizzle and then evaporate, and then the coconut will start to toast on the hot surface. Keep stirring, so that as it starts to brown you get an even toasting with no scorching. Once the coconut is an even golden brown, turn it out into a bowl to cool, then use in recipes as directed.

To make coconut milk: The flesh of the coconut is grated, then mashed with warm water (most easily in a food processor; traditionally by hand), squeezed, and pressed. The warm water emulsifies the oil and washes it out of the flesh. This water-oil mixture is what is called coconut milk. It is a largely saturated fat that will become solid if refrigerated. The process of adding warm water, kneading the flesh, and then pressing out the liquid is repeated a number of times. The "first pressing" yields the richest, thickest coconut milk (in Burmese, *ohn no*); the "second pressing" is less rich. **Canned coconut milk** is a reasonable substitute. I find Mae Ploy and Aroy D brands from Thailand the most reliable. Make sure it is unsweetened and contains nothing but water and coconut milk. Often canned milk separates into thicker, oilier, almost solid coconut cream and thinner, more watery liquid beneath. (You can assist this process by placing a can of coconut milk in the refriegerator for half an hour.) Use the thick upper layer when "**thick coconut milk**" is called for, or use first-pressing coconut milk.

CORIANDER LEAVES; ROOTS; SEEDS: The leaves of the plant *Coriandrum sativum,* often known in the United States by its Mexican name, cilantro, are widely used in Burma and in fact all over Southeast Asia, usually as a last-minute fresh addition to a curry or a soup or salad. The Burmese word for coriander is *nunun;* the leaves are *nunun pin* and the seeds *nunun si.* The **roots** of coriander plants are used, pounded, in Tai Koen dishes as

CORIANDER SEEDS

well as in Thai curry pastes. Look for bunches of coriander with the roots still on. Store them in water, in the refrigerator, with the tops loosely covered with a plastic bag. When finished with the leaves and stems, store the roots in the freezer, wrapped in plastic. Add to your stock of roots whenever you have a chance. You can substitute the stems of coriander plants for the roots if necessary. **Coriander seeds,** round and off-white, are a savory spice in South Asian cooking and in a few Shan and Kachin dishes; in the West they are more often used in sweet baking.

CUCUMBER TENDRILS; CUCUMBER SHOOTS: The Bamar, Shan, Tai Koen, and Kachin all cook and eat the growing tips of vegetable vines such as peas (pea tendrils), cucumbers, and other similar vegetables like summer squash and gourds. They are parboiled and dressed as salads or added to soups, or lightly stir-fried and served as a vegetable dish. In Kengtung I heard cucumber and pumpkin tendrils called *pak payang* by both Shan and Tai Koen vendors; the Burmese word is *payon ywet.* They are sometimes available at farmers' markets in North America. Just chop them crosswise into 1- to 2-inch lengths and stir-fry them or add them to soups or curries.

CURRY; CURRIES: The moist main dishes that accompany rice in Burma are known in Burmese as *hin.* In English the usual word used for them is *curry.* The term comes from British India, where it came to denote any sauced dish of vegetables or meat or a mixture. The flavor base for Burmese curries is neither a "curry paste" such as people use when making some of the classic Thai curries, nor any version of "curry powder" that people in the West associate with dishes from India. Like many sauced dishes, Burmese curries start with flavors cooked in oil. Usually the early flavorings include chopped shallots, turmeric powder, perhaps some dried red chiles reduced to a paste or a powder, and often ginger or garlic. Whole spices such as those used in Bengali cooking are rarely used in traditional Burmese dishes.

DANDELION GREENS: *Taraxacum officinale.* These dark green leaves with their familiar jagged edges are now much more widely available in grocery stores, for they're being grown commercially in North America. They're rich in iron and in vitamins A and C. Chop them crosswise, discarding any tough stems, then stir-fry or include in any steamed vegetable dish to give a pleasing bitter edge.

DEEP-FRYING: This method of cooking food by immersing it in hot oil is widely used by street vendors in Burma. They usually deep-fry in a large wok, rather than in the deep-fryers used in fast-food restaurants in North America. Deep-frying cooks food by heating the moisture in the food, which both steam-cooks from inside and also escapes out into the hot oil (causing the sizzling sound we hear during deep-frying). The escaping steam pushes outward, which helps prevent the oil from penetrating the food. The important thing with deep-frying is to make sure the pan you are using is stable and that the oil is at the correct temperature: somewhere between 345 and 375°F, depending on the size and nature of the foods being fried. The oil needs to be hot enough to almost immediately create a cooked outer layer on the food, which helps prevent the absorption of oil. If the oil is not hot enough, it will soak into the food, leaving it oily and flaccid. If the oil is too hot, it will smoke and start to break down, creating undesirable compounds and an unpleasant taste and smell. In addition, overly hot oil will burn the outside before the center of the food is cooked.

If you have a cooking thermometer, use it to test the temperature of your oil. I usually use a cook's test instead. There are several of these. I hold a wooden chopstick vertically in the hot oil, with one end touching the bottom of the pan. If oil bubbles up along the chopstick, then the oil is hot enough (a gentle bubbling up is about 345 to 355°F and a more vigorous bubbling up is 360°F or so). Another test calls for dropping a cube of bread into the hot oil; it should take just under a minute to brown. And another option is to drop a small spoonful of batter into the oil. It should sink and then rise, without burning. If it burns or doesn't sink, lower the heat slightly.

Often I **substitute shallow frying** when traditionally deep-frying is called for. This can work well if you are cooking only small amounts for home use. The food must be turned constantly so that all surfaces get exposed to the hot oil.

To **clean oil after deep-frying,** so that you can use it again, toss in a handful of 1-inch (or so) bread cubes, together with several scallions. The bread will help absorb odors. Any oil that has a smell or has overheated to smoking during frying should not be used again but instead discarded or put to another purpose (used cooking oil is being recycled in some places and used as biofuel, for example).

DILL: *Anethum graveolens.* This strong-tasting herb is related to parsley and fennel and is associated with the cooking of northern and eastern Europe. It's not much used in Southeast Asia, except in outlying areas: by the Shan and Tai Koen in Kengtung, where it's called *pak ghee la* and used in soups and stews, and in northern Laos around Luang Prabang, where it flavors stews such as *or lam.*

DIVISIONS: See **political areas.**

DRIED ANCHOVIES: Clear plastic packages of these tiny silvery dried fish are sold in Southeast Asian and Chinese groceries, as well as in Japanese markets, where they're called *niboshi.* They keep well.

DRUMSTICK TREE: See **moringa.**

DUCK EGGS: Larger than hen eggs (about 70 grams) and widely available in Burma, duck eggs are preferred for making the hard-cooked eggs that accompany mohinga and other noodle dishes. In North America, duck eggs are sold at many farmers' markets and specialty stores. Duck eggs have less water and proportionately larger yolks than hen eggs. They can be substituted for hen eggs in baking; the usual substitution is one duck egg for every two medium hen eggs.

EGGPLANT: In Southeast Asia, people grow and eat a wide variety of eggplants, from long green

ASIAN EGGPLANTS

or pale violet or dark purple to round ones that may be white or white with pale green or bright yellow. All are varieties of *Solanum melongena,* a plant native to India that has been cultivated in Asia for millennia. Newcomers to the region find it hard to believe that eggplants can come in such different guises. In North America, a wider variety of eggplants is now available, especially in Southeast Asian grocery stores. In general, the long Asian eggplants are less bitter than the large round purple Mediterranean varieties; they are never presalted to draw out bitterness.

ENDIVE: *Chicorium endiva* is closely related to chicory, *Cichorium intybus,* and both are leafy greens (though they may also be red-colored) with a slightly bitter edge to their flavor. Both are available in well-stocked supermarkets and in Mediterranean groceries, especially in the winter months. I substitute endive or dandelion for the wild-gathered greens used in some Burmese and Kachin and Shan dishes, when I want a bitter note.

FERMENTED SHRIMP PASTE: See **shrimp paste.**

FERMENTED SOYBEANS: See **soybeans.**

FERMENTED TEA LEAVES: See **tea leaves.**

FISH AND SEAFOOD: The world of fish and seafood is a huge one, and bewildering to most of us in its complexity. Not only are there hundreds of species of fish, but there is endless advice about which fish are overfished, which ones endangered, and which ones advisable to eat—not to mention the arguments over health, safety, and sustainability. Rather than abandoning the idea of shopping for fish and seafood, I advise you to engage with it. Start simply, by consulting an online resource, such as www.foodandwaterwatch.org/fish/seafood/guide. Look for fish that are locally available—for example, freshwater fish, if you live far inland—and familiar to you. Then go looking for them at a well-stocked grocery store or fishmonger. When you want to try a fish that is unknown to you, look it up and see whether it's being raised or caught sustainably. Because the fish and seafood situation keeps evolving (some species do return to healthy levels and get moved off the endangered list), check online again from time to time.

FISH SAUCE; FERMENTED FISH; PICKLED FISH; SALTED FISH: Burmese fish sauce is called *ngan pyar yay.* It can be dark and pungent or clearer and red-tinted. The latter is made from shrimp, I am told. I substitute Thai fish sauce for Burmese, since it is easily available in North America; my preference is Squid brand. If you have the time, buy several bottles of different fish sauces and do a taste test. Try to avoid the ones that contain sugar; I find it muddies the flavor. See also **shrimp paste.**

FLOUR: See individual flours, e.g., **rice; semolina; tapioca.**

FRIED PORK SKIN; PORK CRACKLINGS; PORK SKIN: Called *chicharrones* in Mexico and the Philippines, this is a snack food and ingredient among Tai peoples, including the Shan (see Three-Layer Pork with Mustard Greens and Tofu, page 190, for example). It is made by slowly frying pieces of pig skin until the fat is rendered, leaving it crisp and cracker-like. See also Pork Belly Skin, page 189.

FRUITS: In Burma, as in other places in the tropics and subtropics, there's a whole world of amazing sweet fruit for eating. Fruit is a snack and is also "dessert" in Burma, a great way to end a meal. Most of the fruits available in Burma are very seasonal. Some are available only in hot season, others in rainy season, and so on. The fruits include cherimoya (*natawza*), durian (*duyin thi*), jackfruit (*peinne thi*), lychee (*hnin thi*), mango (*thayet thi*), mangosteen (*mingut thi*), papaya (*thimbaw*), pineapple (*nanat thi*), rambutan (*kyetmauk thi*), and watermelon (*paye thi*).

FRYING: See **deep-frying; stir-frying.**

GAI LAN: See **Chinese kale.**

GALANGAL: *Alpinia galanga* is sometimes called Siamese ginger; in Burmese it's *badai gaw*. It's a rhizome with a thinner, paler skin than ginger that is banded at regular intervals with fine lines. The smell and taste is resinous and aromatic. It's used in Shan cooking and in Thai curry pastes. Galangal is now available in Asian grocery stores. A smaller amount of ginger can be substituted, to give a taste hit and a little heat, but it lacks the distinctive earthy resinous flavor of galangal. Dried galangal has no flavor and is not worth buying.

GARLIC; ASIAN GARLIC: The garlic used in Burma, where it's called *kyetthen hpyu*, generally has much smaller cloves than those in North American garlic. Many cooks don't bother peeling individual cloves but just smash them with the flat side of a cleaver, or with a pestle, then add them to hot oil. The skins eventually float off and can be discarded. When the garlic is to be sliced—for making fried garlic, for example—it is peeled first.

The garlic available in the winter and spring in North America is often very dried out and thus

GARLIC

intense and harsh-tasting. *If you are using dried winter garlic,* and if the recipe calls for uncooked garlic, I suggest that you dry-roast it in a skillet or over a flame to soften its strong edge before using it. In Burma, unlike in Thailand, shallots rather than garlic are the primary aromatic used to flavor oil at the start of cooking. But garlic does play a role, and so does garlic oil. Remember that chopped or cooked garlic does not keep well, for it is an inviting home for bacteria; refrigerate cooked garlic (such as the garlic used to flavor Garlic Oil, page 25) and keep for no longer than five days.

GINGER; PICKLED GINGER: *Zingiber officinale* is just one of several rhizomes used for cooking in Burma. Young ginger has a fine, pale skin and sometimes pink tips on the rhizomes and is usually available in North America in late summer and early fall; mature ginger has a thicker brown skin but should still be plump and heavy, not dried out and wrinkled. Peel before using. Ginger is used minced as a flavoring in many dishes. **Pickled ginger** is the main ingredient in the delectable Punchy-Crunchy Ginger Salad (page 48). To make your own pickled ginger (it can be used the day after you make it), buy young ginger or, failing that, the plumpest, freshest mature ginger you can find. Peel it, then slice it very thinly (a benriner is the ideal tool for getting thin shavings; otherwise use a cleaver or a very sharp knife). For ½ pound of ginger, you will need 1 tablespoon sea salt, 1 cup rice vinegar, and ⅓ cup sugar. Add ½ teaspoon or so salt to the ginger slices, mix, and let stand for 15 minutes, then rinse off with boiling water and drain. Heat the vinegar, remaining salt, and the sugar in a small pot, stirring to dissolve the sugar. Pour boiling water into a widemouthed jar, then pour it off; use tongs or chopsticks to add the ginger to the jar. Pour the vinegar mixture over and cover tightly. Let stand at least overnight before using; store in the refrigerator for up to 2 months.

GLUTINOUS RICE: See **rice.**

GOURDS AND SUMMER SQUASHES: The wax gourd *Benincasa hispida*, also known as winter melon, is a large fast-growing gourd with a pale green to white interior. It is grown all over Southeast Asia and in China. In Burma, it is used in curries; in Thailand, in soups and curries. The bottle gourd *Lagenaria siceraria* is another similar vegetable, longer rather than fat, pale green outside, with firm white flesh. There's a gourd in Burma called calabash (*boothi* in Burmese) that is used in curries; it has a narrow neck bulging out into a large round shape and a fuzzy pale-green skin and white flesh. And there's angle-gourd, also known as luffa (*thabut* in Burmese), with seven ridges running lengthwise on its long slender green shape. Chayote and deseeded zucchini, pattypan, and other summer squash can be substituted for these gourds and for one another with some differences in cooking times and textures.

GURKHA: The name taken by soldiers from central Nepal who fought for the British as part of the Indian army and later the British army. The Gurkhas (sometimes spelled Ghurkas or Ghorkas) were famed for their tenacity and fearlessness in many British wars. A number of them served in Burma before and after the Second World War;

some of those settled in Myitkyina and other places in Kachin State, as well as elsewhere in Burma.

HIBISCUS; HIBISCUS FLOWER; HIBISCUS LEAVES; ROSELLE: The hibiscus, *Hibiscus sabdariffa*, is an ornamental shrub native to Africa. In Burma its English-language name is roselle; in Burmese it is

HIBISCUS FLOWERS

chimbaung. Its red flowers, stripped of their petals (so the calyxes only), yield a tart-sweet tea or juice when boiled in water with sugar. The leaves are used as a tart ingredient in curries and in soups.

HOG PLUM: *Spondia pinnata* is a greenish egg-shaped fruit with a large stone; its flesh has a tart astringent taste that sweetens as you chew it. A related fruit, also called hog plum (sometimes olive plum) in English, is *Elaeocarpus madopetalus*, which is called *makawk* in Thai. Both have a tart taste and make a great salsa or chutney. There is no exact substitute, but tomatillos are what I suggest using in the chutney recipe on page 202. You could also use gooseberries or sour plums such as damsons, or another tart fleshy fruit. Finely minced green *makawk* wood is a traditional binding ingredient in Shan meatballs (see Lemongrass-Ginger Sliders, page 192).

INDIAN FOOD: In Burma there is still an important community of South Asian ancestry, even though many in that community left the country after the military coup in 1962. There are South Asian shops and restaurants in Mandalay and in Rangoon especially, and Indian snacks, from samosas to parathas, are available at almost every tea shop. In the Indian restaurants, often referred to as "Chetty" restaurants (a link to the origins of some immigrants in Chettinand on India's east coast), there's a wide variety of pulaus and curries and dals available, especially at lunchtime. There's been a notable adaptation to local tastes, because most of the time the meal comes served with a traditional-style Burmese sour soup and a small Burmese palate-freshening salad of grated lettuce and sliced shallots.

INTHA PEOPLE: The Intha live in settlements near Inle Lake and in "floating villages" on the lake. They speak an old version of Burmese (they probably moved to the Inle region from somewhere south). They are known for cultivating tomatoes hydroponically on their floating islands, as well as for their technique of leg-rowing while standing up.

KACHIN PEOPLE: An umbrella term for a large group of related peoples that includes the Jingpo, Lisu, Trone, Dalaung, Gauri, Hkahku, Duleng, Maru (Lawgore), Rawang, Lashi (La Chid), Lawa Atsi, and Taron, all of whom speak Tibeto-Burman languages. Hilltop dwellers, by tradition hunter-gatherers and swidden agriculturalists, the Kachin peoples gradually migrated south over the centuries from the mountains of Tibet into the hills of the upper Irrawaddy basin, displacing other peoples, including the Shan and the Chin. Many of them were converted to Christianity in the nineteenth and twentieth centuries; some remain animist.

KACHIN STATE: The northernmost state, with a mixed population of people who have over time filtered into the area and whose populations straddle the international borders with neighboring countries. The majority population is Kachin (see above). Others include various peoples from the Indian subcontinent such as Gurkhas and Punjabis, as well as Chinese from Yunnan and elsewhere, Shan, Chin, and Bamar. The capital of Kachin State is Myitkyina; Bhamo is another important town. Both of them lie on the Irrawaddy River, which flows south through the center of the state.

KAFFIR LIMES: See **limes.**

KAPOK FLOWER: The red flower of the kapok tree, *Bombex ceiba*, is used dried in soups in Burma and northern Thailand. In Burmese it's called *lepan bwin.* The tree is tall and blooms in dry season (February); the fruits contain a soft fiber (kapok) that is used for stuffing quilts and mattresses.

KAREN (ALSO CALLED KAYIN) PEOPLE; KAYIN (FORMERLY KAREN) STATE: The Karen are a Sino-Tibetan people with many subgroups. They speak a Tibeto-Burman language and are rice-growing agriculturalists. Karen live in many parts of Burma and are also settled in Thailand along the Burma border. During the British colonial era, many Karen were moved to the Irrawaddy Delta to establish rice cultivation there. Karen still live in the delta around Pathein and east from there. The Karen "homeland" area is Karen State (now called Kayin State), bordered on the east by Thailand, on the north by Kayah State, and on the west by Mon State. The Salween River flows through the capital, Hpa'an. Many Karen were converted to Christianity by missionaries in the last 150 years; others are Buddhists or animists. The Karen were the first group to take up arms against the central government after independence. That struggle continues. As a result, there are many Karen who are internally displaced people, and many more have sought refuge across the Thai border in the area around Mae Sot.

KAYAH PEOPLE; KARENNI; PADAUNG; KAYAH STATE: The Kayah, also known as Karenni, Red Karen, or **Padaung,** are a Sino-Tibetan people who live in the mountains of eastern Burma. The state is bordered by Shan State on the north, Thailand on the east, and Kayin State on the south; the capital is Loikaw. The Karenni have been battling the central government of Burma for years, and many have become refugees on the Thai border (in the Mae Hong Son area) or remain in Kayah State as internally displaced people. Kayah State is still closed to foreign travelers.

LEEK ROOT: The root of *Allium tuberosum* is grown in Yunnan, in northern Thailand, and in the Shan areas of Burma, where it's known as *jumyit*. It looks like a bunch of white spidery roots. The Shan and other peoples in the region use it chopped in sour soups and in pickles, or eat it raw with rice. The flavor is oniony and earthy, the texture chewy.

LEMONGRASS: *Cymbopogon citratus* is an aromatic herb that is widely used in Southeast Asian cooking, from Burma (where it's called *zabalin*) to Vietnam. To use it, cut off the tough root end and peel off the outer layer or two of stem. Only the bottom two inches or so of the stem have intense flavor; the rest can be discarded. Lemongrass is used crushed (smashed a little with the flat side of a cleaver) to infuse its flavor into soups, or minced (a cleaver is the easiest tool for slicing it finely crosswise) as part of a flavor paste. It is now widely available in well-stocked supermarkets as well as in Southeast Asian groceries. Look for firm fat stems; if they are very light and dried out they will have less flavor and will be tougher to slice. Store in the refrigerator.

LIMES; WILD LIMES; KAFFIR LIMES; MAKRUT LIMES; LIME LEAVES; CITRON: All limes and citrons originated in northeast India, according to botanists. Wild limes, also called **kaffir limes** (an objectionable name, given the meaning of "kaffir") or makrut limes, *Citrus hystrix*, have a rough, bumpy green skin and are lemon-sized. They are used in Southeast Asia for their zest, which is very aromatic. (In Burma a related fruit, called citron in English and *shauk thi* in Burmese, is used to make a salad; see Succulent Grapefruit [or Pomelo] Salad, page 45.) The **leaves of the wild lime** are double-lobed and very aromatic. Very tender leaves are used whole in salads in Burma, or if coarser are deveined, sliced into a fine chiffonade, and used as a topping and flavoring. When you find wild lime leaves (in Southeast Asian markets), buy generously, then store them in the freezer in a well-sealed plastic bag. Use them straight from the freezer. **Common lime,** *tham ba*, is a hybrid with a smooth skin that turns from green to yellow when it is completely ripe. The limes in Burma, like those in Thailand, are small, round, and juicy; freshly squeezed lime juice is used to give a sour highlight in salads and in condiment sauces.

LONG BEANS: See **yard-long beans.**

MANGO: *Mangifera indica* is a fruit-bearing tree native to Asia that has been cultivated there for millennia. It is now widely grown in the tropical and subtropical Americas too. Mango trees grow tall. They flower in the dry season and bear fruit in the hot season just before the start of the rains (in Burma and the rest of Southeast Asia, that means from April through June, depending on the variety). Like apples, mangoes do not grow true from seed but are propagated vegetatively to maintain varietal characteristics. The fruit may be sweet or sour when ripe. Sweet mangoes are usually orange yellow when ripe, and sour ones green. Unripe sweet mangoes are also tart and green, but then sweeten as they ripen. In Burma tart mangoes are eaten as a vegetable, usually in salads (see Green Mango Salad, page 63), but also as part of a Raw and Cooked Vegetable Plate (page 217). Sweet mangoes are eaten in great quantity in mango season, as a sweet snack at any time of day.

To prepare a mango, cut it lengthwise by standing it on its side and cutting just off the center line. The seed inside is flat, and you want to cut down close to the seed. Repeat on the other side of the seed. The two hemispheres can then be peeled. Or the flesh can be cut in a cross-hatch pattern, the skin inverted to press the fruit out in a curve; the fruit is then eaten directly off the skin.

MEALS; THE DAY IN FOOD: In Burma most people start the day with an early breakfast, then have a big rice meal for lunch, a snack in the late afternoon, and a light supper.

Breakfast varies, as it does in many parts of the world. It may be rice (often left over from the previous day) lightly stir-fried with shallots or with cooked chickpeas, eaten plain or topped with a fried egg and/or a little meat. Another possibility is mohinga, noodles with broth and flavorings, often topped with crispy fritters. And yet another is a South Asian–inflected breakfast called *nan-piar bei*, which is a tandoor-baked unleavened flatbread topped with tender cooked chickpeas or cowpeas and sometimes a little sugar too.

Lunch is the main meal. Around noontime, friends or even strangers will inquire, "Have you eaten lunch?," for the meal anchors the day. Given a choice, most people sit down to a classic lunch of rice and one or more curries served with a soup and with several condiments and salsas, as well as a plate of raw and/or steamed vegetables; see Rice Meals (page 16).

For supper, a smaller meal than lunch, people eat leftovers, with rice and some of the flavorings and curries from lunch. There may be an omelet made fresh for the meal, or another vegetable dish to round things out.

Tea shops are meeting places where people talk and sip tea or coffee at all hours. In Rangoon the shops often serve a wide variety of foods, from samosas, *nan-piar*, and parathas to simple steamed dim sum (dumplings of various kinds) and omelets. It's like a survey course of the main culinary threads in Burma: Burmese, Chinese, Indian, all subtly altered and cross-influenced by one another.

MINT: *Mentha spicatai* (*butinan* in Burmese) is widely used as a fresh herb, especially in non-Bamar households. Perhaps that reflects the fact that mint grows best in slightly cool environments, so that the dry hot Irrawaddy Valley, the heartland of Bamar culture, doesn't suit it as well. Use a regular spearmint in any recipes that call for mint. Even though the flavor is very different, feel free to substitute it for coriander leaves if you prefer, when they are called for as a fresh garnish.

MISO PASTE; BROWN MISO: Miso is a Japanese flavoring and ingredient. It is sometimes called fermented soybean paste, though in fact it can be made from barley and from rice as well as from soybeans. It is rooted in the same tradition of fermenting soybeans to preserve their food value as the Shan fermented soybeans are. A number of the Shan recipes in this book call for fermented soybeans or for Soybean Disks (page 40). Miso paste—which has the advantage of being readily available in supermarkets and health food stores—is given as a substitute, for those who do not have access to fermented soybeans or the inclination to prepare them.

Miso comes in many colors and flavors, from sweet pale yellow miso to very dark and strong-tasting miso made from barley. The closest substitute for fermented soybeans is a miso that is a medium brown (sometimes labeled "red miso"), not sweet, made from rice and soybeans or just soybeans. When you shop for miso, look for a medium-brown paste and then be sure to store it in the refrigerator. When you are making miso soup, the instructions are to bring water to the boil, then remove it from the heat and stir in the miso paste, not letting it cook over the heat. But when miso is used as a flavoring, as it is in these recipes, it is added before the end of cooking and allowed to blend in with other ingredients.

MIXING BY HAND: In Burma both salads and noodle dishes are mixed and blended by hand, either by the cook just before serving, or by the person eating before starting to eat. The gestures used, and the care taken to mix everything meticulously and thoroughly, are distinctive, not a technique I have seen anywhere else. So for example the ingredients for a salad will be assembled in a shallow bowl and then blended by hand, the fingers working to massage the ingredients together with care, so that flavorings and textures are evenly distributed.

MON PEOPLE; MON STATE: In the third century B.C. the emperor Ashoka sent a Buddhist delegation to visit and bring news of Buddhism to the Mon, who dominated the southern coast of Burma. Beginning about 1,300 years ago, the Mon had a huge trading kingdom along the Andaman Sea coast that stretched across the Irrawaddy Delta and all the way south nearly to Dawei (Tavoy). In the sixteenth century there was a Mon kingdom with a capital at Pegu (Bago). In modern Burma, Mon State lies south of Bago and is centered around the Salween River as it reaches the coast at Moulmein, the state's capital. Mon State is bordered by Kayin (Karen) State on the east and Tenasserim (Tanintharyi) to the south; to the north lies the Bago region. The Mon alphabet, together with Pali writing, is the origin of modern Bamar script. Mon-style Buddhist structures, *chedis*, and payas, including Shwedagon, are found in Bagan, Rangoon, and south of there. But present-day Mon people are slowly being assimilated and losing their language (a member of the Mon-Khmer language family, and unrelated to Burmese, Shan, or Karen). The Mon State army has been fighting the central government for decades.

MORINGA: The moringa tree (*Moringa oleifera;* commonly called a **drumstick tree**) yields long, baton-shaped podlike fruit that is picked young, chopped crosswise, and eaten boiled as a vegetable, both in Burma and in the Indian subcontinent. The tree's leaves are cooked and eaten like spinach; high in calcium and iron, they are used medicinally to lower blood pressure. The seeds of ripe drumsticks yield a good-tasting oil, moringa oil (also known as **ben oil**), that can also be applied to the skin.

MORNING GLORY GREENS; WATER MORNING GLORY; WATER CONVOLVULUS: The hollow stems and long tender leaves of *Ipomoea aquatica* are chopped and stir-fried all over Southeast Asia, for the plant grows wild in ditches and ponds, so it's widely available. Sometimes in Burma small pieces of stem and leaf are part of the vegetable plate, either steamed or raw. In Burmese the vegetable is called *gazun ywet;* in Thai, *pak boong;* and in Vietnamese, *rau muong.* The version sold in Asian grocery stores in North America is a slightly tougher Chinese variety that needs less watery growing conditions.

MSG (MONOSODIUM GLUTAMATE): A white crystalline powder, MSG is an industrial product developed as a flavor enhancer at the end of the nineteenth century. It gives a taste of meatiness, umami, to dishes. It replaces long-simmered bone broths and mushroom broths. Its use has been associated with various long-term illnesses, and in addition many people have a reaction to it, getting a headache or becoming dizzy when, for example, they eat a soup that has been heavily flavored with MSG. Many cooks in Burma still use it, for they have limited access to meat, and they believe that MSG gives their food a better, deeper flavor. Whenever I have said that I don't use it, Burmese cooks suggest that I compensate by increasing the amount of fish sauce. This is not because MSG is salty, but in order to replace its umami-flavor-giving properties (see "Umami," page 31).

MUSHROOMS; OYSTER MUSHROOMS; SHIITAKE MUSHROOMS: Mushrooms are fungi that live off decomposing matter. There are many wild edible mushrooms in Southeast Asia that are especially valued by people living in outlying areas. Oyster mushrooms (there are various subspecies, but all are members of the species *Pleurotus*) are cultivated mushrooms that grow in clumps (on sawdust or rice straw) and are widely available. They have broad flat tops, and the gills underneath extend all the way down the stems. Shiitake mushrooms, *Lentinula edodes*, grow on wood and have been cultivated for centuries in China and Japan. Shiitakes have an intense flavor and are reported to help lower cholesterol. They are often sold dried and are available in that form in large clear bags in Asian grocery stores. Soak for fifteen minutes to soften before trimming and cooking.

MUSSELS: See **shelling oysters; shelling mussels.**

MUSTARD GREENS; PICKLED MUSTARD GREENS: Like gailan and broccoli and cabbage, mustard is a *Brassica*, a member of the cabbage family. In Burmese it is *mohn nyin ywet*. It is used as a vegetable in stir-fries but gets even wider play in pickled form. Pickled mustard greens are available in Chinese groceries. They are made by mashing the greens a little to crush them, letting them dry in the sun, then pickling them with salt. This is a

MASHING GREENS WITH SALT

classic Chinese method of pickling, but in Burma there are often other flavors added too, such as ginger and turmeric. ***Pak som*** and ***pakkat som*** are the Shan and Thai terms, respectively, for pickled greens, usually made by letting the greens dry in the sun or air, then packing them with salt in a sealed container. They give off their liquid and keep indefinitely. They're used as a table condiment, a useful vegetable when there are none around. In the Shan hills near Hsipaw I came upon a Shan household that prepared preserved greens in a related way. They mashed them with salt, shaped them into small nest-like coils, and put them on a rack in the sun to dry out for a day or two. The dry nests that result are then available to be tossed into soup.

MYANMAR: See **Bamar.**

NAGA PEOPLE: There is a sizable Naga population in Burma around the upper Chindwin River; just across the Indian border is Nagaland, where the majority of the Naga live. Traditionally tribal and with a history of headhunting, the Naga were feared by the British and by lowlanders in general. Many Naga were converted to Christianity by missionaries in the nineteenth and twentieth centuries. The Naga are renowned for their fine textile traditions.

NAPA CABBAGE; CHINESE CABBAGE: This member of the *Brassicas, Brassica pekinensis* var. *cylindrica*, is very pale green with long leaves that form a solid long head. It is also known as celery cabbage in Southeast Asia; the Burmese name is *monyin pyu*. It can be eaten raw or cooked, and is a useful winter vegetable. Napa cabbage is now widely available in North America.

NASTURTIUM: *Tropeaolum majus* has edible leaves with a strong, distinctive taste and is one of the options when you are looking for leaves to add to Burmese soups, salads, or curries (to

Mimi's Bean Soup with Tender Leaves, page 98, for example). Watercress is a related plant.

NGAPI: See **shrimp paste.**

NOODLES

Bean Threads: Bean threads, also known as glass noodles, are *chan sen* in Burmese and *wun sen* in Thai. They are made from mung beans that are processed to make a paste, then extruded in thin threads and dried. Before they are cooked, they are tough white strands that are most often sold in coils. Soak before using and then cut into lengths with scissors if you wish. Some bean threads contain tapioca starch as well as mung bean starch. Some bean threads soften very quickly in cooking; others are more resilient and may take 5 minutes or more to soften.

Egg Noodles: Made from wheat flour strengthened with eggs, egg noodles are the base of several noodle dishes that consist of noodles, a sauce, and a broth, as well as toppings. Store egg noodles in the refrigerator; they have a very short shelf life.

Flat Rice Noodles, Fresh; Dried Rice Noodles; Rice Stick: Fresh **rice noodles** are a real treat, tender yet a little elastic. You can find them in well-stocked Chinese and Southeast Asian groceries, in the cooler section. They harden if refrigerated, so are best used within two days. Rinse off any oil; they are often lightly coated with oil to prevent them from sticking together. If you can't find rice noodles, you may find **rice noodle sheets** (often labeled "sa-ho" noodles)—just slice them into ribbons and proceed. The easiest rice noodles for the cook are **dried rice noodles,** also known as **rice stick**. They come in narrow and medium widths, in clear cellophane packages weighing 1 pound. Soak them in lukewarm water as directed before stir-frying. If using in soup, dip them into boiling water until just softened, then serve.

Rice Vermicelli: Called *kanom jiin* by the Tai Koen and in Thailand, and *khao sien'* by the Shan

in Kengtung, these fine hand-made fresh rice noodles are the essential element in mohinga. The noodles are made from a lightly fermented dough of rice and water that is pressed through small holes into boiling water. The fine white strands cook and set in the hot water, then are coiled up and cooled before going to the market to be sold.

Round Rice Noodles, Fresh: Known as *mondi* or *monti* in Mandalay, where they are a specialty, these fatter-than-spaghetti round rice noodles have a pleasing bite. You may find a version of them in the cooler of Asian grocery stores; use immediately, since they have a short shelf life.

NUTMEG: The nutmeg tree, *Myristica fragrans,* is native to the Moluccas, the Spice Islands of Indonesia, but is now grown elsewhere too. Nutmeg spice is the seed or nut of the fruit of the tree. The seed is covered by a lacy outer layer, which is the spice called mace. The aromatic nut is best freshly ground on a fine grater.

OILS: See specific oils.

OKRA: A member of the mallow family, *Abelmoschus esculentus* is a green vegetable that is also known as lady's fingers or gumbo, and in Burmese is *yonbaday thi.* The green pods contain a lot of white seeds in a sticky paste. Okra can be cooked whole or chopped and fried (see Okra-Shallot Stir-Fry, page 102). Steamed whole okra is often served as part of a Raw and Cooked Vegetable Plate (page 217), and very tender young okra is sometimes one of the raw vegetables there.

OYSTERS: See **shelling oysters.**

OYSTER SAUCE: A dark-colored liquid flavoring widely used in Cantonese cooking and also in Chinese-influenced Southeast Asian cooking. Originally made of cooked-down oyster-cooking broth, it is now usually made of water flavored with oyster extract, sugar, and salt. It adds depth of flavor to stir-fried greens. Oyster sauce is sold in Asian grocery stores.

PADAUNG PEOPLE: See **Kayah.**

PAK SOM; PAKKAT SOM: See **mustard greens.**

PALAUNG PEOPLE: A Mon-Khmer group who live in villages in the hills of Shan State, especially near Kalaw and west of Hsipaw. The Palaung grow rice, live in long houses, and are mostly Buddhist, although they are now being targeted by Christian evangelicals.

PALM SUGAR: See **sugar.**

PANEER: A firm fresh cheese made from cow's milk. Paneer stays firm when heated, rather than melting, and is a staple in parts of northern India. It is sold in South Asian groceries. To make ½ pound of firm paneer, you will need a sieve or a colander lined with cheesecloth, 2 quarts whole milk, and some freshly squeezed lemon juice. Heat the milk to a boil in a heavy pot, stirring frequently to prevent scorching. Lower the heat and add the lemon juice a tablespoon at a time, stirring, until (usually after the third tablespoon) the milk turns and the white curds separate from the pale green whey. Remove from the heat. Place the cheesecloth-lined sieve or colander over a bowl and pour in the contents of the pot. The whey will drain through. Pour cold water onto the curds to rinse away the lemon taste. Pull the edges of the cheesecloth together, squeeze out any extra water, and tie up your improvised cheesecloth bag over a bowl, so that the curds can drain further and firm up. After 20 minutes you will have soft cheese. To make firm paneer, leave in the cheesecloth, flatten it into an approximate square, put it in a shallow bowl, and place a weight on top. The weight will squeeze out more moisture and cause the cheese to firm up.

PA-O PEOPLE: The Pa-O are part of the family of

Tibeto-Burman peoples that includes the Karen (Kayin) and Kayah (Karenni and Padaung). The Pa-O population is found mostly in Kayah State and Shan State, but another important community lives around Thamanyat Kuang, a large temple complex east of Hpa'an in Kayin State.

PAPAYA: Native to Central America, the papaya (*Carica papaya*) is now widely grown in subtropical Asia. In Burmese, it's *thimbaw*. Papaya fruit grows in clumps at the top of spindly-looking trees that mature very quickly and produce fruit year-round. The fruits are long and slightly bulbous, green skinned and hard when unripe, with pale green flesh. They ripen and soften to yellow- or orange-colored skin with yellow to almost-red flesh. The

PAPAYAS

skin is fine and supple and inedible; the seeds are black and are an old remedy against intestinal worms.

Green papaya is eaten as a vegetable, usually as a salad, from India to Southeast Asia; ripe papaya is eaten as a fruit, usually with a squeeze of lime juice to balance what traditional medicine believes to be its "heat."

PEANUTS; PEANUT OIL: Although they grow in the ground, peanuts (*Arachis hypogaea*, called *myaypei* in Burmese) are in fact legumes, as the word *pea* indicates. They are rich in oil and a good source of protein. In Burma peanuts are used roasted and crushed as a flavoring and texture in salads, but their main use is for oil. The dry zone in the middle of the country, around Mandalay and Bagan, is ideal for growing peanuts. The oil is pressed from the seeds, and the mass that remains is often dressed with flavorings (finely sliced lime leaves, lime juice, shallots, etc.) and used as the base for a kind of salad.

Most peanut oil available in North America is produced in the United States or in China. The latter is now often sold blended with vegetable oil of some kind, usually safflower. Try to find pure peanut oil to use for deep-frying, or use (unroasted) sesame oil.

The raw peanuts that are called for in the recipe for roasted peanuts (see page 35) are sold in Asian groceries, as well as in health food stores and some large well-stocked supermarkets. Store them in the refrigerator, well-sealed. I like buying the nuts that still have their papery wrappers on because they seem fresher to me, generally, than the bare peanuts. Make sure to read the label when you're shopping: some of the raw-looking peanuts sold in Asian groceries have already been boiled.

Some people are allergic to peanuts, violently so. They can substitute unroasted sesame oil (see **sesame**) for peanut oil in the recipes, and toasted sesame seeds or split soybeans for the peanuts called for in some recipes.

PEA TENDRILS; PEA SHOOTS: All through the Mekong region, pea tendrils—the growing tip of the pea plant *Pisum sativum* var. *saccharatum*— are used as a raw green or a lightly cooked vegetable. They have become much more widely available in North America in the last ten years or so. Some are very fine, for they're the young sprouts of green pea plants; others are coarser and stronger, and look as if they were cut from a tall growing pea plant. The former can be stir-fried after a little chopping; the latter should be chopped into bite-sized lengths before stir-frying.

The former can be eaten raw, or added to soups at the last moment; the latter are much better after being cooked to wilt them thoroughly. See also **cucumber tendrils.**

PENNYROYAL: *Mentha pulegium,* a low-growing member of the mint family with a strong spearmint aroma when crushed. The oil is poisonous, but the leaves were used as an herb flavoring by the Romans and in Europe until several centuries ago. The mint-like herb that I encountered in Kengtung, which was called *pak du'ean,* seemed to me to be a kind of pennyroyal. I was told it was good for sore throats, and usually used by the Tai Koen to flavor pork dishes.

PENNYWORT: *Centella asiatica,* an herb that is often called *gotu kola* in English (the name it goes by in Sri Lanka). In Burma it is called *myin kwa ywet* and the round green leaves are believed to be good for the kidneys, much as dandelion leaves are; they are used fresh to make salads. If you find pennywort in a Southeast Asian or South Asian grocery store, use it in Tender Greens Salad with Crispy Fried Shallots (page 49), but don't cook it at all—just use it well-washed and fresh. Western researchers report that gotu kola leaves seem to have tumor-inhibiting powers.

PEPPER; BLACK PEPPER; PEPPER LEAVES: The pepper (*Piper*) family includes the vine that produces peppercorns (that are processed into black and white peppercorns), as well as the vine (*Piper betle*) whose leaves are used to wrap areca nut and lime to make "betel nut chew" and the pepper vine *Piper sarmentosum.* The latter is the source of the shiny dark green tender pepper leaves that are used in Burma, Thailand, Laos, and Vietnam as raw or cooked greens as well as wrappers for savory snacks (*miang* in Shan and Thai). In Vietnam the leaves are called *la lot;* they're used most famously to wrap ground beef that is grilled as one of the *Bo Bay Mon* (beef seven ways) dishes. Sometimes pepper leaves are available in Southeast Asian groceries. See also **Sichuan pepper.**

PEPPER WOOD; SAKHAN: The stem of a member of the *Piper* family, *Piper interruptum* is used as a flavoring in Shan, Palaung, Lao, and northern Thai cooking. The northern Thai and the Lao call it *sakhan;* the Palaung call it *kham.* The plant is a liana, a twining vine that needs shade and moisture. The stem (sold as small lengths of wood in markets) is used either as a thin slice of wood that flavors a stew or a broth and is inedible (rather as a bay leaf or a cinnamon stick is included as a flavoring to be set aside rather than chewed) or is finely minced so that it blends into other ingredients.

PICKLED MUSTARD GREENS: See **mustard greens.**

PLACE-NAMES: As mentioned on page 3, the names of many towns and political divisions have changed over the centuries in Burma. For example, Rakhine State used to be known as Arakan, and its capital, Sittwe, was called Akyub when the British controlled the area. Similarly, the town of Dawei on the south coast was known as Tavoy under the British; the storied place of ancient monuments and temples, Bagan, is often spelled Pagan on older maps, and the town of Bago is Pegu on British maps. The renaming trend has only accelerated in the five decades since the military takeover of 1962; for example, these days the Irrawaddy River, Burma's main artery, is transcribed into our alphabet as Ayeyawaddy; however, as with the name of the country itself, I use the more familiar spelling.

Complicating matters, as Burmese place-names are transcribed into the Western alphabet, spelling can vary, partly because transliteration standards have changed over time and partly because people use different systems. Just to cite one example, the capital of eastern Shan State,

Kengtung, is also spelled Chiang Tung.

The following list, while not comprehensive, shows the most common changes.

Old	New
Irrawaddy River	Ayeyawaddy River
Pagan	Bagan
Pegu	Bago
Pathein	Bassein
Tavoy	Dawei
Karenni State	Kayah State
Karen State	Kayin State
Moulmein	Mawlamyine
Burma	Myanmar
Yaunghwe	Nyaungshwe
Arakan State	Rakhine State
Akyub	Sittwe
Tenasserim	Tanintharyi
Rangoon	Yangon

PLUM TOMATO: See **Roma tomato.**

POLITICAL AREAS: Burma is divided into two kinds of larger units: states and regions. The seven states are areas where one or more non-Bamar people are in the majority, while the regions (formerly called divisions) are areas whose population is predominantly Bamar. The states are Kachin, Kayah (formerly Karenni), Kayin (formerly

POMELOS

Karen), Chin, Mon, Rakhine (formerly Arakan), and Shan; the regions are Sagaing, Bago, Magway, Mandalay, Yangon, Ayeyarwady, and Tanintharyi (formerly Tenasserim).

POMELO: Also sometimes called shaddock, the pomelo, fruit of *Citrus maxima,* is the largest of the citrus fruits; pomelos can weigh more than 15 pounds. The tree is native to Southeast Asia. The fruit has a very thick skin, and the flesh of the fruit is less juicy than that of grapefruit. (Grapefruit is a hybrid created in Barbados over two hundred years ago by cross-breeding the pomelo and the mandarin orange.)

PORK BELLY; THREE-LAYER PORK: Pork belly looks like pale slab bacon. It has a rind or a skin on it, and underneath are alternating layers of meat and fat. Cut off the skin before trying to slice it. The fat can be rendered from the skin to give you lard and cracklings (see **fried pork skins**). In the last few years, it has become more widely available as Western-trained chefs have discovered its wonderful flavor and texture. Look for it in butcher shops or, failing that, in the meat section of large, well-stocked grocery stores. See also Pork Belly Skin, page 189.

PORK CRACKLINGS; PORK SKIN: See **fried pork skin.**

PUMPKIN; SQUASH: The usual pumpkin in Burma and other parts of Southeast Asia is a flattened globe with dark green skin, hard flesh, and a yellow-orange interior; its Latin name is *Cucurbita moschata,* and in Burmese it's *payon thi.* It is used in making sweets as well as vegetable curries. The tendrils, or tender shoots (*payon ywet*), are used in soups and salads (see **cucumber tendrils**). Other pumpkin or squash can be substituted, including Japanese kabocha and Caribbean pumpkin.

PUNJABIS; PUNJAB: Among those who came from the Subcontinent with the British in the

SQUASH

nineteenth century (see Burma over Time, page 306) and later on, in the course of the Second World War, were a large number of people from the Punjab. That's the area, divided now between India and Pakistan, that is a fertile wheat-growing region watered by five rivers (*panj* in Punjab means five). Although many Punjabis left Burma after the 1962 coup, many others stayed on. Some are Sikh, others Muslim or Hindu. See also "Echoes of the Past," page 134.

QUARRY TILES; UNGLAZED QUARRY TILES: See **baking stone.**

RAKHINE PEOPLE; RAKHINE STATE; ROHINGYA: Rakhine (sometimes transcribed **Rakhaing**) is the modern name for the west coast of Burma, immediately south of the Bangladeshi border. This area was formerly called Arakan. The Arakan people, now the **Rakhine** people, speak a Burmese language that is different from central Burmese. They are predominantly Buddhist, although there are also many Muslims. Some of the Muslims in Rakhine are descended from early Muslim traders and settlers, some are of Bangladeshi origin, and most are labeled Rohingya (also transcribed **Rohinga**). The Rohingya have faced persecution from the Burmese government for years; as a result many have fled to Bangladesh, Thailand, or Malaysia.

RICE: *Oryza sativa* is grown in most regions of Southeast Asia. In well-watered level areas such as valley floors and deltas, rice is grown in level irrigated fields and two crops a year can be grown. In the upland areas, where there is little water available for irrigation, the rice crop is seeded just as the rainy season begins, then harvested at the start of the dry season in October–November. In Burma the main rice resembles Thai **jasmine**, being fine, tender, and aromatic. It is cooked in a measured amount of water. **Sticky rice**, also known as **glutinous rice**, has lower amylose, so it absorbs less water as it cooks (usually by steaming) and is softer and more clinging. It is used for making sweets and for brewing liquor; it is the daily staple rice for the Tai Koen people (and in northern Thailand and Laos). **Black and white sticky rice** is a common breakfast treat in Burma. **Broken rice** is used for rice soups and by people who cannot afford higher-quality rice; it consists of a high proportion of broken grains, so that it does not cook to an even texture. **Brown rice** (rice with the bran still on it) is not a popular food. **Toasted rice powder** is raw rice that has been dry-cooked in a skillet and then ground; it is used as an ingredient in soup by the Kachin and Karen (see page 224).

RICE FLOUR; GLUTINOUS RICE FLOUR; STICKY RICE FLOUR; SWEET RICE FLOUR: When buying rice flour, make sure that you buy the one you need. Sticky rice flour, also called sweet or glutinous rice flour, is made from sticky rice and produces a very soft dough. Regular rice flour has a higher amylose content and so produces a drier, stronger texture. One cannot be substituted for the other.

ROHINGYA; ROHINGA: See **Rakhine.**

ROMA TOMATO: A fleshy, small variety of tomato that is often used to make tomato sauces. Romas grow well in dry heat and so are often grown in Burma in the dry season. Other tomatoes can be substituted, though it's best to cook them down a little, or pour off some of their liquid, since they are generally less fleshy and dense than Romas.

ROSELLE: See **hibiscus.**

SAKHAN: See **pepper wood.**

SALT; SALT WELLS; SEA SALT: The salt used in Burma may be sea salt or salt produced by cooking down water from salt wells. I like to use sea salt or kosher salt; use what pleases you, but unless you have strong reasons for needing iodine, try to avoid iodized salt when cooking Burmese dishes.

SAWTOOTH HERB: *Eryngium foetidum.* Sometimes referred to as "long coriander" or "broad leaf coriander," or by its Mexican name "culantro," sawtooth herb has long green leaves, like a smaller cousin of romaine lettuce, but with a spiky-looking edging. As its Latin name indicates, it has a strong smell. It's not used raw, but is added as an aromatic toward the end of cooking and gives a taste somewhat like coriander leaves. It's usually sold in bundles in Asian grocery stores, often together with other herbs that are used to flavor Vietnamese soups. The Burmese name is *Shan nun nun* (meaning "Shan coriander"); the northern Thai name is *pak pai;* in Vietnam it's *ngo om.*

SEMOLINA FLOUR: This coarse-textured pale-yellow flour is ground from durum wheat. It is used for making pasta and for a number of both savory and sweet dishes in the northern part of the Indian subcontinent. It is sold in Italian groceries and large supermarkets, as well as in Indian groceries, where it is usually labeled *sooji* or *suji.*

SESAME; SESAME OIL; SESAME PASTE; SESAME SEEDS: *Sesamum indicum* is one of the oldest sources of oil. The plant is an annual shrub that grows about 5 feet tall and is cultivated for its seeds and for the oil that can be pressed from them. The seeds are teardrop shaped and can be any color from black or tan to nearly white, but inside the outer husk all seeds are white.

The sesame oil produced and used in Burma is made from unroasted sesame seeds, so it is almost clear and has a light nutty taste. (By contrast, in China and Japan, most sesame oil is brown, because it's made of seeds that have been roasted; the process gives it an intense roasted-sesame flavor.) Sesame oil keeps well, is high in polyunsaturated fatty acids (oleic and linoleic), and is stable when heated. This makes it a very desirable cooking oil. Unroasted sesame oil is sold in South Asian groceries (labeled "gingelly" or "gingili" oil) and is also available in some Middle Eastern groceries.

In places in Burma where sesame oil is processed, women in the markets sell the "grounds," what remains of the sesame seeds once the oil has been pressed from them. It is a delicious slightly crumbly paste that still has a lot of sesame flavor, despite having had the oil pressed out. (I've never seen sesame grounds for sale in North America.) It's usually transformed into a kind of salad or condiment, with the addition of finely sliced lime leaves, chopped peanuts, fried shallots, and often a little drizzle of shallot or garlic oil. The whole thing is mixed together and then eaten as one of many dishes in a rice meal (see page 16).

Sesame seeds are eaten as a topping or a flavoring with both savory and sweet dishes in Burma. They are often lightly toasted and partly ground before being used as a topping. Because they are so rich in oil, sesame seeds should be stored well-sealed in the refrigerator or freezer to prevent them from going rancid.

SHALLOTS; ASIAN SHALLOTS: These small cousins of onions are *Allium ascalonicum*, with purple to red outer skin and a pink-tinted interior. They are less watery than European shallots

SHALLOTS

(which may be substituted) and much less pungent than onions. In Burmese English-language cookbooks, as in Indian cookbooks, they are often called onions. Shallots are the most important flavoring in Burmese cooking, cooked as a paste, minced, or sliced. When they are used raw, they are sliced, soaked briefly in water, then squeezed dry. Sliced shallots fried to a brown crispness are a frequent topping in Burmese salads and other dishes. Store shallots in a cool dark place or in the refrigerator, in paper not plastic bags.

SHAN PEOPLE; SHAN STATE: The name Shan is given to people who call themselves Tai Yai, and derives from the old word for Thailand, "Siam." The Shan live in a large hilly region that stretches from southwestern Yunnan into Kachin State and across the whole of Shan State into the northern hills of Thailand. There are a number of subgroups of Tai Yai, but all speak a Tai language, and like other Tai peoples (Thai, Lao, Dong, Tai Koen, Tai Lu, etc.) are traditionally rice-growing agriculturalists known for their strong social and political organization.

In culinary terms, Shan food is fascinating not only because it is delicious and inventive, but particularly because it uses no fish sauce or fermented shrimp paste, and instead gets depth of flavor from fermented soybeans, used as is or dried into disks (see Soybean Disks, page 40). This makes it a wonderful source of recipes for vegetarians who want to try Southeast Asian food.

The other distinctive Shan food that is now found in many parts of Burma is Pale Yellow Shan Tofu (page 126), which is a dense, savory, pale yellow jelly made of chickpea flour cooked in water and allowed to set.

SHELLING OYSTERS; SHELLING MUSSELS: Oysters and mussels are used as an ingredient in a number of dishes of Chinese origin in Southeast Asia. Consequently, freshly prepared oysters and mussels out of the shell are sold in Chinese and Southeast Asian grocery stores, usually in small 1- and 2-cup plastic containers; you can also find them canned. If you are making the Seafood Noodle Stir-Fry (page 272) and prefer to start with oysters or mussels in the shell, then you'll need to shell them. The best trick for **oysters** is to freeze them for 3 hours; the freezing makes the liquid in the oyster expand, so it forces the top shell to lift. You just need to take it off (instead of using the traditional oyster shucking method: lay the oyster flat side up, narrow [hinge] end toward you, slide the tip of an oyster knife between the two shells, and twist to force the shells apart). **Mussels** need to be scrubbed clean, then put in a pot with a small amount of water over high heat. When the water boils, the mussels will start to open; discard any that don't. Lift the mussels out, remove from the shells, and use as directed.

SHRIMP: See **fish and seafood.**

SHRIMP PASTE: Known to most Burmese as *ngapi*, this staple of the Burmese flavor palate is made of shrimp that have been fermented and processed to a pungent paste. Similar products are used in Thailand (where it is called *kapi*); Indonesia (*trassi*), and Malaysia (*belacan*). It gives an umami depth of flavor to dishes, and when used with a light hand, it is a subtle and delicious addition even for those unaccustomed to it. For outsiders, *ngapi* tastes

strong. Consequently, the amounts called for in this book are at the restrained end of the spectrum. For people who use *ngapi* all the time, it is an appetite stimulant, just as the aroma of garlic or onions cooking in olive oil or butter is to many people in Europe and North America; as Shwe Nwe U said to me in Mrauk U, "It tastes sweet to us, makes us hungry." If you are working from this book to feed *ngapi* lovers, you will want to increase the amount you use, and cut back on salt or fish sauce.

Shrimp paste is used more with vegetable dishes than in meat dishes. Rakhine and Mon people use it with salads; central Burmese tend not to. And the people of the hills—the Karen, Shan, Chin, and Kachin—traditionally do not use it. The Shan get meaty depth of flavor from fermented soybeans (see Soybean Disks, page 40) instead.

Shrimp paste is usually sold in glass jars in East Asian grocery stores and is grayish or pinkish gray in color. (In Burma it's sold from huge pots in the markets.) Some has a smooth, paste-like consistency; other shrimp pastes are firmer and drier in texture. The jars may be labeled "fine shrimp sauce" (like the Koon Chun brand I often use), "shrimp paste," or "fermented shrimp paste." The paste keeps, if well sealed in the refrigerator, for a long time. If you can't find it, or if you don't want to use it, you can omit it from recipes, with some loss of umami; add extra fish sauce to compensate, or some Dried Shrimp Powder (page 30) or a dash of brown miso paste.

To toast shrimp paste: Generally, shrimp paste is cooked, either in the dish it is flavoring, or before it is added to an uncooked dish (see Shallot Chutney with Chiles, page 218, for example). The easiest way to cook it, given that it smells very pungent as it's being heated, is to place it, whether paste-like or firmer, on some aluminum foil, wrap it tightly, and cook in a skillet over medium-high heat, as if you were dry-grilling. Turn the package over after a couple of minutes. Let cool before opening the package. It should have a dry crumbly texture. The Burmese method I've seen used in

FERMENTED SOYBEANS

home kitchens and that I find easier than the aluminum foil technique is to smear the paste on the back of a large metal spoon and hold it over a gas flame, paste side up, until the paste on top cooks and dries on the hot metal.

SHRIMP POWDER: Made from dried shrimp, this is a staple ingredient in many parts of Burma, where it's called *pazun chauk.* Dried shrimp are pounded or ground to a powder (see page 30) that is then used to thicken and give a depth of flavor (umami) to dishes.

SICHUAN PEPPER: Sometimes called fagara (because it was formerly classified in the botanical genus *Fagara*), known in Mandarin as *hua jiao* (meaning flower pepper), this is the dried fruit of *Zanthoxylum simulans,* one species of prickly ash. (The Japanese *sansho* is from another species of prickly ash, *X. piperitum.*) It is one of the oldest spices in recorded history. It has a resinous flavor and numbs the tongue. It is heavily used in Sichuan cooking and also plays an important role in Yunnanese cooking. In Burma it's found in Kachin dishes, and is generally known as "Kachin pepper" in northern Burma. A related spice, probably another species of prickly ash, is also used in parts of Shan State.

SORREL LEAVES: In Burma, the English word that is most often used for hibiscus leaves is *roselle,* but sometimes they are called sorrel. For those, see **hibiscus.**

But in the West, other plants are called sorrel, and they are also tart-tasting: *Rumex acetosa,* with long leaves, and *Rumex scutatus,* with round leaves. I find Western sorrel (usually the long-leafed one is what I have available) a useful substitute in Burmese and Kachin dishes where I want a tart fresh tang, and in Burmese soups.

SOYBEANS; FERMENTED SOYBEANS: Soybeans, *Glycine max,* have been cultivated for about five thousand years in China. Because the soybean is a legume, it fixes nitrogen in the soil, so it's often grown in rotation with rice (soybeans in dry season, rice in rainy season). In Burma soybeans (*peipok si*) are used to make tofu and are also eaten as fresh beans. Soybeans grow in a green pod, and although fresh soybeans can be difficult to find in North America, frozen soybeans, either in their pods or shelled, are sold in Asian groceries and in larger supermarkets too. They are often referred to by their Japanese name, *edamame.* Raw soybeans are not digestible because they contain protease inhibitors, but these disappear with cooking. **Fermented soybeans,** sold in glass jars in Chinese and Southeast Asian groceries, are soft, slightly salty soybeans that give a meaty umami depth of flavor; they may be sold whole or as mashed beans. The Burmese name is *pei ngapi* (bean *ngapi*), which explains their role as equivalent to that of *ngapi,* to give umami (see page 31) in a dish. Look for jars labeled "preserved soybeans," "soybean paste," or "fermented soybeans," and check the list of ingredients: you want them to be limited to salt, water, and soybeans, with no sugar or other flavorings. The beans are a pale brown and very soft. They can be mashed in a mortar with a pestle, but also by placing them in a bowl and pressing them with the back of a spoon, a matter of a couple of minutes. Brown miso paste can be substituted, but since miso has a stronger flavor, use half or less than half the amount called for. See also *tua nao*.

SOY SAUCE: Soy sauce is a standard condiment in China and Japan and is now widely used elsewhere too. In Burma soy sauce is *pei nganpya yay* (meaning bean fish sauce). It is mostly used in Chinese dishes, as a condiment for Chinese food, and in some Kachin dishes. In addition, the fermented soybeans and Soybean Disks (page 40) used by the Shan are first cousins to soy sauce, using fermentation to generate flavor and preserve the food qualities of soybeans.

Soy sauces vary widely. Good soy sauces are brewed, made from soybeans that are fermented with wheat and salted. Tamari sauces from Japan are the only soy sauces that do not contain any wheat. Do a comparative tasting of soy sauces to see which one(s) you prefer. Some are milder and lighter tasting, others are more deeply flavored, and still others, made from lesser ingredients and not brewed properly, are harsh-tasting and should be avoided.

SPIDER: A very useful cooking tool, especially for lifting small objects out of hot oil or hot water, a spider is like an openwork wire basket attached to a long handle. Chinese grocery stores and equipment stores are good places to find them. See photograph, page 301.

SPLIT FRIED SOYBEANS; SPLIT ROASTED SOYBEANS: These bar-snack-like crisp nuts are one of the ingredients in tea-leaf salad. They're sold widely in Burma but can be hard to find in North America. Look for them in Chinese groceries. If you're having no luck, substitute whole roasted peanuts.

STAR ANISE: *Illicium verum.* Used more often in Chinese and Vietnamese cooking (for example, to flavor the beef broth used for *pho*) than in Burma, star anise is a brown-colored, star-shaped spice about ½ inch in diameter, with a penetrating warming anise flavor and aroma. It is sold in Asian groceries and well-stocked specialty shops. Store, like any spice, in a well-sealed jar away from heat and light. Use sparingly, for its flavor is intense.

STATES: See **political areas.**

STICKY RICE FLOUR: See **rice flour.**

STIR-FRYING: Books have been written about the technique of stir-frying. Briefly, it is a method of cooking small-chopped ingredients on the hot oiled surface of a wok by keeping them moving so they do not burn but instead cook evenly and quickly. In Burma cooks use a modified wok-like pan, like a curved deep frying pan, for making vegetable dishes. I use a wok or a wide cast-iron skillet for quickly fried Burmese dishes. See also **wok.**

STUPA: See **chedi;** see also **Buddhism.**

SUGAR; SUGARCANE SUGAR; PALM SUGAR: Sugar is made from boiling down the sweet liquid of various plants, including sugarcane, sugar beet, and sugar palm. In Burma very little sugar is used in savory dishes. For making sweets, most people in the cities use palm sugar or commercially produced (from sugarcane) white sugar, but in the countryside a cruder cooked-down form of sugarcane juice, a brown sugar that is sold in blocks, is often used. It has an appealing smoky rich flavor. See "Travels with Sai," page 283. **Palm sugar,** is made by boiling down the sap of the Palmyra palm (*Borassas flabellifer*), often called the toddy palm. (The same sap is used to make toddy.) This sugar is called *htanyet* in Burmese and may also be referred to by its Indian name, *jaggery.* It's often served, chopped into small lumps, as an afterdinner sweet in Burmese homes and restaurants; it's also used for making desserts where a smoky depth of flavor is wanted. Palm sugar comes in many shades and many degrees of smoky flavor, from pale brown and milder-tasting to dark brown and more intensely flavored. Sold in round, square, or cone-shaped blocks, it is now widely available in Asian grocery stores and specialty shops. The flavor is reminiscent of maple sugar, though not as sweet, and so brown sugar, or maple sugar blended with brown sugar, can be substituted. Blocks of palm sugar must be chopped or sliced. This is most easily done with a cleaver. You will notice that in warm humid weather the sugar softens and is much easier to chop. See also **toddy; toddy palm.**

TAI PEOPLES: The Tai peoples originated in Southern China and then some of them moved down into Southeast Asia, following the Mekong, Red, and other rivers. Anthropologists describe them as highly socially organized rice-growing cultures who settled in fertile river valleys. They speak related languages that have diverged to varying degrees over the centuries. In modern times, the Thais, northern Thais, Lao, Tai Yai (Shan), Tai Koen, Tai Yuan (of northern Laos), Tai Dam, Tai Lu and others all live outside China, while within China the peoples named Dai and Dong are also Tai.

Tai Koen: The Tai Koen (sometimes spelled Tai Kuen), whose cultural capital and "homeland area" is the town of Kengtung in the far eastern part of Shan State, speak a language almost identical to that spoken in the northern Thai provinces of Chiang Mai and Chiang Rai. Their cooking culture is very similar too.

Tai Yai: See **Shan people.**

TAMARIND; TAMARIND PULP; TAMARIND PASTE: *Tamarindus indica.* The tamarind tree is tall and generous, giving shade from Africa to India and Southeast Asia. Its tender leaves are used to make a Burmese salad. Its fruit (*magyi thi* in Burmese) grows in long pale pods, inside which is a sticky brown mass of flesh and seeds.

Some tamarind is tart-sweet and can be eaten as a (rather sticky) snack; and some is just tart. Tart tamarind is used as a souring agent from Vietnam to India and Pakistan. The name comes from the Arabic *tamar-hindi,* meaning "date [*tamir*] from India."

The recipes in this book all call for **tamarind pulp.** It is the unrefined pulp of the fruit, dark brown, nearly black, that includes seeds and a few membranes, as well as the flavorful flesh. It is sold in Asian groceries, usually in small dark rectangular blocks wrapped in clear plastic and labeled *me chua* in Vietnamese and *mak kham* in Thai. Before it is added in cooking, it must be chopped into smaller pieces and soaked in a little hot water for a few minutes to soften (so that the pulp—the flavor—separates from the seeds), then strained through a sieve into a bowl. The tamarind liquid (*magyi thi hnit* in Burmese) is tart and smooth, a wonderful souring agent; the seeds and pulp are discarded. Instructions for this simple process are included with each recipe.

Look for the softest block of tamarind pulp you can find. Once you have used some of your pulp, be sure to wrap it tightly in plastic and refrigerate it, so that it keeps well without drying out.

Do not buy "tamarind paste" instead of pulp. This preprocessed version has an unpleasant metallic taste (from preservatives).

TAPIOCA; TAPIOCA FLOUR; TAPIOCA PEARLS: Tapioca, also known as cassava or manioc, is the tuber of *Manihot esculentai,* an important source of carbohydrates in many places, especially where there are poor soils. It was first cultivated in Brazil over ten thousand years ago. Tapioca can be processed in many ways, but in this book is called for only in the form of tapioca flour and tapioca pearls. Both are sold in Asian grocery stores, in small bags. **Tapioca flour** adds chewiness and strength to rice-flour batters and noodles; it is also sometimes added to bean thread noodles during processing. **Tapioca pearls** are used in desserts and sweet treats such as bubble tea. They cook in liquid until tender, and only then is sugar added, for adding it earlier prevents the pearls from softening. When buying tapioca pearls to make desserts be sure to buy the small ones (they are a little larger than sesame seeds when dried, then expand as they cook in water) rather than the large ones that are used in bubble tea.

TEA LEAVES; FERMENTED TEA LEAVES; PICKLED TEA LEAVES: *Laphet* is the Burmese word for "green tea." It's also the term for tea leaves that have been stored in earthenware jars and left to ferment. They have a distinctive flavor, tart and fresh, that is very appealing, even to foreigners

FERMENTED TEA LEAVES

who have never tried them before. They are the main ingredient in one of Burma's most well-known dishes, *laphet thoke*, or tea-leaf salad (see page 64). They are sold in Burmese groceries and are now becoming available in other Southeast Asian groceries too.

TEA SHOPS: Elsewhere, Burmese tea shops might be called cafés; they are places for people to hang around, chat, sip a cup of something, eat a snack, take a break.

TENASSERIM; TENASSERIM COAST; TENASSERIM DIVISION: Now called Tanintharyi, this is the southernmost region of Burma, the long narrow part that borders Thailand to the east and the Andaman Sea to the west. The region is known for its rubber and areca nuts as well as for its remarkable seafood. The capital is Dawei; other towns are Mergui (Myeik) and, at the southern tip, Kawthoung.

TODDY; TODDY PALM: *Borassus flabellifer* is also known as the Palmyra palm or sugar palm. It's a tall, very slow-growing tree that used to be widespread in the low-lying areas of tropical southeast Asia. There are still palms growing in ones and twos by rice fields in southern Burma, for example in Mon and Karen States and in Tenasserim. The tree is tapped for its sweet sap, the region's first (pre-sugarcane) plant source for sugar. The sap is often fermented into an alcoholic drink known as toddy or distilled into liquor called *arak*, especially in rural villages.

TOFU; FIRM TOFU; PRESSED TOFU: Tofu is called *tohu* in Burmese, or *peipya*. It is made of soybeans that are cooked, ground, pressed, and treated with a coagulant so that the pressed liquid gels. Tofu can be silky soft, with a fragile breakable custard texture. Silken tofu is not called for in this book; in Southeast Asia it is most often eaten as a sweet snack, bathed in a ginger-flavored syrup. Regular tofu is fairly firm; it can be sliced, but it does not stand up well to much stirring. A firmer version of regular tofu is now sold widely in North America, in vacuum-packed plastic bags that hold water and the tofu. **Firm tofu** and **pressed tofu** are both firm like a young cheddar, and can be sliced and stirred without breaking. You can firm up tofu by pressing it: lay it in a shallow bowl and place a cloth on top and then a bread board or other weight. The pressure will push water out of the tofu, causing it to shrink and to firm up. Drain off the water. It takes several hours for the tofu to get very firm.

TODDY PALM

TUA NAO: I call these Soybean Disks (see page 40); *tua nao* is the Shan and Tai Koen name for them, and in Burmese they're *peipok*. They're an essential flavoring in Shan and Tai Koen cooking, and also used by the Kachin and others in Kachin and Shan States such as the Palaung. Miso paste or fermented soybeans can be substituted; for instructions, see individual recipes.

TURMERIC: Like ginger and galangal a rhizome, turmeric (*Curcuma longa*, also called *Curcuma domestica*) is usually sold in the West in its powdered form, a bright yellow to orange powder that stains everything it touches. The Burmese word for it is *hsa nwin*. In this book, turmeric powder is used in many recipes; in only one, from Shan State (Fish Stew with Aromatics, page 145) is turmeric rhizome called for. Whole turmeric is sold in Southeast Asian and South Asian groceries. It is smaller than most ginger, about a baby finger size in thickness, with a dull orange skin and brilliant orange flesh that is crisp and firm. You can stir-fry it, treating it like a vegetable, or mince it like ginger. Turmeric has medicinal properties, being antibacterial (hence the powder is often rubbed on meat or fish before cooking), antiflatulent (hence usually added to dals and legumes of all kinds in South Asian cooking), and anti-inflammatory (hence currently prescribed in the West as an "anti-aging" food). Turmeric powder is shown in the upper right of the photograph on page 18.

UMAMI: The Japanese word that has come to be used by Westerners to denote another category of flavor (a fifth, after salty, sweet, sour, and bitter), the taste that is "meatiness." It's the taste that we associate with ripe tomatoes, deeply flavored mushrooms, grilled meat. See "Umami" (page 31) for details, and for the various sources of umami in the culinary traditions of Burma.

VEGETARIAN OPTIONS: Instead of fish sauce, use salt (1 teaspoon salt is approximately equal to 1 tablespoon fish sauce); instead of dried shrimp powder, use toasted chickpea flour and increase salt or add soy sauce. Remember that adding dried mushrooms to a dish increases depth of flavor, just as shrimp paste and fish sauce and *tua nao* do (see **umami**).

VIETNAMESE CORIANDER: *Polygonum odoratum* (also listed under the name *Persicaria odorata*) is a succulent, a perennial herb that grows best in damp soil. In Vietnamese it is called *rau ram*, and in Burma it's *pe-pei-yuet*. It's more used by the Shan and the Kachin than by the Bamar. The flavor is somewhere in the coriander-to-mint range, and it is particularly delicious with cooked chicken and in salads. The leaves are medium to dark green and tapered, with a darker-colored V on them. The stems are knobby and jointed. Look for it in Southeast Asian markets. If you want to start growing it, place some stems in water, and they will develop rootlets. Plant in moist soil and keep well watered and in partial shade.

VINEGAR; RICE VINEGAR; BLACK RICE VINEGAR; APPLE CIDER VINEGAR: Vinegar is acetic acid.

Most vinegars are diluted to about 3½ percent acetic acid. Vinegar is made by fermenting a sweet liquid such as wine or apple cider. The best rice vinegar is brewed; Japanese brands are very reliable. Try to avoid "seasoned vinegars"; they have salt and sugar in them and so the seasonings in the recipes will no longer be appropriate. Black rice vinegar is made of black rice water and salt. Check the label and avoid any that contain caramel or other non-rice ingredients.

WA PEOPLE: The Wa people live in Yunnan along the Burma border and in northern parts of Shan State as well as in adjacent border areas of Kachin State. They speak a Mon-Khmer language, grow corn and vegetables, and raise pigs and chickens. The British never managed to conquer them completely and referred to them as the "terrible Wa." They are also called Va, Kawa, or Awa. The Wa have a large, relatively well-armed military force that has been battling the central Burmese authorities for years; they are also notorious in modern times for trafficking in opium and other narcotics.

WATERCRESS: *Rorippa nasturtium-aquaticum,* also known as *Nasturtium officinale,* is a leafy green that grows in watercourses, wild and cultivated. It is used for salad in Burma, where it is called *ye monyin.* It has a sharp taste that works beautifully with the sweetness of sliced shallots and fried shallots. It is yet another possible addition to Burmese soups and curries.

WET MARKET: A term used to distinguish markets that sell vegetables and fish and meat from those that sell dry goods, clothing, and packaged foods. At wet markets, the emphasis is on freshness: most produce is locally grown and in many cases the fish and seafood, and sometimes also the chickens and ducks, are brought to the market alive and then prepared for customers when they are purchased. Most food markets in Burma are wet markets, although now there are some large upmarket stores with huge food sections springing up on the outskirts of Rangoon.

WILD LIME LEAVES: See under **limes.**

WINGED BEANS: These attractive long pods with frilled angular edges, *Psophocarpus tetragonolobus,* are also known as Manila pea. The Burmese name is *pezaungya.* They are bright green when cooked, and can be eaten like asparagus, as a tender green vegetable. They are also served raw or lightly parboiled on Burmese vegetable plates or included in salads (see page 68, for example).

WINTER MELON: See **gourds and summer squashes.**

WOK: A curved metal pan that derives from a South Asian pan but was developed further in China, the wok is a wonderful kitchen tool, useful for stir-frying, simmering, and braising. I use my large wok more than once every day. If you don't have a wok, a deep skillet can be substituted for making the recipes in this book, preferably one with a rounded shape, so that it's easier to move ingredients around in the pan. Good spun-steel woks and hand-beaten woks are now available in North America; search online for them if you don't have a kitchen equipment store near you. Have a look at Grace Young's 2004 book, *The Breath of a Wok,* for advice about buying and maintaining a wok. See also **stir-frying.**

YARD-LONG BEANS: *Vigna sesquipedalis.* These attractive green beans, about 18 inches long, are a wonderfully useful and delicious version of bean. They're now widely sold in Asian groceries. The Burmese name is *pei daungshayi.* They can be eaten raw or lightly cooked, chopped into 1- to 2-inch lengths, as part of a vegetable side-plate or as a Burmese salad (see Long-Bean Salad with Roasted Peanuts, page 50); they also make a good addition to curries.

ANNOTATED BIBLIOGRAPHY

This list includes memoirs and novels as well as cookbooks, reference books, and histories, all of them sources of insight and information about the country. I have not listed the many articles, blog posts, and conversations from which I've gleaned information and understanding through the years. And I should mention that my previous books—especially *Hot Sour Salty Sweet*, *Beyond the Great Wall*, and *Mangoes & Curry Leaves* (all co-authored with Jeffrey Alford)—also contributed context and understanding as I worked on this one.

BOOKS

Aye, Nan San San, trans. Ma Thanegi. *Cooking with Love Myanmar Style.* Yangon: Seikku Cho Cho, n.d.

Callahan, Mary P. *Making Enemies: War and State Building in Burma.* Ithaca, N.Y.: Cornell University Press, 2003.
A remarkable analysis of the origins of Burma today, and especially of the lead-up to the 1962 military coup, that describes how the army transformed itself into a powerful force during the 1950s and also how it viewed itself as a necessary stabilizing force.

Chutintaranond, Sunait, and Chris Baker, eds. *Recalling Local Pasts: Autonomous History in Southeast Asia.* Chiang Mai, Thailand: Silkworm Books, 2002.
A collection of essays that look at local history rather than central-authority-centered history, including three on places in Burma: Mrauk U, the Tenasserim coast, and Pegu.

Connelly, Karen. *The Lizard Cage.* Toronto: Random House Canada, 2005.
A novel set in Rangoon's Insein Prison; compelling, heart-wrenching, and beautifully written.

_____. *Burmese Lessons.* Toronto: Random House Canada, 2009.
A poetic memoir of the author's love affair with

Burma, and her time in the refugee camps along the Thai-Burma border, that gives a picture of the democracy movement from outside the country, as well as a feeling for life in the refugee camps and among the opposition forces along the Thai border in the mid-1990s.

Danell, Eric, Anna Kiss, and Martina Stohrova. *Dokmai Garden's Guide to Fruits and Vegetables in Southeast Asian Markets*. Bangkok: White Lotus, 2011.

Davidson, Alan. *The Penguin Companion to Food*. London: Penguin, 2002.

Delisle, Guy. *Burma Chronicles*. Montreal: Drawn and Quarterly, 2008.

A cartoonist who lived in Burma for two years with his wife (who was working there for Médecins sans Frontières) and their baby uses the graphic nonfiction format to detail daily life as he saw it, simplistically but with humor and appreciation.

Elliott, Patricia. *The White Umbrella*. Bangkok: Post Books, 1999.

A story of modern Burma, told through the eyes of a major player, the Sao (wife of the Prince) of Yawnghwe, on Inle Lake. Her husband, the Saobha Prince Shwe Thaik, was the first president of Burma. It is a fascinating glimpse into the hopes and frustrations and heartbreak of the 1945 to 1962 period, which ended in the military coup (and the disappearance and death of the Shan princes). In that coup, the Sao's husband was arrested and killed; one son was also shot. She escaped with her remaining children and then led a Shan insurgent army in the hills of northern Thailand.

Fetherling, George. *Three Pagodas Pass: A Roundabout Journey to Burma*. Bangkok: Asia Books, 2003.

A sympathetic traveler's account.

Fielding-Hall, Harold. *The Soul of a People*. 1898. Reprint, Bangkok: White Orchid, 1995.

An attempt to understand and communicate what Buddhism means to the Burmese people— not what the texts say, but how it is seen and lived on the ground. Amazingly empathetic for the time.

_____. *Thibaw's Queen*. 1907. Available at www.openlibrary.org.

An account of the court before the arrival of the British, starting with King Mindon, the great mid-nineteenth-century king of Burma, who died in 1878 and was succeeded by King Thibaw.

Fink, Christina. *Living Silence in Burma: Surviving Under Military Rule*, 2nd ed. Chiang Mai, Thailand: Silkworm Books, 2009.

An extremely clear and useful introduction to Burma's recent history.

Ghosh, Amitav. *The Glass Palace*. New York: Random House, 2001.

A sweeping historical novel that opens in Mandalay in 1885 and ends in Burma in the 1990s; a great introduction to the colonial and modern eras.

Grabowsky, Volker, and Andrew Turon. *The Gold and Silver Road of Trade and Friendship: The McLeod and Richardson Diplomatic Missions to Tai States in 1837*. Chiang Mai, Thailand: Silkworm Books, 2003.

Hallett, Holt S. *A Thousand Miles on an Elephant in the Shan States*. 1890. Reprint, Bangkok: White Lotus, 2000.

An account of an Englishman's 1876 journey in search of a good route for a railway to connect northern Thailand with Burma's coastal ports, to enable more profitable trade and the exploitation of teak.

Halliday, Robert. *The Mons of Burma and Thailand*. 2 vols. Bangkok: White Lotus, 2000.

Volume 1, The Talaings, is an account of Mon culture and history, based on studies by the author in the first half of the twentieth century. (The Mon were then referred to as Talaing.) Volume 2, Selected Articles, serves as a valuable reminder—given the pressures for assimilation of Mons in Burma—of the age of Mon culture.

Heiss, Mary Lou, and Robert J. Heiss. *The Story of Tea: A Cultural History and Drinking Guide*. Berkeley, Calif.: Ten Speed Press, 2007.

Howard, Michael C. *Textiles of the Highland Peoples of Burma. Vol. 1, The Naga, Chin, Jingpho, and Other Baric-speaking Groups.* Bangkok: White Lotus, 2005.
Color photographs and explanations of the complex textile culture and subcultures of the peoples of the northern and northwestern mountains of Burma.

Hutton, Wendy. *Tropical Herbs & Spices of Thailand.* Bangkok: Asia Books, 1997.

———. *Tropical Vegetables of Thailand.* Bangkok: Asia Books, 1997.

Khaing, Mi Mi. *Cook and Entertain the Burmese Way.* Rangoon: Mayawaddy Press, n.d.

Khoo Thwe, Pascal. *From the Land of Green Ghosts: A Burmese Odyssey.* London: HarperCollins, 2002.
The memoir of a young Padaung (Kayan) man who, with the help of an English academic whom he meets by chance, flees Burma, makes it to Great Britain, and graduates from Cambridge.

Kingdon-Ward, Frank. *Burma's Icy Mountains.* 1949. Reprint, Bangkok: Orchard Press, 2006.
A 1937 botanical expedition to northern Burma that starts in Myitkyina and heads into the mountains and valleys north of the confluence of the two tributaries that come together to form the Irrawaddy River.

———. *Return to the Irrawaddy.* 1956. Reprint, Bangkok: Asia Books, 2004.
This account of another of Kingdon-Ward's botanical trips is full of colorful local detail.

Larkin, Emma. *Finding George Orwell in Burma.* New York: Penguin, 2005.
A graceful nonfiction exploration of life in present-day Burma. The author connects colonial rule and Orwell's change in attitude while he was in Burma in the 1920s (as he became a fierce critic of the British Empire) with his later writings against totalitarianism in the novels 1984 and Animal Farm. She finds that the world he portrays in 1984 is uncannily like the situation under the Burmese government of the 1990s and the early years of the next decade.

———. *Everything Is Broken: A Tale of Catastrophe in Burma.* New York: Penguin, 2010.
A report of the destruction wrought by Cyclone Nargis in May 2008, the failure of the Burmese government to help alleviate people's suffering, the efforts of individuals on the ground, and the ongoing consequences.

Lewis, Norman. *Golden Earth: Travels in Burma.* 1952. Reprint, London: Eland, 2003.
This beautifully written tale of travels in early postwar Burma gives a glimpse of the charm of the country and its people for foreigners, as the author journeys south to Tenasserim and then north into the Shan States and to Myitkyina.

Lintner, Bertil. *Land of Jade: A Journey Through Insurgent Burma.* Bangkok: White Orchid, 1996.
A noted journalist's story about an extraordinary illegal trip he and his partner (a Shan woman from Burma) and their baby made across the northern part of Burma in the mid-1980s. They started in India's Nagaland and ended in China's Yunnan province about eighteen months later. It's a saga that along the way gives a detailed history of the independence movements in Burma from 1948 to the mid-1980s and also an idea of the countryside and way of life of people in the hills.

———. *Burma in Revolt: Opium and Insurgency Since 1948.* Chiang Mai, Thailand: Silkworm Books, 1999.
A useful review of recent border history and politics.

MacGregor, John. *Through the Buffer State: Travels in Borneo, Siam, Cambodia, Malaya and Burma.* 1896. Reprint, Bangkok: White Lotus, 1994.
A Scot's travels through the outlying parts of the British Empire and into Thailand and Cambodia too.

Maclean, Rory. *Under the Dragon: Travels in a Betrayed Land.* London: Flamingo, 1999.
A thoughtful and creative memoir of travels in Burma in the late 1990s that manages to connect emotionally with the human landscape of the counry at its most repressive and painful.

Malcom, Howard. *Travels in the Burman Empire.* 1840. Reprint, Bangkok: Ava House, 1997. *An account of the travels of an American Baptist missionary in 1836, in Arakan (Rakhine) and central Burma, noting customs and geography and the possibilities for missionary work.*

Mannin, Ethel. *Land of the Crested Lion: A Journey Through Modern Burma.* London: Jarrolds, 1955. *A postindependence account of travels in Burma.*

Maugham, W. Somerset. *The Gentleman in the Parlour.* 1930. Reprint, Bangkok: White Orchid, 1995. *In 1922, Maugham traveled on horseback from Taunggyi, near Inle Lake in Shan State, all the way east to Kengtung, then an independent Shan kingdom. It took him more than two months. His book about the journey is a straight travel memoir that gives a rare glimpse of the region that lies east of the Salween River in Shan State.*

Mesher, Gene. *Burmese for Beginners.* Bangkok: Paiboon, 2005.

Milne, Leslie. *Shans at Home.* 1910. Reprint, Bangkok: White Lotus, 2001. *Among my favorites, written by an Englishwoman who lived in two different Shan kingdoms, Hsipaw and Namshan, for a total of eighteen months in 1910–11. Milne was a clear-eyed, appreciative observer of customs and culture, and the book includes line drawings as well as black-and-white photographs.*

_____. *The Home of an Eastern Clan: A Study of the Palaungs of the Shan States.* 1924. Reprint, Bangkok: White Lotus, 2004. *Like Milne's Shan book, a closely observed description, and an appreciative one, of the Palaung people.*

Mirante, Edith T. *Burmese Looking Glass: A Human Rights Adventure and a Jungle Revolution.* New York: Atlantic Monthly Press, 1993. *An American artist who got bitten by the injustices in Burma travels with rebel forces into Shan State and Karen State; with the Mons all the way to the coast in Tenasserim; and then with the Kachin in the north. She gives detailed useful background on all the insurgency struggles.*

_____. *Down the Rat Hole: Adventures Underground on Burma's Frontiers.* Bangkok: Orchid Press, 2005. *In her second book, Mirante travels into Burmese territory from China's Yunnan and from Manipur in India. She also goes to Bangladesh to meet and learn about Rakhine and Rohingya resistance. As in her earlier book, she is impassioned, wanting revolution. She also sees the fragmentation and weakness of the opposition, as well as the valor.*

MoMo and BoBo's Kitchen: A Burmese Cookbook. Mae Sot, Thailand: Borderline, 2010. *A small book of recipes contributed by refugees living on the Thai–Burma border and published there.*

Myint-U, Thant. *The River of Lost Footsteps.* New York: Farrar Straus and Giroux, 2006. *A modern retelling of Burma's history, from the perspective of an insider who is also a historian with an international perspective. Thant gives us privileged access to the point of view of the people on the ground; it's refreshing to get a Burma-centric perspective rather than that of a colonial writer.*

_____. *Where China Meets India: Burma and the New Crossroads of Asia.* New York: Farrar Straus and Giroux, 2011.

Orwell, George. *Burmese Days.* 1934. Reprint, New York: Mariner, 1974. *This early novel draws on Orwell's experiences as a colonial officer in towns all over Burma (it's set in a place very like the small town of Katha, on the Irrawaddy River between Mandalay and Myitkyina, where he was posted for a time). It gives a sense of the brutality of British rule and the lack of respect the British had for Burmese people and culture.*

Phan, Zoya, and Damien Lewis. *Little Daughter: A Memoir of Survival in Burma and the West.* London: Simon & Schuster, 2009.

A young Karen woman who is now a spokeperson for the pro-democracy movement, gives a detailed picture of her life in a Karen village, and then of the horrors of flight from the Burmese army as it overran Karen-held territory in the mid-1990s. She describes her life in the camps along the Thai border and her eventual success in getting access to education and legal status in England.

Po, San C. *Burma and the Karens.* 1928. Reprint, Bangkok: White Lotus, 2001.

An account of Karen history and the relations between Burma and the Karen, from a Karen scholar writing long before independence.

Reid, Robert, Joe Bindloss, and Stuart Butler. *Lonely Planet Myanmar (Burma),* 11th ed. Victoria, Australia: Lonely Planet, 2009.

Robert, Claudia Saw Lwin, Wendy Hutton, San Lwin, and Win Pe. *The Food of Myanmar: Authentic Recipes from the Land of the Golden Pagodas.* Hong Kong: Periplus, 1999.

Sargent, Inge. *Twilight over Burma: My Life as a Shan Princess.* With a foreword by Bertil Lintner. Honolulu: University of Hawaii Press, 1994.

The story of a foreigner who married a Shan prince and then was forced to flee the country.

Southeast Asia Neighbors Press. *28 Colourful Ethnic Recipes from Burma.* Chiang Mai, Thailand: Southeast Asia Neighbors Press, 2008.

Suu Kyi, Aung San, and Fergal Keane. *Letters from Burma.* New York: Penguin, 2010.

A reissue with new foreword by Fergal Keane of a collection of letters by the Nobel Laureate that ran as articles in a Japanese newspaper in the mid-1990s. Gives a clear sense of Burmese culture and the aspirations of the pro-democracy movement under the repressive authoritarian regime of the time.

Taik, Aung Aung. *The Best of Burmese Cooking.* San Francisco: Chronicle, 1993.

Thanegi, Ma. *An Introduction to Myanmar Cuisine.* Rangoon: U Kyaw Hin, 2004.

_____. *Defiled on the Ayeyarwaddy: One Woman's Mid-Life Travel Adventures on Myanmar's Great River.* San Francisco: Things Asian, 2010.

_____. *The Native Tourist: In Search of Turtle Eggs.* Rangoon: Swiftwinds, 2000.

Ma Thanegi is an artist and writer with a special interest in and knowledge of food who lives in Rangoon. Her cookbook is reliable and very good. Her two books of travel in Burma are nuanced and entertaining introductions to Burmese culture, with small illuminating asides and lively line drawings.

Vaughan, J. G., and C. A. Geissler. *The New Oxford Book of Food Plants,* 2nd ed. New York: Oxford University Press, 2009.

Williams, Lt.-Col. J. D. *Elephant Bill.* 1952. Reprint, London: Long Riders' Guild Press, 2001.

This engaging memoir tells the story of a young man from Britain who worked in the Burma Company's logging camps after the First World War, and then was in charge of the elephants as the British retreated to India after the Japanese conquered Burma in 1942. The day-to-day realities and relationships in the logging camps and the extraordinary role played by elephants and their oozies (handlers) during the war makes a fascinating read.

Win, Daw Ena. *Myanmar Cook Book.* 1999, n.p.

Younghusband, G. J. *The Trans-Salwin Shan State of Kiang Tung.* 1888. Edited and with an introduction by David K. Wyatt. Reprint, Chiang Mai, Thailand: Silkworm Books, 2005.

An explorer's travels through the Eastern Shan states shortly after the British conquest of Mandalay. Younghusband is best known for his later expedition (really an invasion) into Tibet in 1903–1904.

WEB SITES AND ARTICLES

Ghosh, Amitav. "Burma." *The New Yorker*, August 12, 1996.

A report of life in Burma in the decade following the pro-democracy demonstrations and the repression of the democracy movement by the government, including interviews with Aung San Suu Kyi.

Packer, George. "Drowning: Can the Burmese People Rescue Themselves?" *The New Yorker*, August 25, 2008.

_____. "Burma's Opposition Boycotts," in "Interesting Times" blog, *The New Yorker* online, April 2010: http://www.newyorker.com/online/blogs/georgepacker/2010/04/burmas-opposition-boycotts.html.

http://www.culturalsurvival.org/Burma+Country+Profile?gclid=CJDtpPzlqKgCFUMUKgodFWRiIQ

A good resource for cultural information about the peoples of Burma.

http://www.irrawaddy.org/

Current news written by dissidents and Burmese in exile.

http://www.mizzima.com/

Like the Irrawaddy web site, this is produced and written mostly by exiled Burmese.

http://www.uni-graz.at/~katzer/engl/spice_index.html

Gernot Katzer's incredible web pages about spices and herbs, with names for plants in many languages, etc. A great resource.

ACKNOWLEDGMENTS

When I began thinking about this book, in 2008, Burma had been locked away under totalitarian rule for decades. But food is about pleasure, warmth, and welcome. How would I learn enough? I wondered. And would people feel safe talking to me?

Now that Burma is opening up and liberalizing and people there feel at ease, rather than afraid, talking to a foreigner, it's strange to look back at how oppressive things were just a few years ago. When I headed into Burma on my first trip for the book, in February 2009, I felt anxious, not wanting to put people at risk and yet needing to learn so much.

That feeling of anxiety soon fled as I walked the streets of Rangoon, chatted with the people who worked in my guesthouse, hung out in tea shops, and spent hours up at Shwedagon. People were warm and welcoming. They were cautious about talking much to me in public but generous in spirit, and quick to help and offer suggestions or insights about food and culture. I relaxed into their welcome, soaked up their warmth, and began to feel new life and optimism about Burma and its people.

I traveled to Rakhine State, near Bangladesh, and to the far north, in Kachin State. And in those far-flung and complicated places with limited resources and a history of both neglect and active repression by the central government, I found vibrant food culture and daily life. In my many return trips to Burma, wherever I traveled I had the same experience: people were tolerant of my photographing and of my questions, and generous about sharing with a complete stranger.

So my first thanks goes to all those people in Burma who individually and cumulatively helped me gain an understanding of their foods and food traditions, and much else in their daily lives. Specifically, I am grateful to many people who generously opened their homes and kitchens to me: Mi Mi, who taught me a number of traditional dishes in her Rangoon kitchen; Cho Cho, outside Bagan; Mya Mya, KoKo, and family in Pakokku; Sai in Hsipaw; YinYin in Yaunghwe; and Shwe Nwe U and family at the Prince Hotel in Mrauk U. Each time I see Ma Thanegi (who lives in Rangoon and writes wittily about food, culture, and travel) as we eat and talk for hours, I gain insights into Burmese food, culture, and history—a huge thanks for everything Thanegi (and thanks to James Oseland for insisting that we meet). I am very grateful to U Cin Lamh Mang and Daw Khun Shwe, who have patiently explained many aspects of Chin culture to me over the years. Warm thanks to Min Min for ongoing advice and help, to his father for insights about language, to Tyler Dillon for introducing us, and to Bagan Min Min for his help. In Dawei I was taken in hand by a number of the supporters of the Sitagu Sayadaw and the Sitagu Foundation; many thanks to all for that generosity and for conversations about Burma, food, and more. Special thanks to Howng Lam and thanks to Sister Mary Dillon, Labya Turing, Nkumla, Howng Lam, Zenah, and Mohammed Khan in Myitkyina; and Simon of World Vision, Trudy, and Bessie and Kyle, for Burma conversations.

I am also grateful to many unnamed men and women in Burma for answering my questions about food and agriculture and history; they include many of the people who work in the guesthouses and small hotels I have stayed in all around the country, many monks encountered along the way, market people, and fellow passengers in trains, boats, and buses.

Some of my research about Tai Koen and Shan food happened in northern Thailand. In Immerse Through, the "cultural immersion through food" course I coordinate each winter in Chiang Mai, we engage hands-on with Tai Koen and Shan recipes and food traditions. Huge thanks to Fern Somraks, my good friend and partner in Immerse Through, for helping hold it all together. Warm thanks also to Kun Mae, Fern's mother, for her endless patience in transmitting village-level Tai Koen food wisdom, and to Jam and Boon-Ma, who teach Shan food. I have learned so much from all of them over the years. And thanks to the students who've come to Immerse Through for their active, inquiring participation.

I've made all but one of my recent trips into Burma on my own. Traveling solo means I meet lots of people, locals and also other foreigners, with whom I can explore and ask questions, and who have great insights. Thanks to the indomitable Annie Kemp, for her company in Rangoon and the Irrawaddy Delta and for many conversations about Burma. Thanks to Paul Copeland for his good company on a trip to Kengtung, to Matt Goulding and Nathan Thornburgh, and to many chance-met travelers, including Alison Fuglsang, Ko Doo, Ol Schwarzbach, Sam and Suezan Aitken, Clément and Maëlle, Dr. Luc Beaucourt, Justin Brown, and Dieter Wertz.

Burma watchers and supporters who share information about the situation in the country and surrounding region become a kind of community. Their insights and opinions have been a great help. Many thanks to all, including Pattie Walker, Karen Connelly, Anne Bayin, Coleen Scott, Paul Hilts, and (once more) Paul Copeland and Annie Kemp. Thanks also to Bill Harrison, Ron Hoffman, Guy Horton, Bertil Lintner, Bob Tilley, and members of the LIFT team I met in Kalaymyo, for recent conversations.

Friends in Toronto and elsewhere have been very supportive and generous-minded. The list is a long one, and so I'll just say, they know who they are, lovely people. I thank them all, for everything. Special thanks to longtime friends in Chiang Mai for their friendship and for listening to my enthusiastic talk about Burma each time I return from a trip, and to Aye and Jack, whose engagement with Burma is deep. I am grateful to the Social Science faculty at Chiang Mai University and to the Friends Library for the talks they sponsor about Thai-Burma border issues.

The cross-linkages with other people around the world who are interested in food, culture, and food history have grown stronger because of the Internet; I am grateful for comments and suggestions from many people on Facebook and Twitter, and elsewhere online. And as the bibliography indicates, I am indebted for understanding and background to the authors of many books with a Burma focus.

After figuring out recipes in my kitchen I'm always happy to feed them to people, and also to have other people test-drive them. Many thanks to friends in Toronto for willingly and enthusiastically eating and discussing what I set in front of them. Big thanks to Dina Fayerman, who is always prepared to discuss the project and recipes with her usual clarity. For recipe-testing and the resulting thoughtful feedback, I owe much to Hilary Buttrick, Robyn Eckhardt, Anne MacKenzie, Cameron Stauch, Kathy Wazana, and Dawn Woodward. Thanks too to *Cooking Light*, *Food & Wine*, and the Australian magazine *Feast*, which have tested and published versions of several of the recipes here.

In the summer of 2008 I began to shoot with a digital camera (a Nikon 700), and I used it for all the photo work on this book. It's been an adventure getting comfortable with digital photography after years of shooting slides, not so much with the camera and photographing out in the field, but with the post-production part of the process. I am very grateful to Thomas Wong for his help and to Nicole Regina Wong for rescuing me and helping get my photo files in order. Thanks too to David Hagerman and Edmund Rek for advice and encouragement.

As always, when it comes time to talk of acknowledgments, Ann Bramson has a halo around her, for her confidence in me and her ability to push things until they feel right and beautiful—I am very lucky to have her support and guidance. Trent Duffy did the detailed editing of the manuscript, in tandem with the superb copy editor Judith Sutton; he made the sometimes scary process feel harmonious as he pushed me to figure out the unclarities in my thinking and writing.

I am so fortunate that the talented and hardworking Richard Jung was available to make the glowing studio photos for the book. He was assisted by the wonderful Linda Tubby, who styled, and by props from Roísín Nield.

The edited manuscript, Richard's photographs, and my location shots were put together by Artisan's Susan Baldaserini and Laurin Lucaire, who provided a lovely design. At Artisan I also benefited from the efforts of Lia Ronnen, Allison McGeehon, Nancy Murray, Michelle Ishay, Bridget Heiking, and Barbara Peragine.

I am very grateful to Anne Collins of Random House Canada for being so confident about this project and pushing hard for it, and also to Sharon Klein for her care.

Finally of course I owe a huge debt to Dominic and Tashi, now grown up and just as fabulous as they were as kids in the late nineties, when we all traveled to Inle Lake, Kalaw, and Mandalay. Even though they were anxious when I headed out on my first few trips in 2009, they've been very supportive through the years of making this book. And as a non-tech-generation person, I've been very happy to be able to rely on them and on their friends to help sort out tech glitches from time to time.

INDEX

Note: Page numbers in *italics*
refer to illustrations.

CONVERSION CHARTS

Here are rounded-off equivalents between the metric system and the traditional systems that are used in the United States to measure weight and volume.

WEIGHTS

US/UK	METRIC
1 oz	30 g
2 oz	55 g
3 oz	85 g
4 oz (¼ lb)	115 g
5 oz	140 g
6 oz	170 g
7 oz	200 g
8 oz (½ lb)	225 g
9 oz	255 g
10 oz	285 g
11 oz	310 g
12 oz	340 g
13 oz	370 g
14 oz	395 g
15 oz	425 g
16 oz (1 lb)	455 g

VOLUME

AMERICAN	IMPERIAL	METRIC
¼ tsp		1.25 ml
½ tsp		2.5 ml
1 tsp		5 ml
½ Tbsp (1½ tsp)		7.5 ml
1 Tbsp (3 tsp)		15 ml
¼ cup (4 Tbsp)	2 fl oz	60 ml
⅓ cup (5 Tbsp)	2½ fl oz	75 ml
½ cup (8 Tbsp)	4 fl oz	125 ml
⅔ cup (10 Tbsp)	5 fl oz	150 ml
¾ cup (12 Tbsp)	6 fl oz	175 ml
1 cup (16 Tbsp)	8 fl oz	250 ml
1¼ cups	10 fl oz	300 ml
1½ cups	12 fl oz	350 ml
2 cups (1 pint)	16 fl oz	500 ml
2½ cups	20 fl oz (1 pint)	625 ml
5 cups	40 fl oz (1 qt)	1.25 l

OVEN TEMPERATURES

	°F	°C	GAS MARK
very cool	250–275	130–140	½–1
cool	300	148	2
warm	325	163	3
moderate	350	177	4
moderately hot	375–400	190–204	5–6
hot	425	218	7
very hot	450–475	232–245	8–9